Seeing the Social Context

READINGS TO ACCOMPANY
SOCIAL PROBLEMS

Edited by
James M. Henslin
Southern Illinois University, Edwardsville

Boston ■ New York ■ San Francisco
Mexico City ■ Montreal ■ Toronto ■ London ■ Madrid ■ Munich ■ Paris
Hong Kong ■ Singapore ■ Tokyo ■ Cape Town ■ Sydney

Executive Editor: Jeff Lasser
Editorial Assistant: Lauren Houlihan
Senior Marketing Manager: Kelly May
Editorial Production Service: Omegatype Typography, Inc.
Composition Buyer: Linda Cox
Manufacturing Manager: Debbi Rossi
Electronic Composition: Omegatype Typography, Inc.
Cover Administrator: Linda Knowles

For related titles and support materials, visit our online catalog at www.ablongman.com.

Between the time website information is gathered and then published, it is not unusual for some sites to have closed. Also, the transcription of URLs can result in typographical errors. The publisher would appreciate notification where these errors occur so that they may be corrected in subsequent editions.

ISBN-13:   978-0-205-56875-8
ISBN-10:   0-205-56875-0

Library of Congress Cataloging-in-Publication Data

Seeing the social context : readings to accompany social problems /
edited by James M. Henslin.
    p.   cm.
  Includes bibliographical references and index.
  ISBN-13: 978-0-205-56875-8 (pbk.)
  ISBN-10: 0-205-56875-0 (pbk.)
  1. Social problems—United States.   2. Social structure—United
States.   3. United States—Social conditions—1980–   I. Henslin, James M.
II. Title: Social problems.
  HN59.2.S44 2008
  361.10973—dc22

                                                    2007017468

Printed in the United States of America

10   9   8   7   6   5   4   3   2   1   11   10   09   08   07

Contents

Preface ■

Because this is a short book, the preface will be short—and unpretentious.

Here is an overview of the book's structure and a little flavor of its contents: To introduce the sociological perspective and raise our consciousness to better perceive the broader forces that create social problems, the first selection examines poverty in its social context. We then turn our lens on individuals as they struggle with growing old. In the second part, we examine social problems that center on norm violations. The authors of these selections analyze violations of norms of sexual behavior, drugs, and violence. Their focus on violations of norms of violence includes both violence against women and violence by the police. In the third part, we examine problems of social inequality. The authors of these selections focus on the lives of homeless women, racists who preach hatred, women's experience of the military, and the meaning of "insanity." In the concluding part, we look at how families adjust to the severe strains that come when they uproot themselves and migrate to a strange land, background factors of taken-for-granted legislation, the lingering effects of past colonialism, a case of environmental abuse so extensive that it destroyed a people's entire way of life, and the current brutal practice of using children as soldiers of war and terrorism.

I hope that you enjoy these selections. They have the potential to change your angle of vision, helping to make more visible the underlying social forces that create social problems, factors that impinge on your life and on those of the rest of us.

Jim Henslin
Henslin@aol.com

The Sociology of Social Problems

Personal troubles, said C. Wright Mills, are the difficulties that people experience as they live their lives. We all have them—and most of us experience a lot of them. For some, it seems that one personal trouble is hardly finished before another two, waiting in the sidelines, eagerly rush in to take its place. Sometimes we have so many personal troubles that life seems to consist only of a series of them.

Social problems, in contrast, said Mills, are large-scale disruptions in society. These dislocations, which have serious effects on many people, come about because the social institutions are having difficulty adjusting to social change. At times it can seem that there are so many social disruptions that life seems to consist only of a series of them.

After pointing out this distinction—that individuals experience personal troubles and societies experience social problems—Mills made this observation: The personal troubles of individuals are connected to the social problems of society. What we personally experience as troubles are reflections of the dislocations that our society is undergoing. As an example, Mills pointed to unemployment.

If an individual is unemployed, it is only a personal trouble. If jobs are available, the cause of that person's situation could be personal characteristics or failings—health problems, laziness, or failing to perceive or seize opportunities. If small groups of people are unemployed, this can still be an instance of personal troubles. If, in contrast, a lot of people who want to work can't find jobs, we have a social problem. Their misery, embarrassment, and inability to contribute to their family's economic survival as they did previously have nothing to do with personal characteristics. Their situation is due to external factors, to economic arrangements that have made jobs dry up. Social problems go beyond individuals, reaching into the social structure. In this example, some dislocation in society is making jobs unavailable to large numbers of people. Social problems, such as widespread unemployment, reverberate throughout society, affecting both large numbers of people and social institutions.

The experiencing of personal troubles can be called *biography*, said Mills, while that of social problems can be called *history*. It is the connecting of biography and history that lies at the heart of the sociological perspective. This connection between personal troubles and social problems, though, often eludes us. Our eyes are usually placed on the events that we personally experience. The broad social forces that lead to our personal troubles—even if we are aware of them—seem remote and inconsequential. To see the sociological perspective, it is precisely this connection that we must train ourselves to make.

Although Mills drew these distinctions back in the 1960s, they remain as valid today as when he made them. We continue to have difficulty perceiving these connections. We still tend to see our personal troubles as only individual matters. Social problems seem to be things "out there," with their impact on our own lives continuing to remain outside our awareness.

To remedy this situation, at least partially, is one of the primary goals of the course in social problems. After taking this course, you should have a much better perception of how large-scale events in society have a direct and ongoing impact on your own life.

In this first part of the book, we focus on the sociological perspective. In the selection that opens this part, Allan Johnson does a great job of raising our perception so we can move beyond the individual level to those broader forces that have such dramatic influences on our own well-being. In the second selection, David Unruh focuses on how the elderly adjust to their impending death, allowing us to see how individuals grapple with broader social forces.

The Forest for the Trees

Allan G. Johnson

introduction

Our views of social problems are almost always quite limited. What we are usually aware of are the events that come directly into our line of vision—those things that we experience personally or that we see going on around us. The connections that link these personal experiences with the broader social forces that bring them about usually lie so far beyond our line of vision that they remain invisible to us. With our consciousness formed by our personal experiences and our understanding limited, we have the need of the sociological perspective.

But what is the sociological perspective? It is an angle of vision, a way of perceiving and connecting the broader events in society to our personal experiences. Placing our personal troubles and other experiences in this broader context helps us to understand how and why we are experiencing difficulties in life. Our problems at work, at school, or in relationships or marriages might seem to be due to our personal characteristics or to some unique situation that we are facing. If we raise our angle of vision, though, we will see that the way work is organized, how education is structured, and what is expected of us in our relationships are connected to our social institutions. These connections set the context for the situations we experience.

When you are first introduced to it, the term sociological perspective can seem vague, making it difficult to grasp. This selection by Allan Johnson should make the interconnections between personal experiences and larger-scale social events more apparent.

Thinking Critically

As you read this selection, ask yourself:

- How can I change my angle of vision so I can see the impacts that broader social forces are having on my own life?

■ ■ ■ PUTTING THE "SOCIAL" BACK INTO SOCIAL PROBLEMS

Reading the daily newspaper and seeing the many problems that face modern societies such as the United States, it is difficult to avoid the impression that nothing seems to work. Governments and their programs come and go, as do debates between opposing political parties, but the problems remain and, if anything, grow worse along with people's feelings of collective frustration and despair.

It is fair to say that the problems are not solved partly because they are so broad in scope and complexity. But sociologists are drawn to a deeper explanation too often overlooked and rarely examined in a critical way: solving social problems requires that first they be understood as *social* problems with causes or consequences that are characteristics of social systems. Consider, for example, the case of poverty, perhaps the most far-reaching, long-standing, and devastating social problem of them all. Given the enormous wealth produced in the United States, the level of poverty and near-poverty is quite high.... Roughly 15 percent of the population lives below the poverty level, and if we include the near-poor, the percentage rises easily to 20 percent or more. Among children, the poor and near-poor include one out of every four. Even the middle class is increasingly insecure, as the cost of buying a house or paying for college education escalates beyond the means of most families, even when both parents work.

How do we explain such levels of poverty and financial insecurity in the midst of an abundant wealth unprecedented in human history? From a sociological perspective, the distribution of wealth and income is a structural characteristic of social systems, and as such, can be understood as a consequence of those systems. As a capitalist society, for example, the United States allows a minority to control most capital, forcing the working majority to live on wages. This facilitates the accumulation of wealth, with a small elite controlling the vast majority of wealth and income, and leaving a relatively small portion for the rest of the population. With a majority of the population competing for a disproportionately small share of the resources, a portion of that population will inevitably come up short and live in poverty. Part of the cause of poverty, then, lies in the nature of an economic system that facilitates and encourages the accumulation and concentration of wealth.

The level of poverty is also linked to basic ways in which industrial capitalism operates as a social system. The primary importance that capitalism places on competition, efficiency, and profit, for example, encourages control over costs by keeping wages low, the use of machines to replace workers, the introduction of high technology that renders obsolete the less sophisticated skills of many workers, moving jobs to locations where labor is cheaper and more easily managed (especially to Third World countries), and closing operations whose level of profit is insufficient to retain the interest of investors looking for a maximum return on their funds. These imperatives arise from the normal operation of capitalism as an economic sys-

From *The Forest for the Trees: An Introduction to Sociological Thinking* by Allan G. Johnson. 1991. Reprinted by permission.

tem, and they result in dislocation, anxiety, and hardship for millions of workers. Even those employed full time often find that capitalist competition between firms forces wages so low that their families fall near or below the poverty line.

To these social factors we can add others, such as government policies that increase interest rates—resulting in higher unemployment—to fight inflation; the high divorce rate and the corresponding increase in single-parent families; the inevitable business cycle of boom and recession that throws people out of work without picking them all up again when the economy swings upward; the centuries-old legacies of racism in the form of poor education, despair, prejudice, and discrimination; and the simple fact that the vast majority of people own no productive property and, as such, have little direct control over any means of making a living other than to make themselves attractive in a changing job market.

Although these are by no means offered as a last word on the causes of poverty, this discussion illustrates how poverty in a society can be understood as a consequence produced by that society. At the level of collective action and understanding, however, relatively little use is made of this kind of analysis in the U.S. Instead, most approaches to poverty take one of two basic forms, perhaps best described as liberal and conservative. A perfect example of the conservative approach is found in Charles Murray's book *Losing Ground.* . . . Murray argued that the world is like a merry-go-round on which the goal is to make sure that "everyone has a reasonably equal chance at the brass ring—or at least a reasonably equal chance to get on the merry-go-round." After reviewing thirty years of federal programs intended to eliminate poverty, Murray concluded the failure of these policies indicates that individual initiative and effort lie at the core of both the causes of poverty and any successful attempt to eliminate it. He would do away with affirmative action programs as well as all federal welfare and income-support systems, including "AFDC, Medicaid, food stamps, unemployment insurance, and the rest. It would leave the working-aged person with no recourse whatsoever except the job market, family members, friends, and public or private locally funded services." The result, he argued, would "make it possible to get as far as one can go on one's merit."

Although the U.S. has not adopted the kind of draconian measures Murray prescribes, his argument touches a deep nerve in the nation's cultural consciousness. There is widespread acceptance of his view of society and the causes of inequality, yet at the same time there is little support for the kinds of policies they would lead to. The belief that individuals are basically responsible for their own outcomes, for example, has not led to a widespread demand to eradicate programs that benefit the needy. One explanation for this inconsistency between belief and action is that although Murray's views resonate with the ideology of individualism that is so powerful in the United States, there is the nagging but largely unarticulated recognition that it does not tell the whole story. This conflict rests on a basic confusion between two very different aspects of social inequality in general and poverty in particular.

On the one hand is the question of how individuals are sorted into different social class categories—the kind of question that is the focus of most sociological research on social mobility and status attainment: What individual characteristics best predict occupation and income? Who gets ahead? These are questions people are most familiar with because they reflect their own attempts to make the most of their lives. Although it may seem counterintuitive, however, these kinds of questions have relatively little to do with the larger questions of why inequality in general and poverty in particular exist and persist.

Imagine that income is distributed according to the outcome of a footrace. All of the income for a year is put in a pool from which people draw according to their place: the first fifth of the field splits 45 percent of the pool, the second fifth wins 25 percent, the third fifth gets 16 percent, the fourth fifth splits 10 percent, and the last fifth collects just 4 percent. The result of such a system would be an unequal distribution of income with roughly the apportionment by population fifths found in the United States.

If we then ask, "Why is there inequality; why is there so much poverty?" one obvious answer—and, to many, the only answer—is that some people get more because they run faster. If we want to explain why two people have different or similar outcomes, this explanation would suffice, although we would probably ask why some people can run faster than others. But if we want to understand why one-fifth must survive on only 4 percent of the income, the answer that they are the slowest runners is inadequate, for this ignores the terms of the race itself that require *some* fifth of the population to live in poverty. If the prize money were distributed more evenly by fifths, there would be less poverty regardless of how fast people could run. [If, for example, the first fifth split 22 percent, the second 21 percent, the third 20 percent, the fourth 19 percent, and the fifth 18 percent, there would still be inequality, but since the share going to the top and bottom fifths would be very close to what would be an equal share of the total pot, the system would allow for far fewer extremes of wealth and poverty.]

There are two very different phenomena involved here. On the one hand are the choices and abilities that affect how well people can live: going to college, for example, tends to have a positive effect on income. On the other hand are the limitations social systems impose which produce patterns of inequality among individuals regardless of what they do: the cost of college places it beyond the reach of most, and given a limited number of well-paid jobs for college graduates, even those who earn degrees may find themselves unemployed or working in jobs far below their training and abilities. To the extent that we confuse the former with the latter (by reducing the race and its outcome to the ability and behavior of the runners) we conceal the social dynamics that produce social problems. In the U.S., this tendency is so entrenched that even those who think they are attributing social problems to social causes often wind up attributing them to individuals instead.

This can be seen both in Murray's analysis and in the responses of many of his critics. Murray's greatest mistake lies not in his selective reading of the data on poverty and federal programs but with his conclusion that if poverty persists [despite] federal antipoverty programs, then the causes of poverty must lie with individuals and their responses to reward and punishment, not with social systems. But the failure of such programs cannot be used to reject the idea that social systems produce poverty because these programs were not grounded in a sociological analysis of the causes of inequality and poverty to begin with. Even liberals, who are most likely to attribute poverty to social causes, focus on what amounts to a slightly more complex version of individualism. By "social," they seem to mean that problems affect many people or that social institutions have some responsibility to do something, but this is a far cry from understanding how systems produce the problem in the first place. Governmental programs have failed not because the idea that poverty is produced by social systems is incorrect, but because policymakers have not understood the meaning of that idea or, therefore, how to act on it. Like most people in the United States, both liberals and conservatives have not known how to get beyond individualistic, personal achievement models of social/inequality.

This inability is very much in evidence in the two major types of antipoverty programs. The first, best exemplified by job training and other educational programs, holds individuals ultimately responsible for social inequality by assuming that the distribution of poverty and wealth result solely from differences in qualifications and behavior. The only new twist introduced by these programs is that social institutions are taking some responsibility for changing the distribution of individual ability and motivation. To return to the analogy of the footrace, this amounts to making physical training more widely available, but without changing the rules of the race that produce the patterns of inequality by attaching different outcomes to where one happens to finish. The result is a certain amount of reshuffling of individuals among the different fifths, but without changing the overall distribution of outcomes, since the standards will still ensure that a certain proportion will be poor.

The second type of program assumes that social systems produce inequality and poverty, but is justified as humanitarian compassion for the victims. In either case, instead of changing the social systems that produce inequality and poverty, these programs try to compensate for their negative consequences. This category includes all welfare and income-transfer programs, from unemployment compensation and food stamps to Medicaid and subsidized housing. There is much to recommend them, since they alleviate some harmful consequences, but in the long run they do little to alter the scope of poverty in the society as a whole. This approach is analogous to the doctor whose patient is bleeding to death, and who gives one transfusion after another without locating or repairing the wound. Murray's position amounts to arguing that transfusions just throw good blood after bad, and in the long run, he may be correct. But if he is right, it is for the wrong reasons, since his alternative—leaving patients to their own devices to avoid an unhealthy dependency—makes it no more likely that the source of the bleeding will be identified, much less healed. He simply shifts the responsibility for the loss of blood elsewhere.

Attempts to solve social problems have often rested on an individualistic approach to social life cloaked in pseudosociological terms, which is to say, they reflect a profound misunderstanding of what makes social problems "social." It is a very narrow view to argue that society is responsible for social problems only in the sense that institutions have a general humanitarian obligation to assist those who suffer as a result. And that view is broadened only slightly by including the responsibility to assist individuals as they struggle not to be the ones who must finish last in the race (which, inevitably, leaves that position to others so long as the social system is structured as it is). Insofar as social problems are more than an accumulation of individual woes, solutions will be found only among the workings of social systems themselves. It will mean raising difficult critical questions about major social institutions, from corporate capitalism and politics to education and the family. It will mean considering the possibility that industrial capitalism may be fundamentally incompatible with the idea of a just society. It will mean seeing schools as more than a means to upward mobility, as institutions in which class, gender, and racial inequality is reproduced in each generation. Putting the "social" back into our approach to social problems promises to be an arduous and at times even frightening process; but it is most likely the only way these problems will ever be solved.

Maintaining Identity While Preparing for Death

David R. Unruh

introduction ■ ■ ■ ■

When you are under age 25 and in college, being old seems a long way off. And it is—about 40 years or so away. But if you talk to your grandparents or anyone else who has made it to their 60s or even to a more advanced age, you will find one thing in common: They will say that they can't believe that the years have gone by so quickly. "Why, it seems like just yesterday that . . . ," and then they will go on to talk about some event that took place 20 or 30 years ago. To them, the event is so fresh in their minds that it does seem like yesterday.

If you are young, this seems strange. How can things that took place such a long time ago—in some cases, even years before you were born—seem so recent to the elderly? You can remember when you were a young child, and *that* was a long time back—maybe 10 years ago. You are likely to shrug off such statements the elderly make as not quite real, as something said by someone who seems to live in a different world.

In many ways, the elderly do live in different worlds. Their perceptions of life are filtered through lenses that have been shaped by experiences quite different from yours. Consequently, they perceive events and evaluate the world differently than you do. A major characteristic of the elderly that separates them from younger people is their awareness of impending death. It isn't that death seems like it will happen tomorrow, but with the death of friends and acquaintances and changes in their own health, the elderly are aware that death is looming—that it can take place at any time. With this awareness, they begin to make preparations that, as David Unruh analyzes in this article, influence their evaluations and perceptions of life.

Thinking Critically

As you read this selection, ask yourself:

- How are the experiences of the elderly that are reported in this article related to large-scale events in society?

*W*hen death occurs, relationships and attachments between the living and the dead are physically if not emotionally severed. The literature on bereavement and survivorship focuses on the social and psychological processes by which survivors cope with the loss, reorganize their lives, and try to reintegrate into society (Berardo 1970; Harvey and Bahr 1974; Hochschild 1978; Kalish 1981; Lopata 1973, 1979). However, survivors often maintain an attachment to the deceased that may never be completely lost; they continue to experience recurring images, thoughts, and memories of the deceased, though these usually decrease in intensity, emotional impact, and centrality to their daily lives (Bornstein et al. 1973; Clayton 1973; Glick et al. 1974; Kastenbaum and Aisenberg 1972; Lindemann 1944; Lofland 1982; Marshall 1980; Volkhart and Michael 1976). This emotional attachment is reinforced by actions on the part of people before they die and their survivors which preserve some of the deceased's multiple identities—often, long after death has occurred.

In this paper, I look at the kinds of activities that encourage continued emotional attachment. I do not assess whether continued attachment is normal or pathological, nor whether the preserved identities which reinforce attachment accurately reflect the deceased's life. Instead, I focus on how identity preservation and the resulting emotional attachment are socially accomplished. The accomplishment of emotional attachment of survivor to deceased is interactional in the sense that survivors interpret and act upon information, actions, traits, and behaviors that were part of the deceased when alive. That is, before they die, people interpret and apportion cues to their personal identities for those who will survive (Butler 1963; Marshall 1980). Dying people hope they will be remembered as good fathers, competent women, successful businessmen, creative artists, or peacemakers. Survivors are left with bundles of images, materials, objects, and wishes of the deceased. Their task is to make sense of this amalgam and selectively preserve certain identities of the deceased. Aspects of the self other than those which directly reflect personal identities may also be preserved: idiosyncrasies, habits, qualities, and characteristics of the deceased may live on in the minds of survivors. The dead may be remembered as loving, obnoxious, volatile, or scornful, whether or not they viewed themselves as such while alive. However, the fact that survivors focus on *personal identity* implies that the deceased held certain images of themselves while alive which others accepted. In this context, what is being preserved after death is a self-concept which existed during life, was acknowledged by others, and had become a significant aspect of the dead person's self (Gross and Stone 1981; Stone 1962).

Dying people and their survivors use a "hierarchy of prominence" to give some identities preference over others (Heiss 1981). McCall and Simmons (1978) and Stryker (1968) note some factors which affect these priorities. Some identities offer greater rewards, provide access to relationships, or dramatize great personal sacrifices. This is crucial since it is impossible for the dying or their survivors to pre-

From David Unruh, "Death and Personal History." *Social Problems, 30,* February 3, 1983, pp. 340–351. Reprinted by permission.

serve all of the dying person's multiple identities. They preserve some identities and downplay, ignore, or discard others. I use the term *strategies of identity preservation* to refer to the activities by which both the dying and survivors keep certain identities intact and alive for the future.

The focus on strategies of identity preservation by the dying and their survivors relies on reminiscence as conceived in the gerontological literature. However, while many authors focus on types of reminiscence (Butler 1970, 1980; Coleman 1974; Lo Gerfo 1980), the relationship between reminiscence and mental health (Boylin et al., 1976; Costa and Kastenbaum 1967; Meacham 1977; Myerhoff and Tufte 1975), and how reminiscences are affected by individual circumstances (Cameron 1971; Havig-hurst and Glasser 1972; Revere and Tobin 1980), I examine the outward, observable actions of the dying and their survivors who seek to structure the frequency and context of some reminiscences. Not all attempts to structure reminiscences are successful and not every memory, image, and thought of the deceased is preserved. Therefore, I focus on how a portion of survivors' reminiscences are preserved.

This paper addresses three questions: (1) What are the strategies by which identities are preserved? (2) How do these strategies promote continued emotional attachment of survivor to deceased? (3) How are the reminiscences of survivors structured by these processes? I have drawn insight, ideas, and materials from a number of sources. First, I interviewed 25 people during 1979 and 1980 to explore their reminiscences and social involvements. The interviews were part of a study of the social lives and involvements of older people in and around a middle-sized northern California city. The people I interviewed represented a broad range of interests, living conditions, economic levels, and physical capabilities. They ranged in age from 62 to 85 years. Second, I analyzed the personal letters, mementos, and conversations of the dying and their survivors. In some instances, these materials were gathered from the older people I interviewed, but I also drew upon contacts and conversations with friends, relatives, and acquaintances. Finally, I examined popular and scholarly materials which address these processes, including autobiographies, newspaper accounts, journalistic interviews, and scholarly studies.

This paper is divided into two parts. The first examines three strategies used by the dying to preserve and communicate how they should be remembered by survivors. The second looks at four strategies that survivors use to preserve the identities of the deceased as they sort through their own thoughts and possessions left to them by the deceased.

■ ■ ■ STRATEGIES OF THE DYING

Dying broadly describes the status of two categories of people: (1) those who have a disease or physical condition which most likely will lead to death in a short or predictable period of time; and (2) those not medically defined as dying, but who have acquired an awareness that "their life will end in the not-too-distant-future" (Marshall 1980:127). The first group have entered a "dying trajectory," a probability statement that death will occur in a specified number of weeks, months, or years (Glaser and Strauss 1968, 1965). While these projections may not reflect the actual course of the dying process, they influence the person's use of existing time, energy, and resources (Lofland 1978). The dying person's belief that death is near is the essential criterion. People in the second category may increasingly think of death as they grow aware of their passage through the life cycle; are exposed to the deaths of others (Tolor and Murphy 1967); compare their age to life expectancy in their cohort (Cain 1978; Reynolds and Kalish 1974); compare their own age to the age that their parents died (Marshall 1975); and consider their occupational risks (Teahan and Kastenbaum 1970). Such awareness of death may stimulate more frequent reflection on the past—especially on matters of self and personal identity. The dying—in either of the above categories—interpret and apportion their identities to survivors through the use of three strategies: solidifying identities, accumulating artifacts, and distributing artifacts.

1) Solidifying Identities

Intensive self-reflection with increasing awareness of impending death is the foundation of Butler's (1963, 1980) life review concept, Myerhoff's (1975, 1978) life history technique, and Marshall's (1980) "last chapters metaphor." Common to all three is the notion that dying people begin to make sense of their lives by accentuating portions of their personal histories for which they wish to be remembered. Solidifying identities emphasizes and makes explicit the function of these activities for preserving personal identities.

Myerhoff (1978:34), in a study of elderly Jews in Venice, California, found that their reminiscences were not intended to mark successes or unusual merits, but to render coherent lives marked by great ruptures and shifts. In reminiscing they searched for "integrating ideas and characteristics" that helped them to know themselves and communicate to others who they were. Some identities dominated others; those of Jew, survivor, and humanitarian were strongest. Similarly, the older people I interviewed began by focusing on matters of social integration, but quickly redirected the conversation toward the personal circumstances underlying their present situations. They mentioned identities which were often those not immediately apparent in their everyday lives. Instead, they presented themselves as good businessmen, hard workers, loving family members, and self-sufficient individuals long after the situations which supplied them with these identities faded away. They indicated which identities were worth remembering by their survivors.

The people I interviewed solidified these identities through memos, letters, notes, journals, poems, and spontaneous reflections they planned to leave behind. When people think they are dying, they begin documenting pieces of their personal history through autobiographies, diary entries, and stories which leave portions of themselves with survivors. A major figure in Myerhoff's (1978) study concluded his written life history with instructions that it be read at family and senior center gatherings after his death. He hoped people would remember him through his writing, which would evoke a modicum of nostalgia, empathy, and continued emotional attachment.

There are other ways the dying supply survivors with information about what should be preserved. Some of these ways simultaneously create and preserve identities. One way is planning for the disposal of one's body. Another is donating an organ so others might live, or so that those still alive won't have to jeopardize their lives by giving an organ. This "priceless gift," as Fox and Swazey (1974) term it, invokes the identity of "self-sacrificing humanitarian" which will live long after the donor dies. Solidifying an identity is not the only reason people become donors, but the act overshadows those negative, suspicious, or simply mundane aspects of the person's history.

One older woman studied by Matthews (1979:161) planned to have her body cremated after death. While she viewed cremation as a sensible, if slightly frightening, act which would allow her finances to be better spent elsewhere, she felt her daughter would not have the courage to make such plans on her own. She, therefore, left this gesture of practicality and self-sufficiency in her will by which her daughter might remember her. Glick et al. (1974) report numerous examples of husbands who made funeral, burial, and financial arrangements before their death. As one widow remembered her husband:

> Jack had gone out and bought his own lot a year-and-a-half ago at the cemetery. He had made all the arrangements, what he wanted and what he didn't want. People were shocked by this, that a man could go and do this, but that's the type of man he was. He said, "I'm making arrangements so that when it happens everybody won't be up in the air and not know what they're going to do" (1974:41).

The funeral arrangements represented a final act of foresight which would be publicly acknowledged after death. Other dying husbands left instructions about how their families should behave at their funeral. For some, the appearance of stoic, composed, and restrained families meant others would perceive them keeping the family unit together even after death. As one widow recalled:

> Last year he said to me, "If anything ever happens to me I don't want you to go to pieces. I want you to act like Jacqueline Kennedy—you know, very brave and courageous. You've got to have class," he said. "I just don't want screaming and hollering" (Glick et al. 1974:60).

Further, by leaving specific instructions about their survivors' behavior at the funeral, these dying husbands and fathers were acting as if their family might be an embarrassment to them even after death.

In a study of the life insurance industry, Zelizer (1979) implies that insurance was marketed—and eventually accepted—as a way the deceased could solidify the identities of good provider and loving husband. Monetary payments are ways such identities are preserved after death.

2) Accumulating Artifacts

Throughout their lives, people acquire objects and imbue them with personal meanings which represent past accomplishments, talents, journeys, and sentiments. When people are dying, some objects become artifacts of their personal history. The accumulation of artifacts is a strategy by which the dying preserve identities over time and communicate their importance to survivors. In Goffman's (1961) terms, artifacts are components of an "identity kit" in which personal identities and feelings about oneself are located, invested, and stored in material possessions. These include scrapbooks, photo albums, mementoes, souvenirs, and jewelry which symbolize personal histories (as well as shared biographies) of the elderly and others. One person I interviewed was an active cross-country cyclist while still in his late 70s. He and his wife compiled scrapbooks of magazine and newspaper articles and sporting programs which chronicled his post-retirement cycling career. They devoted a corner of their mobile home to the display of tour badges, photographs, and trophies. During our interview, the elderly cyclist noted that the utility of these artifacts in the here-and-now was not as crucial as their value for future reference.

> You know, I won't always be as active as I am now. I'm getting up there in years and so it is important for my wife and me to record these good memories and experiences. God forbid, I may get to the point where I start forgetting things, and these things will help me and my children remember these activities.

Many of the people I interviewed recalled past events and important junctures in their lives by using physical objects in their homes to stimulate memories and "stories." The meaning of these objects, and the identities they represented, would be imparted to survivors when death approached or occurred. One woman gave reprints of historic family photographs to her grandchildren with personalized narrations on the back. Phrases like "this may not seem important to you now, but it may someday" and "I am telling you these facts so they will not be lost when I die" reveal her self-identity as family matriarch and the wish to leave her sense of family history to survivors. Sherman and Newman (1977) found that 81 percent of their sample of 94 older people in community senior centers and nursing homes could identify a "most cherished possession." For the elderly, these objects often represent the last symbolic remnants of who and what they once were. Most of the senior center participants and nursing home residents studied by Sherman and Newman associated symbolic jewelry with a spouse and used photographs to evoke memories of their children. The identities of spouse and parent took precedence and were preserved over others.

The possessions of a person—a stamp collection, favorite painting, wedding band, or family Bible—symbolize identities which may become the objects of reminiscences by survivors. However, the full import of an artifact can never completely be transferred from the dying person to a survivor. Collections of personal treasures rarely evoke memories of the same intensity for survivors that they had for the deceased. Auctions and antique stores are full of unwanted objects stripped of the cherished meanings they once held (Taylor 1981). However, if survivors know the "stories" behind an acquired object and the meaning it once had for the deceased, reminiscences will be formed and organized around that knowledge. An acquired rocking chair may be described to visitors as "the one my grandmother used for 60 years as she raised her family." Thus, the grandmother's identity of caring mother may become intertwined with the object itself.

3) Distributing Artifacts

Wills and testaments are the most obvious devices used by the dying to apportion and dispense objects in which personal identities and feelings about oneself are stored. However, wills and testaments also selectively communicate to survivors which identities should be remembered, and the partial content of those reminiscences. Wills generally follow traditional kinship lines with spouses, offspring, and relatives receiving the bulk of possessions. However, variations exist which highlight the ordering of multiple identities on a hierarchy of prominence. Rosenfeld (1979) has noted the modern trend of leaving one's personal estate to the surviving spouse and, at least partially, excluding one's children. In many instances, this decision illustrates preeminence of the identity of generous husband or wife over those of father, mother, community leader, or religious person. The implication of this decision is that the surviving spouse was the major supplier of personal meaning and identity for the deceased.

Most interesting and revealing are instances where the dying bequeath specific artifacts to survivors, or make unorthodox provisions for distribution. Bryant and Snizek (1975:224) noted the obligations and conditions of stewardship of those receiving "special" objects from the dying or deceased. To receive grandmother's pearl brooch or grandfather's favorite shotgun may make emotionally mandatory compliance with other stipulations or expectations. One obligation may be the survivor's desire to preserve and protect specific memories or images of the deceased—that is, to become a guardian of the deceased's persona. These include identities preserved through bequests to dogs, cats, showgirls, under-privileged groups, or complete strangers. The personal identity of one Englishman as an "Irish-hater" was preserved through a provision in his will to have Irishmen assemble at his grave on the anniversary of his death and be supplied with liquor and weapons; the dying Englishman believed they would become drunk, violent, and eventually destroy themselves (Bryant and Snizek 1975:222). The intent of these bequests may be not only to preserve the identities of cat-lover, Irish-hater, liberal, or philanderer, but also that of unpredictable eccentric. Through wills and testaments the dying may best reveal their "true" identities or aspects of their "real" selves (Turner 1976). The concierge of San Francisco's Opera House between 1932 and 1972 would never reveal to anyone which he preferred—the opera or the symphony. Only after his death at the age of 88 was it revealed that he willed $10,000 to the symphony rather than the opera. People who move to nursing homes or retirement communities may develop new friendships, peer groups, and organizational loyalties which are unknown to family members. Rosenfeld (1979, 1980) has analyzed the degree to which friends and loyalties developed in old age have supplanted traditional kinship lines in the distribution of artifacts. One-third to one-half of the elderly residents in three settings Rosenfeld (1980) studied made bequests outside the family. There were many bequests to neighbors and friends from the retirement settings where, in a comparative sense, the older people had brief but intense social lives. Thus, the deceased's will revealed for the first time—and preserved—the newly formed identities of retirement community resident and best friend to other residents.

Disinheritance, the other side of this issue, also preserves identities. Conscious exclusion of an award to legal heirs demonstrates assertiveness, independence, or publicly metes out punishment. One dying woman sought to preserve her identities of mother and homemaker through her will, despite the perceived inadequacies of her daughter:

> I give and bequeath to my daughter, Florence, the sum of One Dollar, and no more; reason for this is due to her not living at home and doing her share to maintain our home, and also due to her having caused me undue worry and trouble for the past couple of years (Rosenfeld 1979:85).

Statements like this may create family polarization, conflict, or feelings of shame (Sussman et al. 1970). The following excerpt from a will reveals an expression of disappointment which must have affected the nature of the surviving brother's reminiscences of the deceased:

> My bequest to _____, my brother, is limited because of his unconcerned attitude and actions with respect to my late wife's illness, as well as having failed to induce his very arrogant physician son, with whom I had repeatedly pleaded, unsuccessfully, to intercede and collaborate with the physicians assigned to the case of my severely ailing wife shortly before her death (Rosenfeld 1979:91).

Finally, while I have focused on distributing artifacts—whether they be objects, property, or money—through formal processes, distribution can also occur informally. The dying often distribute artifacts to friends and family in a casual way. This is a way of allocating personal explanations of the meaning and identity associated with the objects to those receiving them—as well as those excluded.

■ ■ ■ STRATEGIES OF THE SURVIVORS

Survivors maintain an emotional attachment to those who precede them in death by drawing from two sources of information. First, they reinterpret past experiences and knowledge of the deceased and imbue them with personal meaning. Second, the dying supply survivors with information, requests, and desires regarding how they themselves wish to be remembered. Four strategies enable survivors to preserve an emotional attachment: reinterpreting the mundane; redefining the negative; continued bonding activities; and sanctifying meaningful symbols.

1) Reinterpreting the Mundane

Survivors are left with a plethora of images, thoughts, and memories. Some exceptional feats or characteristics of the deceased may live on in the minds of survivors, but much of what remains is ordinary and mundane. The literature on survivorship contains many accounts of survivors who continually remembered such ordinary things as how the deceased ordered wine in a restaurant, told jokes to friends, showed affection to family, dealt with children, or left clothes about the house (Cain 1974; Charmaz 1980; Lopata 1979; Parkes 1972). Conventional wisdom might view such lingering thoughts and memories as signs of continued emotional distress. However, they also maintain an emotional attachment which influences reminiscences for many years. Reinterpreting the mundane emphasizes how survivors sift through the deceased's life to preserve—and create—identities.

The journalist Martha Lear gave her dying husband's possessions to the survivors for which they seemed most meaningful. She anticipated reinterpretation of the mundane by her husband's children, friends, and relatives after his death:

> I went into his closet and closed the door and stood in the dark embracing his clothes, smelling him. Who will take his clothes if he dies? His son, Jon? They won't fit. But as mementos, maybe. Yes, Jon will want his clothes. His books, his desk, his easy chair. Judy will want his bathrobe—as a child, she loved to cuddle in his bathrobe—his granny glasses, his collection of petrified wood. His pictures? How will they divide the pictures? Oh, God, the pictures, hanging on walls, crammed into albums, stashed in boxes on closet floors . . . Hal sailing his Sunfish in our beautiful Provincetown harbor. Hal fighting the bull in some Mexican town. . . . They staged a bullfight for the doctors and then asked for volunteers. And suddenly there was Hal, bounding out onto the field, I yelling, "Are you crazy? Come back here?" (Lear 1980:31).

Lear alludes to two identities of her husband Hal which were preserved in this manner—those of father and adventurer. Similarly, Glick et al. (1974:143) recounted one widow's reminiscences which (despite the obvious idealization) were organized around her husband's identities of family man and thoughtful husband:

> We had a beautiful marriage. I'm not saying this because he's gone but we did, we got along beautifully. I think we were really envied by people because we got along so well. We were always together. . . . He was full of fun. He was a tease with the kids. My nieces and nephews loved him. . . . He didn't deprive his family of anything. We were always together. We had a very nice social life, he took us places, he took the kids. . . .

The evidence consisted of "little things" which most likely escaped attention or comment while the husband was alive. After death, many practices or habits may symbolize identities and thereby stimulate reminiscences about activities of the deceased. In a published interview, Yoko Ono remarked that her swearing sparked reminiscences of her husband John Lennon, as father, who preferred they not swear in the presence of their son. Eating chocolate reminded her of Lennon the songwriter who consumed countless Hershey bars while recording their last record album (Norman 1981).

There are many cues which stimulate reminiscences of the deceased in a specific time and place. The number of mundane activities, traits, or events reinterpreted will likely be high shortly after death and decrease in number and intensity over time. This change is probably due to two factors: the rate of reinterpretation may be higher shortly after death and with passing time there may be fewer things left to reinterpret with regard to the deceased's life. However, attachments based on the mundane remain. Identities preserved in this manner may be less central to survivors' reminiscences than identities preserved in other ways. In other words, this strategy preserves identities that are low on the hierarchy of prominence. One widow I interviewed reminisced about her husband who had died 40 years earlier.

> Every time I go out dancing and have to worry about finding a suitable partner, I have to think about what a really good dancer my husband was. We had a lot of things in common . . . you know, the children, our family, our house, and our friends, but he was such a good dancer that I'm still reminded of it when the subject of dance comes up.

2) Redefining the Negative

Just as dying people engage in self-reflection and interpret their pasts before death, survivors tend to "idealize" the deceased, thereby simultaneously increasing the deceased's status and helping alleviate grief (Charmaz 1980; Glick et al. 1974; Lopata 1979; Neugarten 1968; Rees 1975). Some view idealization as unrealistic and pathological. I prefer to emphasize its function in preserving identities, structuring reminiscences, and sustaining emotional attachment. The point is not that actions or qualities viewed as negative when the deceased was alive are positively redefined. Rather, the negative provides additional evidence for an identity which—good or bad—is part of the survivor's memory. Thoughts about negative qualities may spark reminiscences which keep the survivor and deceased emotionally connected. One elderly widower I interviewed described the following reminiscences of his deceased wife, whose "nagging" and watchful eye later became evidence for her preserved identity as family matriarch:

> I have been living in this apartment by myself for five years now. I get lonely now and then. . . . When my wife was here, she wanted to know where I was and what I was doing all the time. She did this with the kids and me for many years. I guess it was sort of a bone of contention for some time, and we argued about it. Now that I'm by myself, I kind of miss it.

> You know, all she was trying to do was be a good wife. At least, that's what she always said. She was raised to think that a good wife and mother always kept close track of her family. It's funny, but from time to time for several years after she died, I would remember her nearly every time I left the house to go someplace. . . .

For other survivors I interviewed, a lack of economic success became evidence for the preserved identity of honest and benevolent businessman; jealous actions were confirmation of a lover's devotion; and memories of an abrasive manner suggested the preserved identity of aggressive, self-made man. When these traits were observed in others, survivors felt "pangs" of emotional attachment to the deceased (Weiss 1973). Emotional attachment does not always consist of warm and pleasant feelings: survivors may feel hate, guilt, relief, shame, or elation, based on reminiscences of the deceased's negative qualities.

3) Continued Bonding Activities

People create shared biographies through joint activities, processes, events, and acts. Horseback riding, singing, going to the theater, shopping, conversing, or making love all bond aspects of the self with those of others (Lofland 1982). Upon death, these activities may stimulate memories, thoughts, and images of the deceased, and the accompanying identities. Continued bonding activities represent both conscious and unconscious actions. One widow occasionally set a place at the dinner table for her deceased husband on Sundays. When she caught herself, she felt a "funny feeling" running through her for some time afterward. Not only did this act remind her of loneliness and loss, it also sparked reminiscences of the deceased based on his encouragement of "togetherness" at Sunday dinners (Glick et al. 1974:150).

Some survivors continue visiting a summer cabin their partner loved, use opera tickets that were so difficult to obtain, maintain joint group memberships, and walk the same routes the deceased once traveled (Lopata 1973, 1979). Attitudes and reactions to these actions differ. Some survivors find the reminiscences haunting, while others revel in continued ties to the deceased. Continued bonding activities are exemplified by the actions of the surviving friends and family members of two murdered college lovers. The lovers devoted much of their activity and energy toward a city recreation program. They coordinated activities and supervised events sponsored by their city's Department of Parks and Recreation. Some months after their deaths, the survivors organized a "warm remembrance festival" at which friends and family gathered to reminisce about the couple. The event included many of the same activities in which the couple had engaged while involved in the recreation program.

> The mood at the event was anything but sad. Wide-eyed children were scattered throughout the block-long park climbing over an earth ball, gorging on watermelon, or throwing softballs at a dunk tank. Many of the relatives and friends of the slain couple picnicked on the grass. . . . Although certainly many were thinking of the pair, none seemed to be saddened by the tragedy. [According to the father of one of the pair] "It's the best way to remember them." He said, however, that it was impossible to cope with the loss of his son through such tragic circumstances (*California Aggie* 1981:1).

While this event was termed the "first annual warm remembrance festival," it was not held in the succeeding year. However, it was a dramatic example of survivors collectively bonding to the deceased.

4) Sanctifying Meaningful Symbols

Some survivors imbue a small number of objects with meanings symbolic of "special" or exemplary identities of the deceased. In effect, these objects are viewed as "sacred" symbols of the deceased's life. Grave sites and markers are the most obvious examples: accompanying icons and epitaphs cue observers to exemplary identities or traits. However, survivors also sanctify many objects or spaces and preserve other identities. Untouched bedrooms preserve memories of sons, daughters, or spouses; places of birth are places for pilgrimages regardless of current inhabitants; paintings, furniture, needlepoint projects and the like may be sacred embodiments of the identities of artist, woodworker, and craftsperson. Further, portraits or photographs may become objects of "worship" or felt communication with the dead (Parkes 1972). A small number of objects become sanctified to such a degree that their loss would be as tragic for the survivors as was the death of the deceased.

Sanctifying symbols may be a collective endeavor rather than an individual or family act. This is especially true when the deceased is well known to large numbers of people. Special funds in the name of the deceased to combat the fatal disease, or to carry on exemplary work, preserve the identities of cancer victim, murdered leader, literary figure, or philosopher. The collective sanctification surrounding what many fans perceived as the important identities of John Lennon further illustrates this point. In 1981, on the first anniversary of his death, fans gathered outside the Dakota Apartments in New York City where he was murdered, at the Cavern Club in Liverpool where the Beatles were discovered, and at many other symbolic places.

> At vigils and concerts—in Liverpool, New York, and around the world—fans recalled Lennon as a *rock 'n' roll dream-weaver, working-class hero,* and *househusband.* . . . In Liverpool, thousands of Beatles fans paid tribute to Lennon at an outdoor concert and vigil. . . . "I'm memory laning, if not Penny Laning tonight," said disc jockey Bob Wooler, emcee of the free concert (*San Francisco Chronicle* 1981:3, italics added).

Collective efforts to preserve Lennon's identities were instituted by his wife, fans, and New York City officials through plans to refurbish a three-acre "island" in Central Park christened "Strawberry Fields." As a young child in Liverpool, Lennon played in an area known as Strawberry Fields, later wrote a song of the same name, and took his last walk through this area of Central Park. Materials for the refurbishment consisted of plants, trees, and stones donated by fans from many nations; these would be unified into a single "sanctified" symbol. Lennon's identities of working-class child, songwriter, and social visionary would be symbolized and located in this single location, which would become a mecca for fans. However, as planning and construction began, Yoko Ono was said to be frustrated by New York City regulations which forced her to scale down her original design. According to a New York City Parks Department official, "We hope Strawberry Fields will be a very lovely landscape, but it must be in keeping with the rest of the park" (*Rolling Stone* 1982:34).

Collective sanctification highlights the problem not only in achieving consensus on the identities to be preserved, but in the consensual meaning of the symbols used in the process. Conflict between Yoko Ono and representatives of the New York City Parks Department hints at problems in achieving consensus, but the furor surrounding a sculpture by the San Francisco Arts Commission to symbolize that city's assassinated mayor, George Moscone, is instructive. Based on submitted drawings, the Art Commission approved Robert Arneson's plan for a bust of Moscone. The completed sculpture was placed on a pedestal covered with graffiti-like inscriptions, including bullet holes, the profiles of a .38 caliber pistol, blood-like spatters of red glaze, and the name of Dan White, the city supervisor convicted of murdering Moscone and supervisor Harvey Milk. City officials, the deceased mayor's wife, and most of the public expressed shock, not only at the pedestal, but at the facial expression on the bust. One art critic described it as "a grotesquely inane smile. . . . The entire expression has the feeling of a mask . . . that politicians characteristically wear when they are up for election, shaking hands, kissing babies, speaking on the tube" (Albright 1981:25). The furor centered on the artist choosing to preserve the identities of assassinated public figure and plastic politician over the preferred identities of family patriarch, liberal Democrat, friend of the poor, and respected politician. Sanctification of the Moscone Convention Center and reminiscences stimulated by the sculpture were expected to contain only "positive and tasteful images." For example, sculptures to honor deceased politicians have traditionally included patriotic slogans, children kneeling around the figure, flags, and warm smiles. Similarly, the continued emotional attachment city leaders hoped to foster toward the deceased mayor was to be "warm and loving" rather than mixed with the unpleasant.

■ ■ ■ ■ IMPLICATIONS

This chapter has explored the interaction between the dying and their survivors as they seek to preserve certain identities. I have shown how the dying preserve and distribute important images of the self. The other side of this interactional process, in which survivors preserve the identities of the deceased, begins to shed light not on how survivors "work through" and dispense with lingering images of those who precede them in death, but how memories of the deceased thrive through social action. Many preserved identities carry with them an emotional component: memories evoke feelings of love, hate, shame, elation, relief, or grief which sustain a measure of emotional attachment. Thus, continued attachment is not something which simply happens as a result of some psychological state, but it often arises out of strategic social action.

Further, this paper highlights how reminiscences are structured, apportioned, and stimulated, both by the dying and survivors. Unlike most psychiatric and psychological conceptions of the process, reminiscences—and the kinds of images they contain—are structured through social action. We need to recognize the sociological nature of these processes which have previously been conceived as internal, spontaneous, and purely personal, for these are the strategic actions of people trying to exercise some personal control over the impact of death on their personal histories.

■ ■ ■ REFERENCES

Albright, Thomas. 1981. "Arneson's View of Life in Sculpture." *San Francisco Chronicle*, December 4, 25.

Berardo, Felix. 1970. "Survivorship and Social Isolation: The Case of the Aged Widower." *The Family Coordinator* 1(1):11–25.

Bornstein, Philip, Paula J. Clayton, James A. Halikas, William L. Maurice, and Eli Robins. 1973. "The Depression of Widowhood after Thirteen Months." *British Journal of Psychiatry* 122(4):561–66.

Boylin, William, Susan K. Gordon, and Milton F. Nehrke. 1976. "Reminiscence and Ego Integrity in Institutionalized Elderly Males" *Gerontologist* 16(1):118–24.

Bryant, Clifton D., and William Snizek. 1975. "The Last Will and Testament: A Neglected Document in Sociological Research." *Sociology and Social Research* 59(2):219–30.

Butler, Robert N. 1963. "The Life Review: An Interpretation of Reminiscence in the Aged." *Psychiatry* 26(1):65–76.

———. 1970. "Looking Forward to What? The Life Review, Legacy, and Excessive Identity versus Change." *American Behavioral Scientist* 14(1):121–28.

———. 1980. "The Life Review: An Unrecognized Bonanza." *International Journal of Aging and Human Development* 12(1):35–38.

Cain, Leonard D. 1978. "Counting Backward from Projected Death: An Alternative to Chronological Age in Assigning Status in the Elderly." Paper presented to the Policy Center on Aging, Maxwell School, Syracuse University, March 22.

Cain, Lynne. 1974. *Widow*. New York: Morrow.

California Aggie (University of California, Davis). 1981. "Friends Gather for Warm Remembrance." September 5, 1.

Cameron, Paul. 1971. "The Generation Gap: Time Orientation." *Gerontologist* 12(2):117–19.

Charmaz, Kathy. 1980. *The Social Reality of Death*. Reading, Mass.: Addison-Wesley.

Clayton, Paula J. 1973. "Anticipatory Grief and Widowhood." *British Journal of Psychiatry* 122(1):47–51.

Coleman, Peter G. 1974. "Measuring Reminiscence Characteristics from Conversation as Adaptive Features of Old Age." *International Journal of Aging and Human Development* 5(3):281–94.

Costa, Paul G., and Robert Kastenbaum. 1967. "Some Aspects of Memories and Ambition in Centenarians." *The Journal of Genetic Psychology* 110(1):3–16.

Fox, Renee, and Judith Swazey. 1974. *The Courage to Fail*. Chicago: The University of Chicago Press.

Glaser, Barney, and Anselm Strauss. 1965. *Time for Dying*. Chicago: Aldine.

———. 1968. *Awareness of Dying*. Chicago: Aldine.

Glick, Ira O., Robert Weiss, and C. Murray Parkes. 1974. *The First Year of Bereavement*. New York: Columbia University Press.

Goffman, Erving. 1961. *Asylums*. Garden City, N.Y.: Doubleday-Anchor.

Gross, Edward, and Gregory Stone. 1981. "Embarrassment and the Analysis of Role Requirements." In *Social Psychology through Symbolic Interaction*. 2nd ed., edited by Gregory Stone and Harvey Farberman, 115–30. New York: Wiley.

Harvey, Carol D., and Howard M. Bahr. 1974. "Widowhood, Morale, and Affiliation." *Journal of Marriage and the Family* 36(1):95–106.

Havighurst, Robert, and Richard Glasser. 1972. "An Exploratory Study of Reminiscence." *Journal of Gerontology* 27(2):245–53.

Heiss, Jerold. 1981. *The Social Psychology of Interaction*. Englewood Cliffs, N.J.: Prentice-Hall.

Hochschild, Arlie Russell. 1978. *The Unexpected Community*. Berkeley: University of California Press.

Kalish, Richard. 1981. *Death, Grief, and Caring Relationships*. Belmont, Calif.: Brooks-Cole.

Kastenbaum, Robert, and Ruth Aisenberg. 1972. *The Psychology of Death*. New York: Springer.

Lear, Martha Weinman. 1980. *Heartsounds: The Story of a Love and Loss*. New York: Simon and Schuster.

Lindemann, Erich. 1944. "Symptomatology and Management of Acute Grief." *The American Journal of Psychiatry* 101(4):141–48.

Lofland, Lyn. 1978. *The Craft of Dying*. Beverly Hills, Calif.: Sage.

———. 1982. "Relational Loss and Social Bonds: An Exploration into Human Connection." In *Personality, Roles, and Social Behavior*, edited by William Ickes and Eric S. Knowles, 219–42. New York: Springer-Verlag.

Lo Gerfo, Marianne. 1980. "Three Ways of Reminiscence in Theory and Practice." *International Journal of Aging and Human Development* 12(1):39–48.

Lopata, Helena Z. 1973. *Widowhood in an American City*. Cambridge, Mass.: Schenkman.

———. 1979. *Women as Widows*. New York: Elsevier.

McCall, George, and J. L. Simmons. 1978. *Identities and Interactions*. Rev. ed. New York: Free Press.

Marshall, Victor W. 1975. "Age and Awareness of Finitude in Developmental Gerontology." *Omega* 6(2):113–29.

———. 1980. *Last Chapters: A Sociology of Aging and Dying*. Monterey, Calif.: Brooks-Cole.

Matthews, Sarah H. 1979. *The Social World of Old Women*. Beverly Hills, Calif.: Sage.

Meacham, James A. 1977. "A Transactional Model of Remembering." In *Life Span Developmental Psychology*, edited by Nancy Datan and Hayne Reese, 81–95. New York: Academic.

Myerhoff, Barbara. 1978. *Number Our Days*. New York: Simon and Schuster.

———, and Virginia Tufte. 1975. "Life History as Integration." *Gerontologist* 15(4):541–43.

Neugarten, Bernice. 1968. *Middle Age and Aging*. Chicago: University of Chicago Press.

Norman, Philip. 1981. "A Talk with Yoko." *New York* 12(May 25):32–40.

Parkes, C. Murray. 1972. *Bereavement: Studies of Grief in Adult Life*. New York: Basic.

Rees, W. Dewi. 1975. "The Bereaved and Their Hallucinations." In *Bereavement: Its Psychological Aspects*, edited by Bernard Schoenbert, Irwin Gerber, Alfred Wiener, Austin Kutscher, David Peretz, and Arthur Carr, 66–71. New York: Columbia University Press.

Revere, Virginia, and Sheldon Tobin. 1980. "Myth and Reality: The Older Person's Relationship to His Past." *International Journal of Aging and Human Development* 12(1):15–26.

Reynolds, David, and Richard A. Kalish. 1974. "Anticipation of Futurity as a Function of Ethnicity and Age." *Journal of Gerontology* 29(2):224–31.

Rolling Stone. 1982. "Random Notes." Issue 383:34.

Rosenfeld, Jeffrey P. 1979. *The Legacy of Aging: Inheritance and Disinheritance in Social Perspective*. Norwood, N.J.: Ablex.

———. 1980. "Old Age, New Beneficiaries: Kinship, Friendship, and (Dis)inheritance." *Sociology and Social Research* 64(1):86–95.

San Francisco Chronicle. 1981. "Fans Gather for Lennon Tribute." December 11:3.

Sherman, Edmund, and Evelyn Newman. 1977. "The Meaning of Cherished Personal Possessions for the Elderly." *International Journal of Aging and Human Development* 8(2):181–92.

Stone, Gregory. 1962. "Appearance and the Self." In *Human Behavior and Social Processes*, edited by Arnold Rose, 86–118. Boston: Houghton Mifflin.

Stryker, Sheldon. 1968. "Identity Salience and Role Performance: The Relevance of Symbolic Interaction Theory for Family Research." *Journal of Marriage and the Family* 30(4): 558–64.

Sussman, Marvin B., Judith Cates, and David Smith. 1970. *Family and Inheritance*. New York: Russell Sage Foundation.

Taylor, Lisa. 1981. "Collections of Memories." *Architectural Digest* 38(4):36–42.

Teahan, James, and Robert Kastenbaum. 1970. "Subjective Life Expectancy and Future Time Perspective as Predictors of Job Success in the Hard-Core Unemployed." *Omega* 1(2):189–200.

Tolor, Alexander, and Vincent Murphy. 1967. "Some Psychological Correlates of Subjective Life Expectancy." *Journal of Clinical Psychology* 23(1):21–24.

Turner, Ralph H. 1976. "The Real Self: From Institution to Impulse." *American Journal of Sociology* 81(6):989–1016.

Volkhard, Edmund, and Stanley Michael. 1976. "Bereavement and Mental Health." In *Death and Identity*, edited by Robert Fulton, 239–57. Bowie, Md.: Charles Press.

Weiss, Robert S., ed. 1973. *Loneliness: The Experience of Emotional and Social Isolation.* Cambridge, Mass.: MIT Press.

Zelizer, Viviana. 1979. *Morals and Markets: The Development of Life Insurance in the United States.* New York: Columbia University Press.

II Norm Violations in Social Context

As sociologist Emile Durkheim pointed out so long ago, it is inevitable that every society will be filled with deviants. It is impossible for it to be otherwise, he said. To paraphrase Durkheim: To exist, every society has to have rules, and this means that every society will have rule breakers. He said that even if we consider a society of saints—a group of good, sincere, God-fearing men or women, cloistered in a place separated from the world, where they spend their lives reflecting on their sinful condition, singing hymns, and worshipping God—even there, you will find rule breakers. The rules that will be broken will seem trivial to us—not spending enough time in prayer, having bad thoughts, envy of a spiritual brother or sister who has been given more recognition, and the like. Nevertheless, those are rule breakers, or deviants, in sociological terminology.

In a technical sense, such rule-breaking could be considered a social problem. That is, if members of this group of "saints" become upset about some behavior of their members and want to change it, *for them* it would be a social problem. Ordinarily, however, the term social problem refers to the larger group, to that vague thing called "society." To be a social problem, large numbers of people must be upset about some condition of society and want it changed.

In this second part of the book, we look at norm violations—specifically violations of norms that upset large numbers of people. Many find the topic of the first selection to be a surprise. They have difficulty understanding why homosexuality is included as a topic in social problems. Unlike years past, when almost all homosexuals hid their sexual orientation, in Western society today many are open about their sexual orientation and work in highly visible positions. Unlike the past, when the legal system was harnessed to harass and prosecute homosexual behavior, many of today's laws protect homosexuals from discrimination. In some legal jurisdictions, homosexuals are able to marry and to receive from their employers health insurance for their partners. Despite such significant changes, large numbers of people remain upset about homosexuality. Issues of non-closeted homosexuals teaching in schools, homosexuals serving in the military, special legal protection for homosexuals, and the right to marry someone of one's own sex remain hot issues. Therefore, discrimination continues.

The social situation of homosexuals, immersed in prejudice and discrimination, is similar to that of some racial–ethnic groups. To say this is not to take a position on whether homosexuals are born with their sexual orientation; this remains an open, empirical question. Rather, this statement is meant to stress the similarity of these groups' *social* situations. Because of differences from the dominant group (in this instance, not skin color but sexual orientation), people find themselves the object of discrimination in housing, employment, and recreation. Accordingly, homosexuality remains a topic in social problems. In the selection that opens this part of the book, Nancy Naples, a sociologist who is a lesbian, reports on her experiences of emotional rejection and discrimination within her own family—and the longing she has to integrate her two disparate worlds.

In the second topic of this part, illegal drugs, the social problem is much more salient. Almost everyone is upset by the sale and use of illegal drugs. People are bothered by the violence that surrounds the illegal drug trade, the deaths from adulterated drugs, the unreported and untaxed incomes from drug dealing, and the corruption of legal agents from police and prosecutors to judges and prison guards. I say *almost* everyone, because there is another side to the problem. Some experts—a minority, to be sure, as their position is highly unpopular—say that the problem is *not* the drugs but the fact that these drugs are illegal. Making it illegal to possess drugs that are in high demand makes it highly profitable to import, manufacture, and distribute them. Take away their illegality (that is, strike down the laws that make these substances illegal) and you remove the profits to be made in dealing these drugs. When those profits dry up, so does the money that corrupts the legal system—and the violence that surrounds the drugs.

As I said, this view is unpopular. Anyone who expresses it runs the risk of being thought ill-informed, morally misguided, or perhaps a secret user of illegal drugs who wants his or her drugs to be purer, available legally, and cheaper. Yet it is the illegal nature of these drugs that underlies the huge profits to be made in importing, manufacturing, and selling them.

Whether it is the drugs or the laws against them that make drugs a social problem remains an ongoing debate among experts. People of good will find themselves on opposite sides of this debate. Some take the position that we should repeal the laws that make some drugs illegal, while others, equally concerned with solving this problem, take the position that we should increase the penalties for the manufacture, sale, or possession of these drugs and even expand these laws to other drugs that are currently legal. While people debate the merits of such contrary positions, an extensive black market has developed to deliver illegal drugs to consumers. This is the focus of the selection by Patricia and Peter Adler, a husband and wife team of sociologists who report on their study of upper-level drug dealers.

The third topic in this part takes us to a social problem about which even fewer people disagree. No one I know takes the position that anyone has the right to rape women, men, or children. I don't even see this position in the radical literature. This, then, seems to be a social problem on which almost all of us agree. Again, however, I must say *almost*, because, as you will read in the selection on this topic, some rapists defend their actions. They place the blame on their victims or on some situation outside of themselves that absolves them of blame. Diana Scully and Joseph Marolla, who explore the motivations of rapists, introduce us to a different world of reality.

In the final article we examine the criminal justice system, the agency set up to deal with the social problem of crime. It is often the case, however, that the criminal justice system becomes part of the problem. In some countries, corruption is so pervasive that people are as afraid of the police as they are of criminals. In these countries, the police are simply the *uniformed* criminals. When I lived in Mexico, I found that regular, law-abiding Mexicans were expected to pay bribes (*mordido*, "the bite") if they were stopped for a traffic violation. They simply paid the cop some amount they negotiated on the spot and then went on their way. This was an orderly system of corruption, though, as the police did not stop people arbitrarily. The driver had to be guilty of some traffic violation. If not, the citizen would report the officer.

In the United States, the corruption of the police—with payoffs and bribery—is the exception. The U.S. police are monitored well, by citizens and by internal affairs officers. It is not that police corruption is unknown in the United States, but that it is unlikely. Violence, in contrast, plagues U.S police departments. Violence among the police seems to be less than it was 50 or 75 years ago, when "third-degree" confessions (those gained through beatings) were common, but it persists. Reasons for this persistence are rooted not in some psychological personality of police officers but in the occupational subculture, as Jennifer Hunt documents in the selection that closes this part.

Reactions to Being a Lesbian

Nancy Naples

introduction ▪ ▪ ▪ ▪ ▪

A basic principle of symbolic interactionism, one of the major theoretical orientations of sociology, is that human behavior has no inherent meaning. To have meaning, any and all behavior must be interpreted. The ways we interpret behavior depend on the conceptual frameworks provided by our society, or more specifically, by the ways of thinking that we learn from the social groups to which we belong or to which we are exposed.

This simple principle—that the meaning of behavior does not come from the behavior but from its interpretation—has far-reaching implications. It lies at the root of determining which behaviors or conditions of society are considered social problems. Homosexuality, for example, is not a social problem unless it is so defined. If in one society homosexuality is defined as an alternative, acceptable form of sexual behavior, then that is the definition it has in that society. If in another society homosexuality is defined as a social problem, then that is the meaning it has in that society.

These frameworks of thought by which we evaluate human behavior, like all other social aspects of our being, are learned, not innate. Pluralistic societies, such as ours, are made up of many groups, and some of these groups have competing and incompatible definitions of reality. Groups whose definitions contrast sharply, ordinarily maintain sharp boundaries among themselves. By keeping themselves separate, the members feel more comfortable. This helps them to avoid a clash of definitions and the discomfort that people experience when they encounter conflictive worlds.

In this selection, a sociologist recounts the conflicts she experienced when her worlds collided—worlds she had tried to keep separate, but which she wanted so desperately to merge.

Thinking Critically

As you read this selection, ask yourself:

▪ Based on the experiences reported here, what reasons underlie hostility toward homosexuals?

Standing at my father's freshly dug grave holding the American flag the funeral director had just handed to me, I had the feeling I was in a bad made-for-TV movie. Since my mother was too sick with Alzheimer's to attend and I was the oldest of the six siblings, I was given the "honor." I thought it was especially odd since, given my left-leaning politics, I would be the least likely member of my family to fly the flag on the major military and other national holidays. As I watched my three sisters, two brothers, their spouses, and my fifteen nieces and nephews slowly make their way back to the cars with other members of my large "heteronormal" extended family, I at once ached to be accepted as a part of their world and longed for my "real" family.

I flashed back to the last time I stood by this graveside. It was also a somewhat dreary fall day. My brother Donald, who was the nearest in age to me (born less than a year and a half after me) and who was closest to me in other ways as well, had died in a car crash. At this time, my father decided to buy a plot in the local cemetery in their suburban community just north of New York City that would fit eight family members—less than needed if all of us wanted to be buried there, more if everyone else was buried with their own nuclear family. So now two of the plots are inhabited. I wondered who besides my mother would join them. I presumed that all the other siblings would be buried with their nuclear families. Maybe my father thought that since I was "single," namely had no "family" of my own, it would make sense for me to join them when the time came.

The significance of my singleness in the context of all the two-parent male and female families who made up the funeral procession was not lost on my two aunts. Earlier at the funeral parlor I overheard one of my aunts say to another aunt, "You know, the one I feel the most sorry for is Nancy. She has nobody." Their hushed and worried exchange amused me somewhat, although I also felt a great deal of sadness since, as many gays and lesbians, I am rich with loving and intimate friends whom I consider my "real" family. Yet in fact I was indeed alone at my father's funeral. Where was everybody?

When my brother Donald died in 1985, two of my most treasured "real" family were there for me. My lover Nina, who died in 1987 of breast cancer, and Peter, my brother-in-spirit who died of AIDS in 1996, were with me and were important witnesses over the years to the difficulties I had negotiating relationships with my family. Nina and Peter most assuredly would have been by my side had they been alive. Yet since neither Nina nor Peter were my legal or biological relations, their presence would have done little to shake the perception of my aloneness in the heteronormative world of my family.

Nina was my first female lover. We met in graduate school and I fell madly in love with her. When I "came out" to a lesbian friend about our relationship, she expressed great pleasure at my "coming to consciousness" or something to that effect. She made me feel that my more than fifteen years as a practicing heterosexual was

From Nancy Naples, "A member of the funeral." *Queer Families, Queer Politics*, Mary Bernstein and Renate Reimann, eds., pp. 21–34. 2001. Reprinted by permission of Columbia University Press.

something akin to false sexual consciousness. I resisted the revised grand narrative she attempted to impose on my sexual identity. I asserted that my relationships with men, as troubled as they were, were authentic expressions of my sexual desire. However, as I made this statement I remember feeling uncomfortable about laying claim to some authentic self.

Maybe my long heterosexual history has made it difficult for my siblings to accept my claim to a lesbian identity. Nina was incorporated into my family as my "best friend." No questions were asked about why I was no longer seeing my boyfriend Mark, nor did anyone ever ask why I never had another boyfriend after him. This seemed like an obvious question since I had dated boys since eighth grade, been married once, and lived with another man for several years. Nor did I take the initiative to explain. I just believed deep in my bones that coming out to my parents and siblings at the time would only strain my already conflict-ridden relationship with them. I did not feel that I had anything to gain from doing so and had much more to lose. I remember having drinks with Donald one Christmas eve. When he said he wanted to ask me something important about Nina, I held my breath for what I thought would be the inevitable question: Are you and Nina lovers? I remember how perversely relieved I was when he asked me a very different question: Had I ever thought about her dying?—she was in the first of several rounds of chemotherapy treatment for breast cancer.

Not surprisingly, the unspoken but palpable homophobia I felt from my family was deeply woven into my own psyche. I colluded in the silence about it while Nina was alive. However, after she died I desperately wanted them to acknowledge who she was in my life and what her loss meant for me. I remember my mother commenting on what a good friend and social worker (my previous career) I was, given my central role in Nina's care, which included taking her to doctors' appointments and chemo treatments, sleeping over at the hospital during the last months of her life, and acting as executor of her will. Not even the fact that she left me all her worldly possessions, the money from the successful lawsuit against the breast surgeon who misdiagnosed the cancer, and her precious dog, Lucy, could shake my family's construction of my "friendship" with Nina.

Given the diversity among my siblings, coming out to them was much easier as well as much harder than I anticipated. The reactions ranged from downright hostility and rejection to ambivalent acceptance (the subtle message was that as long as I did not speak too much about my life as a lesbian, they could accept it). My brother John, the most hostile one, was violently angry and said in an attacking tone that having a sister who was a lesbian was a great embarrassment for him and that he would surely lose friends because of it. My brother Paul refused to hear it at all. Lisa and Melissa, the youngest of the clan, were mildly accepting, although over the years it became clear that, as Lisa put it, they would rather "not think about it.". . .

Religion also served as a main wedge between my other siblings and me. We were brought up by a devout Catholic mother, and all of my siblings—with the exception of my sister Karen, who became a member of a conservative Christian church—continued to attend mass regularly and participate in all the Catholic sacraments. They baptized each of their children in the Catholic Church. I attended most of the baptisms but became increasingly pained by the way this ritual further marginalized me in the family. My lack of religious affiliation and unmarried status made me unfit, in my siblings' eyes, to be godparent to any of my fifteen nieces and nephews.

Regardless of their individual responses to my coming out as a lesbian, each sibling strongly warned me against telling my parents. I think they all firmly believed that, as my brother John said, "it would kill daddy"—a projection of their own fears and a threat that is frequently used to keep gays and lesbians in the closet. Of course I did not really believe that the simple statement about my sexual orientation would kill my father or mother. However, on one level I felt I had nothing to gain by taking the risk and, on another level, I figured my father already knew. After all, he was a firefighter in the West Village for twenty-five years, even helping to put out the fires of Stonewall. I rationalized that if he wanted to deal with my lesbian identity, he would bring it up himself. So we developed an unspoken contract. I would not name my relationships with women as lesbian and he would accept my girlfriends into his home, no questions asked. I thought that was fair for the most part. In retrospect, I realize that I somehow bought into the fear that my lesbian self was a shameful secret that might have the power if not to kill, at least to deeply harm others.

Over the more than ten years since I came out as a lesbian to my siblings, I tried to find a way to be a part of the family while also trying to protect myself from their rejection of my lesbian self. I maintained normalized relationships with all but my brother John and related to the other brother Paul through my sister-in-law, who seemed to be more open. I stopped celebrating Christmas and Thanksgiving with them. I would limit my visits to one or two days, staying over no more than one or two nights. Since my parents had moved from my childhood home on Staten Island to a small town just an hour and a half north of Manhattan, I could stay with my friends and drive up for the day. I did not discuss my relationships with my family and showed up unaccompanied, even when in a relationship, for most events such as christenings, weddings, baby showers, and physical and mental health crises. I sent money or gifts for birthdays and Christmas, but generally kept my worlds separate. When I moved to California, just forty miles south of my sister Lisa, I expected some challenge in balancing the different worlds, but she happened to be one of the two supportive sisters so I was not too concerned about it.

Yet in some ways the geographic closeness did pose some additional dilemmas. I recall the Christmas of 1994 right after my nephew James was born. Wanting to be helpful, I offered to make Christmas dinner for Lisa and her husband, Michael. But Melinda, my lover at the time, did not want to do the holiday thing in this way. What she wanted was a quiet dinner with me at home. Caught between my different families, I decided to make dinner for us at home and later to bring dinner to Lisa and Michael. This seemed doable at the time. The first snag, however, occurred after I described the Santa-Fe-inspired meal I planned to make. Lisa explained that her husband would not eat what Melinda and I had decided on for the main course and that since she was breast-feeding James, she would have to pass on the jalapeno corn bread. Okay, I thought, I need a fall-back plan. I decided to make two dinners, one for Melinda and me, plus one for Lisa and Michael. I made two corn breads, one with and one without the jalapenos. After completing our main course, I put a chicken in the oven to roast. Naturally, all of this took extra time so Melinda and I sat down to eat later than I intended. With the fireplace burning brightly and the candles nicely lit on the table, Melinda was anticipating a very relaxed meal. I, on the other hand, was anxious that we were running late so I could not really enjoy the meal, which was also interrupted several times while I checked the chicken. Then the phone rang. It was my sister wondering where we were. She told me that Michael loved my cooking so that he skipped lunch and was starving. I explained that things were taking a bit longer but that I would be there soon. Melinda, however, did not want to join me on the trip up to my sister's and I struggled with her for a while until the phone rang.

It was Peter wishing me a Merry Christmas. I explained the dilemma to him and complained that Melinda would not come with me to my sister's. Having met many of my family members, he not-so-diplomatically said, "Why should she? Let her stay home if she wants." It did seem such an obvious solution but I now realized how much I wanted to merge my different worlds for that holiday. So out the door I went, telling Melinda I would be back as soon as I could to share dessert with her. Arriving at my sister's, I went into a flurry of activity heating up and then serving the food. I felt like a volunteer for Meals-on-Wheels. And, of course, I could not relax with them much since I felt I needed to get back home or Melinda would start feeling abandoned. I can laugh at the scene now, but it more than symbolized the absurdity and frustration in my attempts to navigate between different family forms.

So, for the most part, my siblings did not have to see me in a relationship with a woman. My long history as a practicing heterosexual was enough to negate my claims to a lesbian identity. How could someone who was involved with men for so long really be a lesbian? I fit none of their stereotypes. My sister Karen rationalized my claim to a lesbian identity as follows: "Well, after all you had such bad relationships with men." The obvious implication was that if I met the right man, I would change my mind. Again I was faced with proving my authentic identity, this time foregrounding my lesbian self....

My siblings have all followed the traditional route. The women have taken their husbands' names and have, for the most part, placed their own careers on hold until all their children are in school. My life as an unmarried college professor of sociology and women's studies was so far from their own lives that they could hardly comprehend it except that they knew I attended a lot of conferences. Furthermore, they never wanted to learn more about it so I rarely discuss what I do with them. I do not think my experience here differs much from other academics who come from the working class. However, I fear that part of my family's reluctance to ask more about my life's work is that for them women's studies equals feminist equals lesbian—and therefore something about my lesbian world might come up. So it is best not to even start down that road.

I continued to keep my worlds relatively separate with a few moments of overlap until 1997 when my mother's Alzheimer's escalated and we had to put her in a nursing home. This precipitated more intense and regular contact with my family. This difficult event overlapped with the start of a new relationship with Sharon, a woman who said that she would not mind being integrated into my family. In fact, she said, "I'm good with lover's families. They like me." I was so pleased to finally have the opportunity to merge my worlds. I neglected to warn her, however, that I had never successfully done so before. She did wonder why I became increasingly anxious as we drove closer to my father's house a week before Christmas. I even passed the turnoff and drove her around the town and several of the surrounding towns before returning to complete the drive to the house. When we arrived at my father's home, my sister Melissa with her son and my hostile brother, John, were there.

My plan was to spend the night and go visit my other brother, Paul's family before making the four-hour drive to Sharon's home the next afternoon. However, shortly after our arrival, as I was wrapping presents in one of the bedrooms, John comes in and asks me in a very accusatory tone: "you're not going to make some big announcement that we should know about? Paul is afraid to come over because he thinks you are planning some big surprise." I was speechless with fury. I now wish I had thought of some clever rejoinder such as: "Oh, you must be watching too many episodes of *Ellen*. If so, you'd know I would only do it in an airport over a loud-speaker." But instead, I was paralyzed with anger and fear. I emerged from the room, didn't say a word to Sharon, went to play with my nephew, and left her to interact with my father and brothers—the second of whom had shown up by this time. Paul proceeded to glare at her from the kitchen. He never spoke to her. It was as though Sharon had a neon sign on her chest that read in bold scarlet letters: BE-WARE, LESBIAN IN THE HOUSE. Later she explained that she felt I had taken her to some anonymous suburban family and dropped her off where she had to introduce herself and be subjected to the critical gaze of the residents. I disappeared emotionally under the homophobic gaze of my brothers. Sharon was angry that I had left her with these "strangers." I tried to explain that I could not have anticipated my reaction since it was the first time I ever really allowed the two worlds to collide so directly. She said that I should have at least warned her that she was the first female lover that I had introduced into the family. I had mistakenly assumed that Nina was the first lover they had met. Since I came out to them after she died, I had wish-fully thought that would count and so my introducing them to Sharon should be no big deal.

The Christmas visit would send me on a very difficult soul-searching journey to confront and effectively eject much of the self-hate I had internalized. This was indeed a very good thing for me in the long run. Unfortunately, in the short run, I was to face a series of painful internal and external crises before I felt purged of some of my own internalized homophobia.

So now fast forward to the week of my father's death, which was quite unexpected. He had problems with his lungs, emphysema, a series of bouts with pneumonia, but until this last week or so no one thought his illness was life-threatening. I won't go into the unfortunate series of medical events that contributed to his death but state simply that I did not have much time to prepare for how I would balance my conflicting worlds while all this was going on.

As a consequence of the previous Christmas I had decided not to stay over with my family if I could avoid it. When I got the call from my youngest sister,

Melissa, that I better get "home" I did not even think about what it would be like to stay with my siblings during the emotionally painful days leading up to my fathers death. Since it involved coming to a collective decision about removing the breathing tube, I assumed it best to stay with them. I also thought I would be criticized harshly if I chose to stay in Manhattan with my friends Jen and Terry, whose apartment was in fact closer to the hospital. I rented a car at the airport and drove to Melissa's home in New Jersey.

The first couple of days were difficult but manageable. All six of us seemed to be getting along pretty well. I remember calling one of my aunts to give her an update and saying how good our communication was as we were debating the pros and cons of removing the ventilator. Each day I spoke to my soon-to-be ex-lover, Sharon (we were in the process of breaking up), who was trying to be supportive. She had initiated the break-up a few weeks earlier. I was resisting vehemently. I had some crazy idea in the back of my mind that this crisis might bring us closer together. Little did I know how wrong I was. Each day Sharon offered to come. I so wanted to take her up on her offer. After all, my siblings all had their spouses and children with them. I had neither lover nor friend. But I also knew, given the view of homosexuality held by my sister Karen, that it would be difficult to have my ex-lover with me, although I had no idea how messy it would become.

When Karen and her children began discussing the possibility of moving up to my father's house so they could be closer to the other cousins, I finally saw an opportunity to invite Sharon to join me. When I mentioned that she was coming, Karen threw a fit. She ranted, "How could you bring this into the family at such a time? What about the children? This is a time for the family to be together. It's not a time for us to have to deal with this." I tried to explain that Sharon was my family and that I needed the support. And, further, I was a lesbian whether my lover was with me or not. She refused to calm down and, in a huff, went up to pack her and her children's bags.

Melissa, the youngest sibling, came to me pleading, "Nancy, do something!" So I took a deep breath, went to my sister Karen and said, "Fine, I'll tell my lover not to come." I thought that this was the only way we could get through the next couple of days. I felt defeated and so alone but I was, after all, the older sister, a role that I performed uncritically for much of my life. After this incident, I could no longer stay with them. I quietly packed my bags and said that I would go stay with my friends in Manhattan. I drove away thinking what a fool I was for forgetting where I really belonged. When I arrived at the airport, I should have gone directly to Jen and Terry's apartment for they were part of my "real" family. How could I have gotten it so wrong?

To make matters worse, Sharon was profoundly offended by my decision to acquiesce to Karen's tantrum. She resented that I placed my need to keep peace in the family over our relationship and told me that if I had discussed my fear of merging the two worlds with her, she might have helped me come up with the solution that eventually I had to turn to anyway—staying with my friends in the city. Further, she painfully exclaimed, how did I think this made her feel as the one defined as a dreaded threat to the moral integrity of my family? I could not find the words to explain what it had been like for me the day before with my sisters.

This conversation took place over the phone. I had just left my father's bed in intensive care when I called her. When I asked her if she would be willing to come after my father died, she initially said, "Why should I? After all, one goes to a funeral to be supportive of the family and your family doesn't want me there." Well, I was devastated to say the least. I called another dear friend and sobbed for an hour. When I returned to my father's bedside, he was dead. So you can see now why I increasingly felt as though the bad TV-movie kept getting worse. Here I was, the only family member left at the hospital, staying through the night to be with my father so that he wouldn't be alone when he died, only to get caught up in a competing drama down the hall. I hope the guilt I feel over this dreadful episode will diminish with time.

After my father died, the nurse contacted my other siblings and they all returned to the hospital. We each said goodbye in our own way and left. It was after 2 A.M. I drove back to Manhattan, exhausted and traumatized by what had just occurred, and I collapsed into bed.

The following day I spent a long time describing the events to Jen and Terry and called some of my other close friends. I also contacted Sharon and asked her once again if she would come to be with me. She finally agreed but we did not decide whether or not she would attend the wake and funeral. I felt a bit aimless that day and thought that, even though it would have been easier to avoid it, I should drive to my father's house and together with my siblings confront the reality of his death. I also resented letting Karen's fear of my lesbian existence keep me away. I did not want her to have that much power over my choices at this point. Anyway, very quickly after I arrived it became clear to me that my lesbianism and the fear that my lover would come to the wake and funeral was the central topic of conversation. I went into the living room and all but my brother Paul were sitting there. John turned to me and said, on behalf of my siblings, that they wanted to talk to me, that they wanted to know what it was going to be like. At first I did not understand what they wanted to now. I thought that maybe since I had experienced so much loss, they wanted me to explain what it would be like at the funeral or the wake. I asked what they meant.

My sister Lisa then turned to me and said, "We want to know what it is going to be like when your lover comes. Are you two going to be touching or whatever?" At this point, I chose not to let them know that Sharon was, in fact, my ex-lover. I thought if I said, "Oh, you don't have to worry. We broke up," it would only feed into their self-righteousness and belief that there was something dangerous about lesbian love. . . .

I, of course, felt attacked, horrified and desperately alone in my father's house. I knew that my siblings only felt free to express their hatred and fear of my lesbian self because he was dead. It made me miss him even more. I got up and started packing my things to leave. Lisa came in and tried to explain why she thought it was a good thing for us to have this discussion, that my lesbianism was no longer a taboo subject, that she loved me, and that my lover would always be welcome in her house. I was appalled at the thought that there should have to be any question about this. I replied that they should deal with their own irrational fears about my sexuality but to leave me out of their conversations in the future. How unloving and hateful could a group of people be—people who are supposed to love me and want the best for me! I understood then that I was tolerated as part of the family as long as they thought I was alone, had no one to love me, to hold me, to comfort me. As I drove back to Manhattan, I understood even more deeply that the precious intimate friendships I had constructed over the years were truer expressions of "real" family than my biological family ever had been.

I missed Nina and Peter more than ever. How different the energy that surrounded Nina's last weeks and her memorial service. Right after Nina died, Peter told me that he had asked her what he was supposed to do with me—since we weren't really "friends," not like he was with Nina. I inherited Peter from Nina, and, I guess, he inherited me as well. He replaced Donald as the brother I could talk to. There was so much I couldn't tell Donald. His own homophobia made him less than the best confidante for me when Nina was first diagnosed with cancer. I am so grateful to Nina for leaving Peter to me and me to him. We were "real" family for each other, Peter with no other kinfolk, me with lots of related kin but none I felt close to or who loved me as freely. Peter was there for me from the time Nina died until his own untimely death.

I so much prefer the version of family I learned from Nina and Peter to the one my biological family embraces. For my biological family, the effort to "do family" takes the form of boundary maintenance—controlling who and what can enter for fear that the family constellation is so fragile any slight disruption will cause permanent damage. Ironically, in their efforts to patrol the borders, the illusive ties that kept me linked to my family have been irrevocably severed. . . .

Well, after my father's funeral everyone returned to his house for a luncheon. I returned with them, flag in hand, and spent my remaining hours in his house talking to my aunts and several of my favorite cousins. After they left, I wasn't sure what to do. I wandered from room to room, looked in closets, found the hardcover copy of my book that I had recently given my father, and took one of his flannel shirts off a hanger. I decided to call my ex-lover. But she was neither at her home nor her work phone. She and my friend Jen had, in fact, made it to the first night of the wake. Need I add that, not surprisingly, nothing dramatic happened. None of my siblings' fears about how our presence together might disrupt the dignified nature of the wake were realized. I did feel compelled to keep my physical distance from her. Sharon decided to leave the next morning. We both agreed that was best. But I was glad she came, even for the one night. The only surprising and touching moment occurred when my sister Melissa introduced herself to Jen and thanked her for taking care of me, her big sister.

When I decided I needed to leave my father's house after the funeral luncheon and return to my "real" family in Manhattan, I put on the flannel shirt and went looking for my brother John, who had been so outraged by my lesbian self. I gave him the flag and my book and told him I didn't expect him to read it but he could have it if he wanted. I drove away while he stood motionless in the driveway. I knew he would miss my father more than anyone since he lived the closest and had followed closely in his footsteps as a New York City firefighter. The house was recently sold and even though I never lived there, I felt the loss of the "family homestead." I also mourned the fantasy that one day I would be an accepted member of my biological family....

In the midst of my family's exaggerated performance of heteronormativity I often felt my lesbian self rendered invisible despite "coming out" to all my siblings. For much of my adult life I could not break through their denial. The events leading up to and surrounding my father's death served to thrust my lesbian self into the center of their consciousness in such a way that it symbolized a threat to the integrity of the family unit. Of course, it was my father's death that fundamentally unraveled the tightly bound net that held us together. In many ways, I was unprepared for the rejection; in other ways, I had been preparing for it most of my conscious life. The crisis led to a reevaluation of my relationship to my family as well as an opportunity to develop a new interpretive framework through which I might be able to construct a family that does not replicate the negative aspects of the earlier formation....

■■■■ ■■■ ■■■ ■■■ ■■■ ■■■ ■■■ ■■■ ■■■ ■■■ ■ ■

Upper-Level Drug Dealers and Smugglers

Patricia A. Adler and Peter Adler

introduction ■ ■ ■ ■

When an item is illegal but in high demand, a black market will develop to supply it. This principle applies to such activities as prostitution and abortion, as well as to such commodities as guns and drugs. The black markets that develop around illegal activities and substances lead to intricate relationships among those who supply an item, those who purchase it, and those whose job it is to enforce the laws against supplying that item. The sociological studies of how these black markets work are fascinating.

Despite laws that provide harsh—sometimes draconian—penalties, illegal drugs are readily available in our society. They are so plentiful that sometimes it is easier to purchase illegal drugs than to buy drugs available by legal prescription. Almost all high school and college students know where to purchase marijuana, for example, or at least they know someone who has this information. In light of the risk of arrest and incarceration because of laws that prescribe stiff penalties for importing, manufacturing, selling, or even possessing illegal drugs, who becomes a drug dealer? How do they smuggle and distribute drugs? What are their personal lives like? Do they ever quit dealing? What do they do with their money? These are some of the questions that Patricia and Peter Adler answer in their research on upper-level drug dealers.

Thinking Critically

As you read this selection, ask yourself:

■ Based on the findings reported here, why does a black market in illegal drugs flourish?

The upper echelons of the marijuana and cocaine trade constitute a world which has never before been researched and analyzed by sociologists. Importing and distributing tons of marijuana and kilos of cocaine at a time, successful operators can earn upwards of a half million dollars per year. Their traffic in these so-called "soft" drugs constitutes a potentially lucrative occupation, yet few participants manage to accumulate any substantial sums of money, and most people envision their involvement in drug trafficking as only temporary. In this study we focus on the career paths followed by members of one upper-level drug dealing and smuggling community. We discuss the various modes of entry into trafficking at these upper levels, contrasting these with entry into middle- and low-level trafficking. We then describe the pattern of shifts and oscillations these dealers and smugglers experience. Once they reach the top rungs of their occupation, they begin periodically quitting and re-entering the field, often changing their degree and type of involvement upon their return. Their careers, therefore, offer insights into the problems involved in leaving deviance....

We begin by describing where our research took place, the people and activities we studied, and the methods we used. Second, we outline the process of becoming a drug trafficker, from initial recruitment through learning the trade. Third, we look at the different types of upward mobility displayed by dealers and smugglers. Fourth, we examine the career shifts and oscillations which veteran dealers and smugglers display, outlining the multiple, conflicting forces which lure them both into and out of drug trafficking. We conclude by suggesting a variety of paths which dealers and smugglers pursue out of drug trafficking and discuss the problems inherent in leaving this deviant world.

■ ■ ■ ■ SETTING AND METHOD

We based our study in "Southwest County," one section of a large metropolitan area in southwestern California near the Mexican border. Southwest County consisted of a handful of beach towns dotting the Pacific Ocean, a location offering a strategic advantage for wholesale drug trafficking.

Southwest County smugglers obtained their marijuana in Mexico by the ton and their cocaine in Colombia, Bolivia, and Peru, purchasing between 10 and 40 kilos at a time. These drugs were imported into the United States along a variety of land, sea, and air routes by organized smuggling crews. Southwest County dealers then purchased these products and either "middled" them directly to another buyer for a small but immediate profit of approximately $2 to $5 per kilo of marijuana and $5,000 per kilo of cocaine, or engaged in "straight dealing." As opposed to middling, straight dealing usually entailed adulterating the cocaine with such "cuts" as manitol, procaine, or inositol, and then dividing the marijuana and cocaine into smaller quantities to sell them to the next-lower level of dealers. Although dealers frequently varied the amounts they bought and sold, a hierarchy of transacting levels could be roughly discerned. "Wholesale" marijuana dealers bought directly from the smugglers, purchasing anywhere from 300 to 1,000 "bricks" (averaging a kilo in weight) at a time and selling in lots of 100 to 300 bricks. "Multi-kilo" dealers, while not the smugglers' first connections, also engaged in upper-level trafficking, buying

From Patricia A. Alder and Peter Alder, "Shifts and Oscillations in Deviant Careers." *Social Problems*, 31, 2, pp. 195–199. 1983. Reprinted by permission.

between 100 to 300 bricks and selling them in 25 to 100 brick quantities. These were then purchased by middle-level dealers who filtered the marijuana through low-level and "ounce" dealers before it reached the ultimate consumer. Each time the marijuana changed hands its price increase was dependent on a number of factors: purchase cost; the distance it was transported (including such transportation costs as packaging, transportation equipment, and payments to employees); the amount of risk assumed; the quality of the marijuana; and the prevailing prices in each local drug market. Prices in the cocaine trade were much more predictable. After purchasing kilos of cocaine in South America for $10,000 each, smugglers sold them to Southwest County "pound" dealers in quantities of one to 10 kilos for $60,000 per kilo. These pound dealers usually cut the cocaine and sold pounds ($30,000) and half-pounds ($15,000) to "ounce" dealers, who in turn cut it again and sold ounces for $2,000 each to middle-level cocaine dealers known as "cut-ounce" dealers. In this fashion the drug was middled, dealt, divided and cut—sometimes as many as five or six times—until it was finally purchased by consumers as grams or half-grams.

Unlike low-level operators, the upper-level dealers and smugglers we studied pursued drug trafficking as a full-time occupation. If they were involved in other businesses, these were usually maintained to provide them with a legitimate front for security purposes. The profits to be made at the upper levels depended on an individual's style of operation, reliability, security, and the amount of product he or she consumed, About half of the 65 smugglers and dealers we observed were successful, some earning up to three-quarters of a million dollars per year. The other half continually struggled in the business, either breaking even or losing money.

Although dealers' and smugglers' business activities varied, they clustered together for business and social relations, forming a moderately well-integrated community whose members pursued a "fast" lifestyle, which emphasized intensive partying, casual sex, extensive travel, abundant drug consumption, and lavish spending on consumer goods. The exact size of Southwest County's upper-level dealing and smuggling community was impossible to estimate due to the secrecy of its members. At these levels, the drug world was quite homogeneous. Participants were predominantly white, came from middle-class backgrounds, and had little previous criminal involvement. While the dealers' and smugglers' social world contained both men and women, most of the serious business was conducted by the men, ranging in age from 25 to 40 years old.

We gained entry to Southwest County's upper-level drug community largely by accident. We had become friendly with a group of our neighbors who turned out to be heavily involved in smuggling marijuana.... Using key informants who helped us gain the trust of other members of the community, we drew upon snowball sampling techniques and a combination of overt and covert roles to widen our network of contacts. We supplemented intensive participant-observation...with unstructured, taped interviews. Throughout, we employed extensive measures to cross-check the reliability of our data, whenever possible. In all, we were able to closely observe 65 dealers and smugglers as well as numerous other drug world members, including dealers' "old ladies" (girlfriends or wives), friends, and family members.

■ ■ ■ BECOMING A DRUG TRAFFICKER

There are three routes into the upper levels of drug dealing and smuggling. First, some drug users become low-level dealers, gradually working their way up to middle-level dealing. It is rare, however, for upper-level dealers to have such meager origins. Second, there are people who enter directly into drug dealing at the middle level, usually from another occupation. Many of these do extremely well right away. Third, a number of individuals are invited into smuggling because of a special skill or character, sometimes from middle-level drug trafficking careers and other times from outside the drug world entirely. We discuss each of these in turn.

Low-Level Entry

People who began dealing at the bottom followed the classic path into dealing portrayed in the literature. They came from among the ranks of regular drug users, since, in practice, using drugs heavily and dealing for "stash" (one's personal supply) are nearly inseparable. Out of this multitude of low-level dealers, however, most abandoned the practice after they encountered their first legal or financial bust, lasting in the business for only a fairly short period. Those who sought bigger profits gradually drifted into a full-time career in drug trafficking, usually between the ages of 15 and 22. Because of this early recruitment into dealing as an occupation, low-level entrants generally developed few, if any, occupational skills other than dealing. One dealer described his early phase of involvement:

> I had dealt a limited amount of lids [ounces of marijuana] and psychedelics in my early college days without hardly taking it seriously. But after awhile something changed in me and I decided to try to work myself up. I probably was a classic case—started out buying a kilo for $150 and selling pounds for $100 each. I did that twice, then I took the money and bought two bricks, then three, then five, then seven.

This type of gradual rise through the ranks was characteristic of low-level dealers; however, few reached the upper levels of dealing from these humble beginnings. Only 20 percent of the dealers we observed in Southwest County got their start in this fashion. Two factors combined to make it less likely for low-level entrants to rise to the top. The first was psychological. People who started small, thought small; most had neither the motivation nor vision to move large quantities of drugs. The second, and more critical factor, was social. People who started at the bottom and tried to work their way up the ladder often had a hard time finding connections at the upper levels. Dealers were suspicious of new customers, preferring, for security reasons, to deal with established outlets or trusted friends. The few people who did rise through the ranks generally began dealing in another part of the country, moving to Southwest County only after they had progressed to the middle levels. These people were lured to southwestern California by its reputation within drug circles as an importation and wholesale dealing market.

Middle-Level Entry

About 75 percent of the smugglers and dealers in Southwest County entered at the middle level. Future big dealers usually jumped into transacting in substantial quantities from the outset, buying 50 kilos of "commercial" (low-grade) marijuana or one to two ounces of cocaine. One dealer explained this phenomenon:

> Someone who thinks of himself as an executive or an entrepreneur is not going to get into the dope business on a small level. The average executive just jumps right into the middle. Or else he's not going to jump.

This was the route taken by Southwest County residents with little or no previous involvement in drug trafficking. For them, entry into dealing followed the establishment of social relationships with local dealers and smugglers. (Naturally, this implies a self-selecting sample of outsiders who become accepted and trusted by these upper-level traffickers, based on their mutual interests, orientation, and values.) Through their friendships with dealers, these individuals were introduced to other members of the dealing scene and to their "fast" lifestyle. Individuals who found this lifestyle attractive became increasingly drawn to the subculture, building networks of social associations within it. Eventually, some of these people decided to participate more actively. This step was usually motivated both by money and lifestyle. One dealer recounted how he fell in with the drug world set:

> I used to be into real estate making good money. I was the only person at my firm renting to longhairs and dealing with their money. I slowly started getting friendly with them, although I didn't realize how heavy they were. I knew ways of buying real estate and putting it under fictitious names, laundering money so that it went in as hot cash and came out as spendable income. I slowly got more and more involved with this one guy until I was neglecting my real estate business and just parrying with him all the time. My spending went up but my income went down, and suddenly I had to look around for another way to make money fast. I took the money I was laundering for him, bought some bricks from another dealer friend of his, and sold them out of state before I gave him back the cash. Within six months I was turning [selling] 100 bricks at a time.

People who entered drug dealing at these middle levels were usually between the ages of 25 and 35 and had been engaged in some other occupation prior to dealing seriously. They came from a wide range of occupational backgrounds. Many drifted into the lifestyle from jobs already concentrated in the night hours, such as bartender, waiter, and nightclub bouncer. Still others came from fields where the working hours were irregular and adaptable to their special schedules, such as acting, real estate, inventing, graduate school, construction, and creative "entrepreneurship" (more aptly called hand-to-mouth survival, for many). The smallest group was tempted into the drug world from structured occupations and the professions.

Middle-level entrants had to learn the trade of drug trafficking. They received "on-the-job training" in such skills as how to establish business connections, organize profitable transactions, avoid arrest, transport illegal goods, and coordinate participants and equipment. Dealers trained on-the-job refined their knowledge and skills by learning from their mistakes. One dealer recalled how he got "burned" with inferior quality marijuana on his first major "cop" [purchase] because of his inexperience:

> I had borrowed around $7,000 from this friend to do a dope deal. I had never bought in that kind of quantity before but I knew three or four guys who I got it from. I was nervous so I got really stoned before I shopped around and I ended up being hardly able to tell about the quality. Turned out you just couldn't get high off the stuff. I ended up having to sell it below cost.

Once they had gotten in and taught themselves the trade, most middle-level entrants strove for upward mobility. About 80 percent of these Southwest County dealers jumped to the upper levels of trafficking. One dealer described her mode of escalation:

> When I started to deal I was mostly looking for a quick buck here or there, something to pay some pressing bill. I was middling 50 or 100 bricks at a time. But then I was introduced to a guy who said he would front me half a pound of coke, and if I turned it fast I could have more, and on a regular basis. Pretty soon I was turning six, seven, eight, nine, 10 pounds a week—they were passing through real fast. I was clearing at least 10 grand a month. It was too much money too fast. I didn't know what to do with it. It got ridiculous, I wasn't relating to anyone anymore, I was never home, always gone. . . . The biggest ego trip for me came when all of a sudden I turned around and was selling to the people I had been buying from. I skipped their level of doing business entirely and stage-jumped right past them.

Southwest County's social milieu, with its concentration of upper-level dealers and smugglers, thus facilitated forming connections and doing business at the upper levels of the drug world.

Smuggling

Only 10 percent of Southwest County drug smugglers were formerly upper-level dealers who made the leap to smuggling on their own; the rest were invited to become smugglers by established operators. About half of those recruited came directly from the drug world's social scene, with no prior involvement in drug dealing. This implies, like middle-level entry into dealing, both an attraction to the drug crowd and its lifestyle, and prior acquaintance with dealers and smugglers. The other half of the recruits were solicited from among the ranks of middle-level Southwest County dealers.

The complex task of importing illegal drugs required more knowledge, experience, equipment, and connections than most non-smugglers possessed. Recruits had some skill or asset which the experienced smuggler needed to put his operation together. This included piloting or navigating ability, equipment, money, or the willingness to handle drugs while they were being transported. One smuggler described some of the criteria he used to screen potential recruits for suitability as employees in smuggling crews:

Pilots are really at a premium. They burn out so fast that I have to replace them every six months to a year. But I'm also looking for people who are cool: people who will carry out their jobs according to the plan, who won't panic if the load arrives late or something goes wrong, 'cause this happens a lot. . . . And I try not to get people who've been to prison before, because they'll be more likely to take foolish risks, the kind that I don't want to have to.

Most novice smugglers were recruited and trained by a sponsor with whom they forged an apprentice-mentor relationship. Those who had been dealers previously knew the rudiments of drug trafficking. What they learned from the smuggler was how to fill a particular role in his or her highly specialized operation.

One smuggler we interviewed had a slightly larger than average crew. Ben's commercial marijuana smuggling organization was composed of seven members, not including himself. Two were drivers who transported the marijuana from the landing strip to its point of destination. One was a pilot. The dual roles of driver and co-pilot were filled by a fourth man. Another pilot, who operated both as a smuggler with his own makeshift crew and as a wholesale marijuana dealer who was supplied by Ben, flew runs for Ben when he wasn't otherwise occupied. The sixth member was Ben's enforcer and "stash house" man; he lived in the place where the marijuana was stored, distributed it to customers, and forcibly extracted payments when Ben deemed it necessary. The seventh member handled the financial and legal aspects of the business. He arranged for lawyers and bail bondsmen when needed, laundered Ben's money, and provided him with a legitimate-looking business front. Most of these family members also dealt drugs on the side, having the choice of taking their payment in cash ($10,000 for pilots; $4,000 for drivers) or in kind. Ben arranged the buying and selling connections, financed the operation, provided the heavy equipment (planes, vans, radios) and recruited, supervised, and replaced his crew.

Relationships between smugglers and their recruits were generally characterized by a benign paternalism, leading apprentices to form an enduring loyalty to their sponsor. Once established in a smuggling crew, recruits gained familiarity with the many other roles, the scope of the whole operation, and began to meet suppliers and customers. Eventually they branched out on their own. To do so, employees of a smuggling crew had to develop the expertise and connections necessary to begin running their own operations. Several things were required to make this move. Acquiring the technical knowledge of equipment, air routes, stopovers, and how to coordinate personnel was relatively easy; this could be picked up after working in a smuggling crew for six months to a year. Putting together one's own crew was more difficult because skilled employees, especially pilots, were hard to find. Most new smugglers borrowed people from other crews until they became sufficiently established to recruit and train their own personnel. Finally, connections to buy from and sell to were needed. Buyers were plentiful, but securing a foreign supplier required special breaks or networks.

Another way for employees to become heads of their own smuggling operations was to take over when their boss retired. This had the advantage of keeping the crew and style of operation intact. Various financial arrangements could be worked out for such a transfer of authority, from straight cash purchases to deals involving residual payments. One marijuana smuggler described how he acquired his operation:

> I had been Jake's main pilot for a year and, after him, I knew the most about his operation. We were really tight, and he had taken me all up and down the coast with him, meeting his connections. Naturally I knew the Mexican end of the operation and his supplier since I used to make the runs, flying down the money and picking up the dope. So when he told me he wanted to get out of the business, we made a deal. I took over the setup and gave him a residual for every run I made. I kept all the drivers, all the connections—everything the guy had—but I found myself a new pilot.

In sum, most dealers and smugglers reached the upper levels not so much as a result of their individual entrepreneurial initiative, but through the social networks they formed in the drug subculture. Their ability to remain in these strata was largely tied to the way they treated these drug world relationships.

■ ■ ■ SHIFTS AND OSCILLATIONS

We have discussed dealers and smugglers separately up to this point because they display distinct career patterns. But once individuals entered the drug trafficking field and rose to its upper levels, they became part of a social world, the Southwest County drug scene, and faced common problems and experiences. Therefore, we discuss them together from here on.

Despite the gratifications which dealers and smugglers originally derived from the easy money, material comfort, freedom, prestige, and power associated with their careers, 90 percent of those we observed decided, at some point, to quit the business. This stemmed, in part, from their initial perceptions of the career as temporary ("Hell, nobody wants to be a drug dealer all their life"). Adding to these early intentions was a process of rapid aging in the career: dealers and smugglers became increasingly aware of the restrictions and sacrifices their occupations required and tired of living the fugitive life. They thought about, talked about, and in many cases took steps toward getting out of the drug business. But as with entering, disengaging from drug trafficking was rarely an abrupt act. Instead, it more often resembled a series of transitions, or oscillations, out of and back into the business. For once out of the drug world, dealers and smugglers were rarely successful in making it in the legitimate world because they failed to cut down on their extravagant lifestyle and drug consumption. Many abandoned their efforts to reform and returned to deviance, sometimes picking up where they left off and other times shifting to a new mode of operating. For example, some shifted from dealing cocaine to dealing marijuana, some dropped to a lower level of dealing, and others shifted their role within the same group of traffickers. This series of phase-outs and re-entries, combined with career shifts, endured for years, dominating the pattern of their remaining involvement with the business. But it also represented the method by which many eventually broke away from drug trafficking, for each phase-out had the potential to be an individual's final departure.

Aging in the Career

Once recruited and established in the drug world, dealers and smugglers entered into a middle phase of aging in the career. This phase was characterized by a progressive loss of enchantment with their occupation. While novice dealers and smugglers found that participation in the drug world brought them thrills and status, the novelty gradually faded. Initial feelings of exhilaration and awe began to dull as individuals became increasingly jaded. This was the result of both an extended exposure to the mundane, everyday business aspects of drug trafficking and to an exorbitant consumption of drugs (especially cocaine). One smuggler described how he eventually came to feel:

> It was fun, those three or four years. I never worried about money or anything. But after awhile it got real boring. There was no feeling or emotion or anything about it. I wasn't even hardly relating to my old lady anymore. Everything was just one big rush.

This frenzy of overstimulation and resulting exhaustion hastened the process of "burnout" which nearly all individuals experienced. As dealers and smugglers aged in the career they became more sensitized to the extreme risks they faced. Cases of friends and associates who were arrested, imprisoned, or killed began to mount. Many individuals became convinced that continued drug trafficking would inevitably lead to arrest ("It's only a matter of time before you get caught"). While dealers and smugglers generally repressed their awareness of danger, treating it as a taken-for-granted part of their daily existence, periodic crises shattered their casual attitudes, evoking strong feelings of fear. They temporarily intensified security precautions and retreated into near-isolation until they felt the "heat" was off.

As a result of these accumulating "scares," dealers and smugglers increasingly integrated feelings of "paranoia" into their everyday lives. One dealer talked about his feelings of paranoia:

> You're always on the line. You don't lead a normal life. You're always looking over your shoulder, wondering who's at the door, having to hide everything. You learn to look behind you so well you could probably bend over and look up your ass. That's paranoia. It's a really scary, hard feeling. That's what makes you get out.

Drug world members also grew progressively weary of their exclusion from the legitimate world and the deceptions they had to manage to sustain that separation. Initially, this separation was surrounded by an alluring mystique. But as they aged in the career, this mystique became replaced by the reality of everyday boundary maintenance and the feeling of being an "expatriated citizen within one's own country." One smuggler who was contemplating quitting described the effects of this separation:

> I'm so sick of looking over my shoulder, having to sit in my house and worry about one of my non-drug world friends stopping in when I'm doing business. Do you know how awful that is? It's like leading a double life. It's ridiculous. That's what makes it not worth it. It'll be a lot less money [to quit], but a lot less pressure.

Thus, while the drug world was somewhat restricted, it was not an encapsulated community, and dealers' and smugglers' continuous involvement with the straight world made the temptation to adhere to normative standards and "go straight" omnipresent. With the occupation's novelty worn off and the "fast life" taken-for-granted, most dealers and smugglers felt that the occupation no longer resembled their early impressions of it. Once they reached the upper levels of the occupation, their experience began to change. Eventually, the rewards of trafficking no longer seemed to justify the strain and risk involved. It was at this point that the straight world's formerly dull ambiance became transformed (at least in theory) into a potential haven.

Phasing-Out

Three factors inhibited dealers and smugglers from leaving the drug world. Primary among these factors were the hedonistic and materialistic satisfactions the drug world provided. Once accustomed to earning vast quantities of money quickly and easily, individuals found it exceedingly difficult to return to the income scale of the straight world. They also were reluctant to abandon the pleasures of the "fast life" and its accompanying drugs, casual sex, and power. Second, dealers and smugglers identified with, and developed a commitment to, the occupation of drug trafficking. Their self-images were tied to that role and could not be easily disengaged. The years invested in their careers (learning the trade, forming connections, building reputations) strengthened their involvement with both the occupation and the drug community. And since their relationships were social as well as business, friendship ties bound individuals to dealing. As one dealer in the midst of struggling to phase-out explained:

> The biggest threat to me is to get caught up sitting around the house with friends that are into dealing. I'm trying to stay away from them, change my habits.

Third, dealers and smugglers hesitated to voluntarily quit the field because of the difficulty involved in finding another way to earn a living. Their years spent in illicit activity made it unlikely for any legitimate organizations to hire them. This narrowed their occupational choices considerably, leaving self-employment as one of the few remaining avenues open.

Dealers and smugglers who tried to leave the drug world generally fell into one of four patterns. The first and most frequent pattern was to postpone quitting until after they could execute one last "big deal." While the intention was sincere, individuals who chose this route rarely succeeded; the "big deal" too often remained elusive. One marijuana smuggler offered a variation of this theme:

> My plan is to make a quarter of a million dollars in four months during the prime smuggling season and get the hell out of the business.

A second pattern we observed was individuals who planned to change immediately, but never did. They announced they were quitting, yet their outward actions never varied. One dealer described his involvement with this syndrome:

> When I wake up I'd say, "Hey, I'm going to quit this cycle and just run my other busi-
> ness." But when you're dealing you constantly have people dropping by ounces and
> asking, "Can you move this?" What's your first response? Always, "Sure, for a toot."

In the third pattern of phasing-out, individuals actually suspended their dealing and smuggling activities, but did not replace them with an alternative source of
income. Such withdrawals were usually spontaneous and prompted by exhaustion,
the influence of a person from outside the drug world, or problems with the police
or other associates. These kinds of phase-outs usually lasted only until the individual's money ran out, as one dealer explained:

> I got into legal trouble with the FBI a while back and I was forced to quit dealing. Ev-
> erybody just cut me off completely, and I saw the danger in continuing, myself. But my
> high-class tastes never dwindled. Before I knew it I was in hock over $30,000. Even
> though I was hot, I was forced to get back into dealing to relieve some of my debts.

In the fourth pattern of phasing-out, dealers and smugglers tried to move into
another line of work. Alternative occupations included: (1) those they had previously pursued; (2) front businesses maintained on the side while dealing or smuggling; and (3) new occupations altogether. While some people accomplished this
transition successfully, there were problems inherent in all three alternatives.

1. Most people who tried resuming their former occupations found that these
had changed too much while they were away. In addition, they themselves had
changed: they enjoyed the self-directed freedom and spontaneity associated with
dealing and smuggling, and were unwilling to relinquish it.

2. Those who turned to their legitimate front business often found that these
businesses were unable to support them. Designed to launder rather than earn
money, most of these ventures were retail outlets with a heavy cash flow (restau-
rants, movie theaters, automobile dealerships, small stores) that had become accustomed to operating under a continuous subsidy from illegal funds. Once their drug
funding was cut off they could not survive for long.

3. Many dealers and smugglers utilized the skills and connections they had developed in the drug business to create a new occupation. They exchanged their illegal
commodity for a legal one and went into import/export, manufacturing, wholesal-
ing, or retailing other merchandise. For some, the decision to prepare a legitimate
career for their future retirement from the drug world followed an unsuccessful attempt to phase-out into a "front" business. One husband-and-wife dealing team explained how these legitimate side businesses differed from front businesses:

> We always had a little legitimate "scam" [scheme] going, like mail-order shirts, wallets,
> jewelry, and the kids were always involved in that. We made a little bit of money on
> them. Their main purpose was for a cover. But [this business] was different; right from
> the start this was going to be a legal thing to push us out of the drug business.

About 10 percent of the dealers and smugglers we observed began tapering off their
drug world involvement gradually, transferring their time and money into a selected

legitimate endeavor. They did not try to quit drug trafficking altogether until they felt confident that their legitimate business could support them. Like spontaneous phase-outs, many of these planned withdrawals into legitimate endeavors failed to generate enough money to keep individuals from being lured into the drug world.

In addition to voluntary phase-outs caused by burnout, about 40 percent of the Southwest County dealers and smugglers we observed experienced a "bustout" at some point in their careers. Forced withdrawals from dealing or smuggling were usually sudden and motivated by external factors, either financial, legal, or reputational. Financial bustouts generally occurred when dealers or smugglers were either "burned" or "ripped-off" by others, leaving them in too much debt to rebuild their base of operation. Legal bustouts followed arrest and possibly incarceration: arrested individuals were so "hot" that few of their former associates would deal with them. Reputational bustouts occurred when individuals "burned" or "ripped-off" others (regardless of whether they intended to do so) and were banned from business by their former circle of associates. One smuggler gave his opinion on the pervasive nature of forced phase-outs:

> Some people are smart enough to get out of it because they realize, physically, they have to. Others realize, monetarily, that they want to get out of this world before this world gets them. Those are the lucky, ones. Then there are the ones who have to get out because they're hot or someone else close to them is so hot that they'd better get out. But in the end when you get out of it, nobody gets out of it out of free choice; you do it because you have to.

Death, of course, was the ultimate bustout. Some pilots met this fate because of the dangerous routes they navigated (hugging mountains, treetops, other aircraft) and the sometimes ill-maintained and overloaded planes they flew. However, despite much talk of violence, few Southwest County drug traffickers died at the hands of fellow dealers.

Re-Entry

Phasing-out of the drug world was more often than not temporary. For many dealers and smugglers, it represented but another stage of their drug careers (although this may not have been their original intention), to be followed by a period of re-involvement. Depending on the individual's perspective, re-entry into the drug world could be viewed as either a comeback (from a forced withdrawal) or a relapse (from a voluntary withdrawal).

Most people forced out of drug trafficking were anxious to return. The decision to phase-out was never theirs, and the desire to get back into dealing or smuggling was based on many of the same reasons which drew them into the field originally. Coming back from financial, legal, and reputational bustouts was possible but difficult and was not always successfully accomplished. They had to reestablish contacts, rebuild their organization and fronting arrangements, and raise the operating capital to resume dealing. More difficult was the problem of overcoming the circumstances surrounding their departure. Once smugglers and dealers resumed operating, they often found their former colleagues suspicious of them. One frustrated dealer described the effects of his prison experience:

> When I first got out of the joint [jail], none of my old friends would have anything to do with me. Finally, one guy who had been my partner told me it was because everyone was suspicious of my getting out early and thought I made a deal [with police to inform on his colleagues].

Dealers and smugglers who returned from bustouts were thus informally subjected to a trial period in which they had to reestablish their trustworthiness and reliability before they could once again move in the drug world with ease.

Re-entry from voluntary withdrawal involved a more difficult decision-making process, but was easier to implement. The factors enticing individuals to re-enter the drug world were not the same as those which motivated their original entry. As we noted above, experienced dealers and smugglers often privately weighed their reasons for wanting to quit and wanting to stay in. Once they left, their images of and hopes for the straight world failed to materialize. They could not make the shift to the norms, values, and lifestyle of the straight society and could not earn a living within it. Thus, dealers and smugglers decided to re-enter the drug business for basic reasons: the material perquisites, the hedonistic gratifications, the social ties, and the fact that they had nowhere else to go.

Once this decision was made, the actual process of re-entry was relatively easy. One dealer described how the door back into dealing remained open for those who left voluntarily:

> I still see my dealer friends, I can still buy grams from them when I want to. It's the respect they have for me because I stepped out of it without being busted or burning someone. I'm coming out with a good reputation, and even though the scene is a whirlwind—people moving up, moving down, in, out—if I didn't see anybody for a year I could call them up and get right back in that day.

People who relapsed thus had little problem obtaining fronts, re-establishing their reputations, or readjusting to the scene.

Career Shifts

Dealers and smugglers who re-entered the drug world, whether from a voluntary or forced phase-out, did not always return to the same level of transacting or commodity which characterized their previous style of operation. Many individuals underwent a "career shift" and became involved in some new segment of the drug world. These shifts were sometimes lateral, as when a member of a smuggling crew took on a new specialization, switching from piloting to operating a stash house, for example. One dealer described how he utilized friendship networks upon his re-entry to shift from cocaine to marijuana trafficking:

> Before, when I was dealing cocaine, I was too caught up in using the drug and people around me were starting to go under from getting into "base" [another form of co-

caine]. That's why I got out. But now I think I've got myself together and even though I'm dealing again I'm staying away from coke. I've switched over to dealing grass. It's a whole different circle of people. I got into it through a close friend I used to know before, but I never did business with him because he did grass and I did coke.

Vertical shifts moved operators to different levels. For example, one former smuggler returned and began dealing; another top-level marijuana dealer came back to find that the smugglers he knew had disappeared and he was forced to buy in smaller quantities from other dealers.

Another type of shift relocated drug traffickers in different styles of operation. One dealer described how, after being arrested, he tightened his security measures:

I just had to cut back after I went through those changes. Hell, I'm not getting any younger and the idea of going to prison bothers me a lot more than it did 10 years ago. The risks are no longer worth it when I can have a comfortable income with less risk. So I only sell to four people now. I don't care if they buy a pound or a gram.

A former smuggler who sold his operation and lost all his money during phase-out returned as a consultant to the industry, selling his expertise to those with new money and fresh manpower:

What I've been doing lately is setting up deals for people. I've got foolproof plans for smuggling cocaine up here from Colombia; I tell them how to modify their airplanes to add on extra fuel tanks and to fit in more weed, coke, or whatever they bring up. Then I set them up with refueling points all up and down Central America, tell them how to bring it up here, what points to come in at, and what kind of receiving unit to use. Then they do it all and I get 10 percent of what they make.

Re-entry did not always involve a shift to a new niche, however. Some dealers and smugglers returned to the same circle of associates, trafficking activity, and commodity they worked with prior to their departure. Thus, drug dealers' careers often peaked early and then displayed a variety of shifts, from lateral mobility, to decline, to holding fairly steady.

A final alternative involved neither completely leaving nor remaining within the deviant world. Many individuals straddled the deviant and respectable worlds forever by continuing to dabble in drug trafficking. As a result of their experiences in the drug world they developed a deviant self-identity and a deviant *modus operandi.* They might not have wanted to bear the social and legal burden of full-time deviant work but neither were they willing to assume the perceived confines and limitations of the straight world. They therefore moved into the entrepreneurial realm, where their daily activities involved some kind of hustling or "wheeling and dealing" in an assortment of legitimate, quasi-legitimate, and deviant ventures, and where they could be their own boss. This enabled them to retain certain elements of the deviant lifestyle, and to socialize on the fringes of the drug community. For these individuals, drug dealing shifted from a primary occupation to a sideline, though they never abandoned it altogether.

■ ■ ■ LEAVING DRUG TRAFFICKING

This career pattern of oscillation into and out of active drug trafficking makes it difficult to speak of leaving drug trafficking in the sense of a final retirement. Clearly, some people succeeded in voluntarily retiring. Of these, a few managed to prepare a post-deviant career for themselves by transferring their drug money into a legitimate enterprise. A larger group was forced out of dealing and either didn't or couldn't return; their bustouts were sufficiently damaging that they never attempted re-entry, or they abandoned efforts after a series of unsuccessful attempts. But there was no way of structurally determining in advance whether an exit from the business would be temporary or permanent. The vacillations in dealers' intentions were compounded by the complexity of operating successfully in the drug world. For many, then, no phase-out could ever be definitely assessed as permanent. As long as individuals had the skills, knowledge, and connections to deal they retained the potential to re-enter the occupation at any time. Leaving drug trafficking may thus be a relative phenomenon, characterized by a trailing-off process where spurts of involvement appear with decreasing frequency and intensity.

■ ■ ■ SUMMARY

Drug dealing and smuggling careers are temporary and fraught with multiple attempts at retirement. Veteran drug traffickers quit their occupation because of the ambivalent feelings they develop toward their deviant life. As they age in the career their experience changes, shifting from a work life that is exhilarating and free to one that becomes increasingly dangerous and confining. But just as their deviant careers are temporary, so too are their retirements. Potential recruits are lured into the drug business by materialism, hedonism, glamor, and excitement. Established dealers are lured away from the deviant life and back into the mainstream by the attractions of security and social ease. Retired dealers and smugglers are lured back in by their expertise, and by their ability to make money quickly and easily. People who have been exposed to the upper levels of drug trafficking therefore find it extremely difficult to quit their deviant occupation permanently. This stems, in part, from their difficulty in moving from the illegitimate to the legitimate business sector. Even more significant is the affinity they form for their deviant values and lifestyle. Thus few, if any, of our subjects were successful in leaving deviance entirely. What dealers and smugglers intend, at the time, to be a permanent withdrawal from drug trafficking can be seen in retrospect as a pervasive occupational pattern of mid-career shifts and oscillations. More research is needed into the complex process of how people get out of deviance and enter the world of legitimate work.

■ ■

"Riding the Bull at Gilley's": Convicted Rapists Describe the Rewards of Rape

Diana Scully and Joseph Marolla

introduction ■ ■ ■ ■ ■

Being raped is certainly one of the worst things that can happen to a person. Beyond the physical injuries, which can be minimal or extensive, are the injuries to the self-concept. An intruder has violated not just one's body but also one's intimate being, slashing and wounding an essential part of one's personal identity. The consequences can be devastating: feelings that one has less moral worth than before the rape, doubts about the self-concept, of who one is in life and in relationships with others. Among the many consequences are feelings of unease, isolation, insecurity, suspicion, and lack of trust.

Why would someone commit this horrible act, inflicting such damage on someone else? Are these attackers mentally unbalanced? Are they deranged fiends? Or do they have such strong sexual desires that they have difficulty controlling themselves? Do some women unintentionally trigger the rape by their appearance or behavior? What prompted the research reported here was the question that is on so many people's minds, "Just why do men rape?"

To try to find the answer, Diana Scully and Joseph Marolla interviewed men who had been sent to prison for rape. In what was a difficult interviewing situation, these researchers established enough rapport that the men felt free to talk about their motives. From this selection, you should gain a better understanding of some of the reasons that men commit this violent act.

Thinking Critically

As you read this selection, ask yourself:

■ Based on the findings reported here, why do men rape and how do you think we can reduce the rape rate?

*O*ver the past several decades, rape has become a "medicalized" social problem. That is to say, the theories used to explain rape are predicated on psychopathological models. They have been generated from clinical experiences with small samples of rapists, often the therapists' own clients. Although these psychiatric explanations are most appropriately applied to the atypical rapist, they have been generalized to all men who rape and have come to inform the public's view on the topic.

Two assumptions are at the core of the psychopathological model: that rape is the result of idiosyncratic mental disease and that it often includes an uncontrollable sexual impulse (Scully and Marolla, 1985*)*. For example, the presumption of psychopathology is evident in the often cited work of Nicholas Groth (1979). While Groth emphasizes the nonsexual nature of rape (power, anger, sadism), he also concludes, "Rape is always a symptom of some psychological dysfunction, either temporary and transient or chronic and repetitive" (Groth, 1979:5). Thus, in the psychopathological view, rapists lack the ability to control their behavior; they are "sick" individuals from the "lunatic fringe" of society.

In contradiction to this model, empirical research has repeatedly failed to find a consistent pattern of personality type or character disorder that reliably discriminates rapists from other groups of men (Fisher and Rivlin, 1971; Hammer and Jacks, 1955; Rada, 1978). Indeed, other research has found that fewer than 5 percent of men were psychotic when they raped (Abel et al., 1980).

Evidence indicates that rape is not a behavior confined to a few "sick" men, but many men have the attitudes and beliefs necessary to commit a sexually aggressive act. In research conducted at a midwestern university, Koss and her coworkers reported that 85 percent of men defined as highly sexually aggressive had victimized women with whom they were romantically involved (Koss and Leonard, 1984). A survey quoted in *The Chronicle of Higher Education* estimates that more than 20 percent of college women are the victims of rape and attempted rape (Meyer, 1984). These findings mirror research published several decades earlier which also concluded that sexual aggression was commonplace in dating relationships (Kanin, 1957, 1965, 1967, 1969; Kirkpatrick and Kanin, 1957). In their study of 53 college males, Malamuth, Haber, and Feshback (1980) found that 51 percent indicated a likelihood that they, themselves, would rape if assured of not being punished.

In addition, the frequency of rape in the United States makes it unlikely that responsibility rests solely with a small lunatic fringe of psychopathic men. Johnson (1980), calculating the lifetime risk of rape to girls and women aged twelve and over, makes a similar observation. Using Law Enforcement Assistance Association and Bureau of Census Crime Victimization Studies, he calculated that, excluding sexual abuse in marriage and assuming equal risk to all women, 20 to 30 percent of girls now 12 years old will suffer a violent sexual attack during the remainder of their lives. Interestingly, the lack of empirical support for the psychopathological model has not resulted in the de-medicalization of rape, nor does it appear to have

From Diana Scully and Joseph Marolla, "'Riding the Bull at Gilley's': Convicted Rapists Describe the Rewards of Rape." *Social Problems, 32*, 3, pp. 251–263. 1985. Reprinted by permission.

diminished the belief that rapists are "sick" aberrations in their own culture. This is significant because of the implications and consequences of the model.

A central assumption in the psychopathological model is that male sexual aggression is unusual or strange. This assumption removes rape from the realm of the everyday or "normal" world and places it in the category of "special" or "sick" behavior. As a consequence, men who rape are cast in the role of outsider and a connection with normative male behavior is avoided. Since, in this view, the source of the behavior is thought to be within the psychology of the individual, attention is diverted away from culture or social structure as contributing factors. Thus, the psychopathological model ignores evidence which links sexual aggression to environmental variables and which suggests that rape, like all behavior, is learned.

▪ ▪ ▪ CULTURAL FACTORS IN RAPE

Culture is a factor in rape, but the precise nature of the relationship between culture and sexual violence remains a topic of discussion. Ethnographic data from pre-industrial societies show the existence of rape-free cultures (Broude and Green, 1976; Sanday, 1979), although explanations for the phenomenon differ. Sanday (1979) relates sexual violence to contempt for female qualities and suggests that rape is part of a culture of violence and an expression of male dominance. In contrast, Blumberg (1979) argues that in pre-industrial societies women are more likely to lack important life options and to be physically and politically oppressed where they lack economic power relative to men. That is, in pre-industrial societies relative economic power enables women to win some immunity from men's use of force against them.

Among modern societies, the frequency of rape varies dramatically, and the United States is among the most rape-prone of all. In 1980, for example, the rate of reported rape and attempted rape for the United States was eighteen times higher than the corresponding rate for England and Wales (West, 1983). Spurred by the Women's Movement, feminists have generated an impressive body of theory regarding the cultural etiology of rape in the United States. Representative of the feminist view, Griffin (1971) called rape "The All American Crime."

The feminist perspective views rape as an act of violence and social control which functions to "keep women in their place" (Brownmiller, 1975; Kasinsky, 1975; Russell, 1975). Feminists see rape as an extension of normative male behavior, the result of conformity or overconformity to the values and prerogatives which define the traditional male sex role. That is, traditional socialization encourages males to associate power, dominance, strength, virility, and superiority with masculinity, and submissiveness, passivity, weakness, and inferiority with femininity. Furthermore, males are taught to have expectations about their level of sexual needs and expectations for corresponding female accessibility which function to justify forcing sexual access. The justification for forced sexual access is buttressed by legal, social, and religious definitions of women as male property and sex as an exchange of goods (Bart, 1979). Socialization prepares women to be "legitimate" victims and men to be potential offenders (Weis and Borges, 1973). Herman (1984) concludes that the United States is a rape culture because both genders are socialized to regard male aggression as a natural and normal part of sexual intercourse.

Feminists view pornography as an important element in a larger system of sexual violence; they see pornography as an expression of a rape-prone culture where women are seen as objects available for use by men (Morgan, 1980; Wheeler, 1985). Based on his content analysis of 428 "adults only" books, Smith (1976) makes a similar observation. He notes that, not only is rape presented as part of normal male/female sexual relations, but the woman, despite her terror, is always depicted as sexually aroused to the point of cooperation. In the end, she is ashamed but physically gratified. The message—women desire and enjoy rape—has more potential for damage than the image of the violence *per se*.

The fusion of these themes—sex as an impersonal act, the victim's uncontrollable orgasm, and the violent infliction of pain—is commonplace in the actual accounts of rapists. Scully and Marolla (1984) demonstrated that many convicted rapists denied their crime and attempted to justify their rapes by arguing that their victim enjoyed herself despite the use of a weapon and the infliction of serious injuries, or even death. In fact, many argued, they had been instrumental in making *her* fantasy come true.

The images projected in pornography contribute to a vocabulary of motive which trivializes and neutralizes rape and which might lessen the internal controls that otherwise would prevent sexually aggressive behavior. Men who rape use this culturally acquired vocabulary to justify their sexual violence.

Another consequence of the application of psychopathology to rape is that it leads one to view sexual violence as a special type of crime in which the motivations are subconscious and uncontrollable rather than overt and deliberate as with other criminal behavior. Black (1983) offers an approach to the analysis of criminal and/or violent behavior which, when applied to rape, avoids this bias. Black suggests that it is theoretically useful to ignore that crime is criminal in order to discover what such behavior has in common with other kinds of conduct. From his perspective, much of the crime in modern societies, as in pre-industrial societies, can be interpreted as a form of "self help" in which the actor is expressing a grievance through aggression and violence. From the actor's perspective, the victim is deviant and his own behavior is a form of social control in which the objective may be conflict management, punishment, or revenge. For example, in societies where women are considered the property of men, rape is sometimes used as a means of avenging the victim's husband or father (Black, 1983). In some cultures rape is used as a form of punishment. Such was the tradition among the puritanical, patriarchal Cheyenne, where men were valued for their ability as warriors. It was Cheyenne custom that a wife suspected of being unfaithful could be "put on the prairie" by her husband. Military confreres then were invited to "feast" on the prairie (Hoebel, 1954; Llewellyn and Hoebel, 1941). The ensuing mass rape was a husband's method of punishing his wife.

Black's (1983) approach is helpful in understanding rape because it forces one to examine the goals that some men have learned to achieve through sexually violent means. Thus, one approach to understanding why some men rape is to shift attention from individual psychopathology to the important question of what rapists gain from sexual aggression and violence in a culture seemingly prone to rape. In this paper, we address this question using data from interviews conducted with 114 convicted, incarcerated rapists.

■ ■ ■ METHODS

Sample

During 1980 and 1981 we interviewed 114 convicted rapists. All of the men had been convicted of the rape or attempted rape of an adult woman and subsequently incarcerated in a Virginia prison. Men convicted of other types of sexual offense were omitted from the sample.

In addition to their convictions for rape, 39 percent of the men also had convictions for burglary or robbery, 29 percent for abduction, 25 percent for sodomy, 11 percent for first or second degree murder, and 12 percent had been convicted of more than one rape. The majority of the men had previous criminal histories, but only 23 percent had a record of past sex offenses and only 26 percent had a history of emotional problems. Their sentences for rape and accompanying crimes ranged from ten years to seven life sentences plus 380 years for one man. Twenty-two percent of the rapists were serving at least one life sentence. Forty-six percent of the rapists were white, 54 percent black. In age, they ranged from 18 to 60 years, but the majority were between 18 and 35 years. Based on a statistical profile of felons in all Virginia prisons prepared by the Virginia Department of Corrections, it appears that this sample of rapists was disproportionately white and, at the time of the research, somewhat better educated and younger than the average inmate.

All participants in this research were volunteers. In constructing the sample, age, education, race, severity of current offense, and past criminal record were balanced within the limitations imposed by the characteristics of the volunteer pool. Obviously the sample was not random and thus may not be typical of all rapists, imprisoned or otherwise.

■ ■ ■ HOW OFFENDERS VIEW THE REWARDS OF RAPE

Revenge and Punishment

As noted earlier, Black's (1983) perspective suggests that a rapist might see his act as a legitimized form of revenge or punishment. Additionally, he asserts that the idea of "collective liability" accounts for much seemingly random violence. "Collective liability" suggests that all people in a particular category are held accountable for the conduct of each of their counterparts. Thus, the victim of a violent act may merely represent the category of individual being punished.

These factors—revenge, punishment, and the collective liability of women—can be used to explain a number of rapes in our research. Several cases will illustrate ways in which these factors combined in various types of rape. Revenge-rapes were among the most brutal and often included beatings, serious injuries, and even murder.

Typically, revenge-rapes included the element of collective liability. That is, from the rapist's perspective, the victim was a substitute for the woman on whom he wanted revenge. As explained elsewhere (Scully and Marolla, 1984), an upsetting event, involving a woman, preceded a significant number of rapes. When they raped, these men were angry because of a perceived indiscretion, typically related to a rigid, moralistic standard of sexual conduct, which they required from "their woman" but, in most cases, did not abide by themselves. Over and over these rapists talked about using rape "to get even" with their wives or some other significant woman. Typical is a young man who, prior to the rape, had a violent argument with his wife over what eventually proved to be her misdiagnosed case of venereal disease. She assumed the disease had been contracted through him, an accusation that infuriated him. After fighting with his wife, he explained that he drove around "thinking about hurting someone." He encountered his victim, a stranger, on the road where her car had broken down. It appears she accepted his offered ride because her car was out of commission. When she realized that rape was pending, she called him "a son of a bitch," and attempted to resist. He reported flying into a rage and beating her, and he confided,

> I have never felt that much anger before. If she had resisted, I would have killed her. . . . The rape was for revenge. I didn't have an orgasm. She was there to get my hostile feelings off on.

Although not the most common form of revenge-rape, sexual assault continues to be used in retaliation against the victim's male partner. In one such case, the offender, angry because the victim's husband owed him money, went to the victim's home to collect. He confided, "I was going to get it one way or another." Finding the victim alone, he explained, they started to argue about the money and,

> I grabbed her and started beating the hell out of her. Then I committed the act. I knew what I was doing. I was mad. I could have stopped, but I didn't. I did it to get even with her and her husband.

Griffin (1971) points out that when women are viewed as commodities, "In raping another man's woman, a man may aggrandize his own manhood and concurrently reduce that of the other man" (p. 33).

Revenge-rapes often contained an element of punishment. In some cases, while the victim was not the initial object of the revenge, the intent was to punish her because of something that transpired after the decision to rape had been made or during the course of the rape itself. This was the case with a young man whose wife had recently left him. Although they were in the process of reconciliation, he remained angry and upset over the separation. The night of the rape, he met the victim and her friend in a bar where he had gone to watch a fight on TV. The two women apparently accepted a ride from him, but after taking her friend home, he drove the victim to his apartment. At his apartment, he found a note from his wife indicating she had stopped by to watch the fight with him. This increased his anger because he preferred his wife's company. Inside his apartment, the victim allegedly remarked that she was sexually interested in his dog, which, he reported, put him in a rage. In the ensuing attack, he raped and pistol-whipped the victim. Then he forced a vacuum cleaner hose, switched on suction, into her vagina and bit her breast, severing the nipple. He stated:

> I hated at the time, but I don't know if it was her (the victim). (Who could it have been?) My wife? Even though we were getting back together. I still didn't trust her.

During his interview, it became clear that this offender, like many of the men, believed men have the right to discipline and punish women. In fact, he argued that most of the men he knew would also have beaten the victim because "that kind of thing (referring to the dog) is not acceptable among my friends."

Finally, in some rapes, both revenge and punishment were directed at victims because they represented women whom these offenders perceived as collectively responsible and liable for their problems. Rape was used "to put women in their place" and as a method of proving their "manhood" by displaying dominance over a female. For example, one multiple rapist believed his actions were related to the feeling that women thought they were better than he was.

> Rape was a feeling of total dominance. Before the rapes, I would always get a feeling of power and anger. I would degrade women so I could feel there was a person of less worth than me.

Another, especially brutal, case involved a young man from an upper middle class background, who spilled out his story in a seven-hour interview conducted in his solitary confinement cell. He described himself as tremendously angry, at the time, with his girlfriend, who he believed was involved with him in a "storybook romance," and from whom he expected complete fidelity. When she went away to college and became involved with another man, his revenge lasted eighteen months and involved the rape and murder of five women, all strangers who lived in his community. Explaining his rape-murders, he stated:

> I wanted to take my anger and frustration out on a stranger, to be in control, to do what I wanted to do. I wanted to use and abuse someone as I felt used and abused. I was killing my girl friend. During the rapes and murders, I would think about my girl friend. I hated the victims because they probably messed men over. I hated women because they were deceitful and I was getting revenge for what happened to me.

An Added Bonus

Burglary and robbery commonly accompany rape. Among our sample, 39 percent of the rapists had also been convicted of one or the other of these crimes committed in connection with rape. In some cases, the original intent was rape, and robbery was an afterthought. However, a number of men indicated that the reverse was true in their situation. That is, the decision to rape was made subsequent to their original intent, which was burglary or robbery.

This was the case with a young offender who stated that he originally intended only to rob the store in which the victim happened to be working. He explained that when he found the victim alone,

> I decided to rape her to prove I had guts. She was just there. It could have been anybody.

Similarly, another offender indicated that he initially broke into his victim's home to burglarize it. When he discovered the victim asleep, he decided to seize the opportunity "to satisfy an urge to go to bed with a white woman, to see if it was different." Indeed a number of men indicated that the decision to rape had been made after they realized they were in control of the situation. This was also true of an unemployed offender who confided that his practice was to steal whenever he needed money. On the day of the rape, he drove to a local supermarket and paced the parking lot, "staking out the situation." His pregnant victim was the first person to come along alone and "she was an easy target." Threatening her with a knife, he reported the victim as saying she would do anything if he didn't harm her. At that point, he decided to force her to drive to a deserted area, where he raped her. He explained:

> I wasn't thinking about sex. But when she said she would do anything not to get hurt, probably because she was pregnant, I thought, "why not?"

The attitude of these men toward rape was similar to their attitude toward burglary and robbery. Quite simply, if the situation is right, "why not?" From the perspective of these rapists, rape was just another part of the crime—an added bonus.

Sexual Access

In an effort to change public attitudes that are damaging to the victims of rape and to reform laws seemingly premised on the assumption that women both ask for and enjoy rape, many writers emphasize the violent and aggressive character of rape. Often such arguments appear to discount the part that sex plays in the crime. The data clearly indicate that from the rapists' point of view, rape is in part sexually motivated. Indeed, it is the sexual aspect of rape that distinguishes it from other forms of assault.

Rape as a means of sexual access also shows the deliberate nature of this crime. When a woman is unwilling or seems unavailable for sex, the rapist can seize what isn't volunteered. In discussing his decision to rape, one man made this clear.

> …a real fox, beautiful shape. She was a beautiful woman and I wanted to see what she had.

The attitude that sex is a male entitlement suggests that when a woman says "no," rape is a suitable method of conquering the "offending" object. If, for example, a woman is picked up at a party or in a bar or while hitchhiking (behavior which a number of the rapists saw as a signal of sexual availability), and the woman later resists sexual advances, rape is presumed to be justified. The same justification operates in what is popularly called "date rape." The belief that sex was their just compensation compelled a number of rapists to insist they had not raped. Such was the case of an offender who raped and seriously beat his victim when, on their second date, she refused his sexual advances.

> I think I was really pissed off at her because it didn't go as planned. I could have been with someone else. She led me on but wouldn't deliver.... I have a male ego that must be fed.

The purpose of such rapes was conquest, to seize what was not offered.

Despite the cultural belief that young women are the most sexually desirable, several rapes involved the deliberate choice of a victim relatively older than the assailant. Since the rapists were themselves rather young (26 to 30 years of age on the average), they were expressing a preference for sexually experienced, rather than elderly, women. Men who chose victims older than themselves often said they did so because they believed that sexually experienced women were more desirable partners. They raped because they also believed that these women would not be sexually attracted to them.

Finally, sexual access emerged as a factor in the accounts of black men who consciously chose to rape white women. The majority of rapes in the United States are intraracial. However, for the past 20 years, according to national data based on reported rapes as well as victimization studies, which include unreported rapes, the rate of black on white (B/W) rape has significantly exceeded the rate of white on black (W/B) rape (La Free, 1982). Indeed, we may be experiencing a historical anomaly, since, as Brownmiller (1975) has documented, white men have freely raped women of color in the past. The current structure of interracial rape, however, reflects contemporary racism and race relations in several ways.

First, the status of black women in the United States today is relatively lower than the status of white women. Further, prejudice, segregation, and other factors continue to militate against interracial coupling. Thus, the desire for sexual access to higher status, unavailable women, an important function in B/W rape, does not motivate white men to rape black women. Equally important, demographic and geographic barriers interact to lower the incidence of W/B rape. Segregation as well as the poverty expected in black neighborhoods undoubtedly discourages many whites from choosing such areas as a target for housebreaking or robbery. Thus, the number of rapes that would occur in conjunction with these crimes is reduced.

Reflecting in part the standards of sexual desirability set by the dominant white society, a number of black rapists indicated they had been curious about white women. Blocked by racial barriers from legitimate sexual relations with white women, they raped to gain access to them. They described raping white women as "the ultimate experience" and "high status among my friends. It gave me a feeling of status, power, macho." For another man, raping a white woman had a special appeal because it violated a "known taboo," making it more dangerous, and thus more exciting to him, than raping a black woman.

Impersonal Sex and Power

The idea that rape is an impersonal rather than an intimate or mutual experience appealed to a number of rapists, some of whom suggested it was their preferred form of sex. The fact that rape allowed them to control rather than care encouraged some to act on this preference. For example, one man explained,

> Rape gave me the power to do what I wanted to do without feeling I had to please a partner or respond to a partner. I felt in control, dominant. Rape was the ability to have sex without caring about the woman's response. I was totally dominant.

Another rapist commented:

> Seeing them laying there helpless gave me the confidence that I could do it. . . . With rape, I felt totally in charge. I'm bashful, timid. When a woman wanted to give in normal sex, I was intimidated. In the rapes, I was totally in command, she totally submissive.

During his interview, another rapist confided that he had been fantasizing about rape for several weeks before committing his offense. His belief was that it would be "an exciting experience—a new high." Most appealing to him was the idea that he could make his victim "do it all for him" and that he would be in control. He fantasized that she "would submit totally and that I could have anything I wanted." Eventually, he decided to act because his older brother told him, "forced sex is great, I wouldn't get caught and, besides, women love it." Though now he admits to his crime, he continues to believe his victim "enjoyed it." Perhaps we should note here that the appeal of impersonal sex is not limited to convicted rapists. The amount of male sexual activity that occurs in homosexual meeting places as well as the widespread use of prostitutes suggests that avoidance of intimacy appeals to a large segment of the male population. Through rape men can experience power and avoid the emotions related to intimacy and tenderness. Further, the popularity of violent pornography suggests that a wide variety of men in this culture have learned to be aroused by sex fused with violence (Smith, 1976). Consistent with this observation, experimental research conducted by Malamuth et al. (1980) demonstrates that men are aroused by images that depict women as orgasmic under conditions of violence and pain. They found that, for female students, arousal was high when the victim experienced an orgasm and *no* pain, whereas male students were highly aroused when the victim experienced an orgasm *and* pain. On the basis of their results, Malamuth et al. suggest that forcing a woman to climax despite her pain and abhorrence of the assailant makes the rapist feel powerful; he has gained control over the only source of power historically associated with women, their bodies. In the final analysis, dominance was the objective of most rapists.

Recreation and Adventure

Among gang rapists, most of whom were in their late teens or early twenties when convicted, rape represented recreation and adventure, another form of delinquent activity. Part of rape's appeal was the sense of male camaraderie engendered by participating collectively in a dangerous activity. To prove one's self capable of "performing" under these circumstances was a substantial challenge and also a source of reward. One gang rapist articulated this feeling very clearly.

> We felt powerful; we were in control. I wanted sex, and there was peer pressure. She wasn't like a person, no personality, just domination on my part. Just to show I could do it—you know, macho.

Our research revealed several forms of gang rape. A common pattern was hitchhike-abduction for the purpose of having sex. Though the intent was rape, a number of men did not view it as such because they were convinced that women hitchhiked primarily to signal sexual availability and only secondarily as a form of transportation. In these cases, the unsuspecting victim was driven to a deserted area, raped, and in the majority of cases physically injured. Sometimes, the victim was not hitchhiking; she was abducted at knife or gun point from the street, usually at night. Some of these men did not view this type of attack as rape either, because they believed a woman walking alone at night to be a prostitute. In addition, they were often convinced "she enjoyed it."

"Gang date" rape was another popular variation. In this pattern, one member of the gang would make a date with the victim. Then, without her knowledge or consent, she would be driven to a predetermined location and forcibly raped by each member of the group. One young man revealed this practice was so much a part of his group's recreational routine, they had rented a house for the purpose. From his perspective, the rape was justified because "usually the girl had a bad reputation, or we knew it was what she liked."

During his interview, another offender confessed to participating in twenty or thirty such "gang date" rapes because his driver's license had been revoked, making it difficult for him to "get girls." Sixty percent of the time, he claimed, "they were girls known to do this kind of thing," but "frequently, the girls didn't want to have sex with all of us." In such cases, he said, "It might start out as rape, but, then, they (the women) would quiet down and none ever reported it to the police." He was convicted for a gang rape, which he described as "the ultimate thing I ever did," because unlike his other rapes, the victim, in this case, was a stranger whom the group abducted as she walked home from the library. He felt the group's past experience with "gang date" rape had prepared them for this crime in which the victim was blindfolded and driven to the mountains where, though it was winter, she was forced to remove her clothing. Lying on the snow, she was raped by each of the four men several times before being abandoned near a farm house. This young man continued to believe that if he had spent the night with her, rather than abandoning her, she would not have reported it to the police.

Solitary rapists also used terms like "exciting," "a challenge," "an adventure" to describe their feelings about rape. Like the gang rapists, these men found the element of danger made rape all the more exciting. Typifying this attitude was one man who described his rape as intentional. He reported:

> It was exciting to get away with it (rape), just being able to beat the system, not women. It was like doing something illegal and getting away with it.

Another rapist confided that for him "rape was just more exciting and compelling" than a normal sexual encounter because it involved forcing a stranger. A multiple rapist asserted, "It was the excitement and fear and the drama that made rape a big kick."

Feeling Good

When the men were asked to recall their feelings immediately following the rape, only eight percent indicated that guilt or feeling bad was part of their emotional response. The majority said they felt good, relieved, or simply nothing at all. Some indicated they had been afraid of being caught or felt sorry for themselves. Only two men out of 114 expressed any concern or feeling for the victim. Feeling good or nothing at all about raping women is not an aberration limited to men in prison. Smithyman (1978), in his study of "undetected rapists"—rapists outside of prison—found that raping women had no impact on their lives, nor did it have a negative effect on their self-image.

Significantly, a number of men volunteered the information that raping had a positive impact on their feelings. For some, the satisfaction was in revenge. For example, the man who had raped and murdered five women:

> It seems like so much bitterness and tension had built up, and this released it. I felt like I had just climbed a mountain and now I could look back.

Another offender characterized rape as habit forming: "Rape is like smoking. You can't stop once you start." Finally, one man expressed the sentiments of many rapists when he stated,

> After rape, I always felt like I had just conquered something, like I had just ridden the bull at Gilley's.

■ ■ ■ CONCLUSIONS

This paper has explored rape from the perspective of a group of convicted, incarcerated rapists. The purpose was to discover how these men viewed sexual violence and what they gained from their behavior.

We found that rape was frequently a means of revenge and punishment. Implicit in revenge-rapes was the notion that women were collectively liable for the rapists' problems. In some cases, victims were substitutes for significant women on whom the men desired to take revenge. In other cases, victims were thought to represent all women, and rape was used to punish, humiliate, and "put them in their place." In both cases women were seen as a class, a category, not as individuals. For some men, rape was almost an afterthought, a bonus added to burglary or robbery. Other men gained access to sexually unavailable or unwilling women through rape. For this group of men, rape was a fantasy come true, a particularly exciting form of impersonal sex which enabled them to dominate and control women, by exercising a singularly male form of power. These rapists talked of the pleasures of raping—how for them it was a challenge, an adventure, a dangerous and "ultimate" experience. Rape made them feel good and, in some cases, even elevated their self-image.

The pleasure these men derived from raping reveals the extreme to which they objectified women. Women were seen as sexual commodities to be used or conquered rather than as human beings with rights and feelings. One young man expressed the extreme of the contemptful view of women when he confided to the female researcher.

> Rape is a man's right. If a woman doesn't want to give it, the man should take it. Women have no right to say no. Women are made to have sex. It's all they are good for. Some women would rather take a beating, but they always give in; it's what they are for.

This man murdered his victim because she wouldn't "give in."

Undoubtedly, some rapes, like some of all crimes, are idiopathic [caused by a condition of unknown origin]. However, it is not necessary to resort to pathological motives to account for all rape or other acts of sexual violence. Indeed, we find that men who rape have something to teach us about the cultural roots of sexual aggression. They force us to acknowledge that rape is more than an idiosyncratic act committed by a few "sick" men. Rather, rape can be viewed as the end point in a continuum of sexually aggressive behaviors that reward men and victimize women. In the way that motives for committing any criminal act can be rationally determined, reasons for rape can also be determined. Our data demonstrate that some men rape because they have learned that in this culture, sexual violence is rewarding. Significantly, the overwhelming majority of these rapists indicated they never thought they would go to prison for what they did. Some did not fear imprisonment because they did not define their behavior as rape. Others knew that women frequently do not report rape and of those cases that are reported, conviction rates are low, and therefore they felt secure. These men perceived rape as a rewarding, low-risk act. Understanding that otherwise normal men can and do rape is critical to the development of strategies for prevention.

We are left with the fact that all men do not rape. In view of the apparent rewards and cultural supports for rape, it is important to ask why some men do not rape. Hirschi (1969) makes a similar observation about delinquency. He argues that the key question is not "Why do they do it?" but rather "Why don't we do it?" (p. 34). Likewise, we may be seeking an answer to the wrong question about sexual assault of women. Instead of asking men who rape "Why?" perhaps we should be asking men who don't "Why not?"

■ ■ ■ ■ **REFERENCES**

Abel, G., J. Becker, and L. Skinner. (1980). "Aggressive Behavior and Sex." *Psychiatric Clinics of North America 3:* 133–151.

Bart, P. (1979). "Rape as a Paradigm of Sexism in Society—Victimization and Its Discontents." *Women's Studies International Quarterly 2:* 347–357.

Black, D. (1983). "Crimes as Social Control." *American Sociological Review* 48: 34–45.

Blumberg, R. L. (1979). "A Paradigm for Predicting the Position of Women: Policy Implications and Problems." In J. Lipman-Blumen and J. Bernard (Eds.), Sex *Roles and Social Policy.* London: Sage Studies in International Sociology, pp. 113–142.

Broude, G., and S. Green (1976). "Cross-Cultural Codes on Twenty Sexual Attitudes and Practices." *Ethnology* 15: 409–428.

Brownmiller, S. (1975). *Against Our Will.* New York: Simon & Schuster.

Fisher, G., and E. Rivlin. (1971). "Psychological Needs of Rapists." *British Journal of Criminology* 11: 182–185.

Griffin, S. (1971, September). "Rape: The All American Crime." *Ramparts* 10: 26–35.

Groth, N. (1979). *Men Who Rape.* New York: Plenum Press.

Hammer, E., and I. Jacks. (1955). "A Study of Rorschach Flexnor and Extensor Human Movements." *Journal of Clinical Psychology* 11: 63–67.

Herman, D. (1984). "The Rape Culture." In J. Freeman (Ed.), *Women: A Feminist Perspective.* Palo Alto, CA: Mayfield, pp. 20–39.

Hirschi, T. (1969). *Causes of Delinquency.* Berkeley: University of California Press.

Hoebel, E. A. (1954). *The Law of Primitive Man.* Boston: Harvard University Press.

Johnson, A. G. (1980). "On the Prevalence of Rape in the United States." *Signs* 6: 136–146.

Kanin, E. (1957). "Male Aggression in Dating-Courtship Relations." *American Journal of Sociology* 63: 197–204.

Kanin, E. (1965). "Male Sex Aggression and Three Psychiatric Hypotheses," *Journal of Sex Research* 1: 227–229.

Kanin, E. (1967). "Reference Groups and Sex Conduct Norm Violation," *Sociological Quarterly* 8: 495–504.

Kanin, E. (1969). "Selected Dyadic Aspects of Male Sex Aggression." *Journal of Research* 5: 12–28.

Kasinsky, R. (1975, September). "Rape: A Normal Act?" *Canadian Forum:* 18.

Kirkpatrick, C., and E. Kanin (1957). "Male Sex Aggression on a University Campus," *American Sociological Review* 22: 52–58.

Koss, M. P., and K. E. Leonard. (1984). "Sexually Aggressive Men: Empirical Findings and Theoretical Implications," In N. M. Malamuth and E. Donnerstein (Eds.), *Pornography and Sexual Aggression.* New York: Academic Press, pp. 213–232.

LaFree, G. (1982). "Male Power and Female Victimization: Towards a Theory of Interracial Rape." *American Journal of Sociology* 88, 311–328.

Llewellyn, K. N., and E. A. Hoebel. (1941). *The Cheyenne Way: Conflict and Case Law in Primitive Jurisprudence.* Norman: University of Oklahoma Press.

Malamuth, N., S. Haber, and S. Feshback. (1980). "Testing Hypotheses Regarding Rape: Exposure to Sexual Violence, Sex Difference, and the 'Normality' Rapists." *Journal of Research in Personality* 14: 121–137.

Meyer, T. J. (1984, December 5). "'Date Rape': A Serious Problem That Few Talk About." *Chronicle of Higher Education.*

Morgan, R. (1980). "Theory and Practice: Pornography and Rape." In L. Lede (Ed.), *Take Back the Night: Women on Pornography.* New York: William M. Morrow, pp. 134–140.

Rada, R. (1978). *Clinical Aspects of Rape,* New York, Grune & Stratton.

Russell, D. (1975). *The Politics of Rape.* New York: Stein & Day.

Sanday, P. R. (1979). *The Socio-Cultural Context of Rape.* Washington, DC: U.S. Department of Commerce, National Technical Information Service.

Scully, D., and J. Marolla. (1984). "Convicted Rapists' Vocabulary of Motive: Excuses and Justifications." *Social Problems* 31: 530–544.

Scully, D., and J. Marolla. (1985). "Rape and Psychiatric Vocabulary of Motive: Alternative Perspectives." In A. W. Burgess (Ed.), *Rape and Sexual Assault: A Research Handbook.* New York: Garland Publishing, pp. 294–312.

Smith, D. (1976). "The Social Context of Pornography." *Journal of Communications 26:* 16–29.

Smithyman, S. (1978). *The Undetected Rapist.* Unpublished dissertation. Claremont Graduate School.

Weis, K., and S. Borges. (1973). "Victimology and Rape: The Case of the Legitimate Victim." *Issues in Criminology 8:* 71–115.

West, D. J. (1983). "Sex Offenses and Offending." In M. Tonry and N. Morris (Eds.), *Crime and Justice: An Annual Review of Research.* Chicago: University of Chicago Press, pp. 1–30.

Wheeler, H. (1985). "Pornography and Rape: A Feminist Perspective." In A. W. Burgess (Ed.), *Rape and Sexual Assault: A Research Handbook.* New York: Garland Publishing, pp. 374–391.

Police Accounts of Normal Force

Jennifer Hunt

introduction ■ ■ ■ ■ ■

Although my personal contacts with the police have been infrequent, I have seen police violence. In St. Louis, I saw an officer handcuff a rape suspect to a tree while he was waiting for a police car to arrive, and then slap him when the man tried to say something. This took place openly, in front of a group of people who had come from nearby apartments when they had heard a disturbance. In a small town in Missouri, I heard a police chief say that he wished a suspect whom he had just arrested would try to escape so he could shoot her and watch her body float down the river.

In Mexico, after my pocket was picked as I was getting off a bus and I began to shout and beat on the bus door, plainclothes officers appeared as though out of nowhere. One man flashed his I.D., got a quick story from me, motioned to fellow plainclothes officers who were standing in the crowd that had gathered. They took off running down the block, and they apprehended one suspect. This man told the officers where he was going to meet the other man to divide the money. The police took me along on their stakeout in a parking lot. (We took a cab, and I had to pay for it.) As we hid behind parked cars waiting for the suspect, I felt as though I had become part of an unfolding TV drama. When the second man appeared, the police jumped out from behind the parked cars and arrested him. Then a surprising thing happened: The officers said they would hold the two men while I beat them. I thought they were joking, but they were quite serious. As the detectives told me, the men deserved to be beaten for the inconvenience they had caused me.

Why should violence by the police be a regular part of their occupation? Is it because the police recruit sadistic people? As sociologists, we do not look for explanations *within* people, such as personality types. Rather, we examine *external* conditions, such as occupational cultures, that affect people's behavior. In this selection, Jennifer Hunt looks at how occupational norms and interactions influence the attitudes and behavior of new police officers.

Thinking Critically

As you read this selection, ask yourself:

■ Based on the findings reported here, how do you think we can reduce police violence?

The police are required to handle a variety of peace-keeping and law enforcement tasks including settling disputes, removing drunks from the street, aiding the sick, controlling crowds, and pursuing criminals. What unifies these diverse activities is the possibility that their resolution might require the use of force. Indeed, the capacity to use force stands at the core of the police mandate (Bittner, 1980). . . . The following research . . . explores how police themselves classify and evaluate acts of force as either legal, normal, or excessive. Legal force is that coercion necessary to subdue, control, and restrain a suspect in order to take him into custody. Although force not accountable in legal terms is technically labeled excessive by the courts and the public, the police perceive many forms of illegal force as normal. Normal force involves coercive acts that specific "cops" on specific occasions formulate as necessary, appropriate, reasonable, or understandable. Although not always legitimated or admired, normal force is depicted as a necessary or natural response of normal police to particular situational exigencies. . . . Brutality is viewed as illegal, illegitimate, and often immoral violence, but the police draw the lines in extremely different ways and at different points [from] either the court system or the public. . . .

The article is based on approximately eighteen months of participant observation in a major urban police department referred to as the Metro City P.D. I attended the police academy with male and female recruits and later rode with individual officers in one-person cars on evening and night shifts in high crime districts.[1] The female officers described in this research were among the first 100 women assigned to the ranks of uniformed patrol as a result of a discrimination suit filed by the Justice Department and a policewoman plaintiff.

■ ■ ■ LEARNING TO USE NORMAL FORCE

The police phrase "it's not done on the street the way that it's taught at the academy" underscores the perceived contradiction between the formal world of the police academy and the informal world of the street. This contradiction permeates the police officer's construction of his world, particularly his view of the rational and moral use of force.

In the formal world of the police academy, the recruit learns to account for force by reference to legality. He or she is issued the regulation instruments and trained to use them to subdue, control, and restrain a suspect. If threatened with great bodily harm, the officer learns that he can justifiably use deadly force and fire his revolver. Yet the recruit is taught that he cannot use his baton, jack, or gun unnecessarily to torture, maim, or kill a suspect.

When recruits leave the formal world of the academy and are assigned to patrol a district, they are introduced to an informal world in which police recognize normal as well as legal and brutal force. Through observation and instruction, rookies gradually learn to apply force and account for its use in terms familiar to the street cop. First, rookies learn to adjust their arsenals to conform to street standards.

Jennifer Hunt, "Police Accounts of Normal Force", from *Urban Life, 13,* 4, copyright © 1985. Reprinted by permission of Sage Publications.

They are encouraged to buy the more powerful weapons worn by veteran colleagues as these colleagues point out the inadequacy of a wooden baton or compare their convoy jacks to vibrators. They quickly discover that their department-issued equipment marks them as new recruits. At any rate, within a few weeks, most rookies have dispensed with the wooden baton and convoy jack and substituted . . . the more powerful plastic nightstick and flat-headed slapjack.[2]

Through experience and informal instruction, the rookie also learns the street use of these weapons. In school, for example, recruits are taught to avoid hitting a person on the head or neck because it could cause lethal damage. On the street, in contrast, police conclude that they must hit wherever it causes the most damage in order to incapacitate the suspect before they themselves are harmed. New officers also learn that they will earn the respect of their veteran co-workers not by observing legal niceties in using force, but by being "aggressive" and using whatever force is necessary in a given situation.

Peer approval helps neutralize the guilt and confusion that rookies often experience when they begin to use force to assert their authority. One female officer, for example, learned she was the object of a brutality suit while listening to the news on television. At first, she felt so mortified that she hesitated to go to work and face her peers. In fact, male colleagues greeted her with a standing ovation and commented, "You can use our urinal now." In their view, any aggressive police officer regularly using normal force might eventually face a brutality suit or civilian complaint. Such accusations confirm the officer's status as a "street cop" rather than an "inside man" who doesn't engage in "real police work."

Whereas male rookies are assumed to be competent dispensers of force unless proven otherwise, women are believed to be physically weak, naturally passive, and emotionally vulnerable.[3] Women officers are assumed to be reluctant to use physical force and are viewed as incompetent "street cops" until they prove otherwise. As a result, women rookies encounter special problems in learning to use normal force in the process of becoming recognized as "real street cops." It becomes crucial for women officers to create or exploit opportunities to display their physical abilities in order to overcome sexual bias and obtain full acceptance from co-workers. As a result, women rookies are encouraged informally to act more aggressively and to display more machismo than male rookies. . . .

For a street cop, it is often a graver error to use too little force and develop a "shaky" reputation than it is to use too much force and be told to calm down. Thus officers, particularly rookies, who do not back up their partners in appropriate ways or who hesitate to use force in circumstances where it is deemed necessary are informally instructed regarding their aberrant ways. If the problematic incident is relatively insignificant and his general reputation is good, a rookie who "freezes" one time is given a second chance before becoming generally known as an untrustworthy partner. However, such incidents become the subject of degrading gossip, gossip that pressures the officer either to use force as expected or risk isolation. Such talk also informs rookies about the general boundaries of legal and normal force.

For example, a female rookie was accused of "freezing" in an incident that came to be referred to as a "Mexican standoff." A pedestrian had complained that "something funny is going on in the drugstore." The officer walked into the pharmacy where she found an armed man committing a robbery. Although he turned his weapon on her when she entered the premises, she still pulled out her gun and pointed it at him. When he ordered her to drop it, claiming that his partner was behind her with a revolver at her head, she refused and told him to drop his.[4] He refused, and the stalemate continued until a sergeant entered the drugstore and ordered the suspect to drop his gun.

Initially, the female officer thought she had acted appropriately and even heroically. She soon discovered, however, that her hesitation to shoot had brought into question her competence with some of her fellow officers. Although many veterans claimed that "she had a lot a balls" to take her gun out at all when the suspect already had a gun on her, most contended "she shoulda shot him." Other policemen confirmed that she committed a "rookie mistake"; she had failed to notice a "lookout" standing outside the store and hence had been unprepared for an armed confrontation. Her sergeant and lieutenant, moreover, even insisted that she had acted in a cowardly manner, despite her reputation as a "gung-ho cop," and cited the incident as evidence of the general inadequacy of policewomen.

In the weeks that followed, this officer became increasingly depressed and angry. She was particularly outraged when she learned that she would not receive a commendation, although such awards were commonly made for "gun pinches" of this nature. Several months later, the officer vehemently expressed the wish that she had killed the suspect and vowed that next time she would "shoot first and ask questions later." The negative sanctions of supervisors and colleagues clearly encouraged her to adopt an attitude favorable to using force with less restraint in future situations. . . .

At the same time that male and female rookies are commended for using force under appropriate circumstances, they are reprimanded if their participation in force is viewed as excessive or inappropriate. In this way, rookies are instructed that although many acts of coercion are accepted and even demanded, not everything goes. They thereby learn to distinguish between normal and brutal force. . . .

■ ■ ■ ACCOUNTING FOR NORMAL FORCE

Police routinely normalize the use of force by two types of accounts: excuses and justifications. . . .

Excuses and Normal Force

Excuses are accounts in which police deny full responsibility for an act but recognize its inappropriateness. Excuses therefore constitute socially approved vocabularies for relieving responsibility when conduct is questionable. Police most often excuse morally problematic force by referring to emotional or physiological states that are precipitated by some circumstances of routine patrol work. These circumstances include shootouts, violent fights, pursuits, and instances in which a police officer mistakenly comes close to killing an unarmed person.

Police work in these circumstances can generate intense excitement in which the officer experiences the "combat high" and "adrenaline rush" familiar to the combat soldier.[5] Foot and car pursuits not only bring on feelings of danger and excitement from the chase, but also a challenge to official authority. As one patrolman commented about a suspect: "Yeh, he got tuned up [beaten] . . . you always tune them up after a car chase." Another officer normalized the use of force after a pursuit in these terms:

> It's my feeling that violence inevitably occurs after a pursuit. . . . The adrenaline . . . and the insult involved when someone flees increases with every foot of the pursuit. I know the two or three times that I felt I lost control of myself . . . was when someone would run on me. The further I had to chase the guy the madder I got. . . . The funny thing is the reason for the pursuit could have been something as minor as a traffic violation or a kid you're chasing who just turned on a fire hydrant. It always ends in violence. You feel obligated to hit or kick the guy just for running.

Police officers also excuse force when it follows an experience of helplessness and confusion that has culminated in a temporary loss of emotional control. This emotional combination occurs most frequently when an officer comes to the brink of using lethal force, drawing a gun and perhaps firing, only to learn there were no "real" grounds for this action. The officer may then "snap out" and hit the suspect.[6] In one such incident, for example, two policemen picked up a complainant who positively identified a suspect as a man who just tried to shoot him. Just as the officers approached the suspect, he suddenly reached for his back pocket for what the officers assumed to be a gun. One officer was close enough to jump the suspect before he pulled his hand from his pocket. As it turned out, the suspect had no weapon, having dropped it several feet away. Although he was unarmed and under control, the suspect was punched and kicked out of anger and frustration by the officer who had almost shot him.

Note that in both these circumstances—pursuit and near-miss mistaken shootings—officers would concede that the ensuing force is inappropriate and unjustifiable when considered abstractly. But although abstractly wrong, the use of force on such occasions is presented as a normal, human reaction to an extreme situation. Although not every officer might react violently in such circumstances, it is understandable and expected that some will.

Situational Justifications

Officers also justify force as normal by reference to interactional situations in which an officer's authority is physically or symbolically threatened. [In contrast to excuses, which deny responsibility for the act but recognize that the act is blameworthy, justifications accept responsibility for the act but deny that the act is blameworthy.—Ed.] In such accounts, the use of force is justified instrumentally—as a means of regaining immediate control in a situation where that control has become tenuous. Here, the officer depicts his primary intent for using force as a need to reestablish immediate control in a problematic encounter, and only incidentally as hurting or punishing the offender.

Few officers will hesitate to assault a suspect who physically threatens or attacks them. In one case, an officer was punched in the face by a prisoner he had just apprehended for allegedly attempting to shoot a friend. The incident occurred in the stationhouse, and several policemen observed the exchange. Immediately, one officer hit the prisoner in the jaw and the rest immediately joined the brawl.

Violations of an officer's property such as his car or hat may signify a more symbolic assault on the officer's authority and self, thus justifying a forceful response to maintain control. Indeed, in the police view, almost any person who verbally challenges a police officer is appropriately subject to force. . . .

On rare occasions, women officers encounter special problems in these regards. Although most suspects view women in the same way as policemen, some seem less inclined to accord female officers *de facto* and symbolic control in street encounters, and on a few occasions seem determined to provoke direct confrontations with such officers, explicitly denying their formal authority and attempting none too subtly to sexualize the encounter. Women officers, then, might use force as a resource for rectifying such insults and for establishing control over such partially sexualized interactions. Consider the following woman officer's extended account providing such situational justifications for the use of force:

> . . . I'm sitting at Second Street, Second and Nassau, writing curfews up. And this silver Thunderbird . . . blows right by a stop sign where I'm sitting. And I look up and think to myself, "Now, do I want to get involved?" And I figure, it was really belligerent doing it right in front of me. So I take off after him, put my lights on and he immediately pulls over. So he jumps out of the car. I jump out of the car right away and I say, "I'm stopping you for that stop sign you just blew through. . . . Let me see your cards, please." Then he starts making these lip smacking noises at me everytime he begins to talk. He said, (smack) "The only way you're seeing my cards is if you lock me up and the only way you're gonna lock me up is if you chase me." And I said to him, "Well, look, I will satisfy you on one account. Now go to your car because I will lock you up. . . . And just sit in your car. I'll be right with you." He smacks his lips, turns around and goes to his car and he sits. And I call a wagon at Second and Nassau. They ask me what I have. I say, "I've got one to go." So as the wagon acknowledges, the car all of a sudden tears out of its spot. And I get on the air and say, "I'm in pursuit." And I give them a description of the car and the direction I'm going. . . . And all of a sudden he pulls over about a block and a half after I started the pursuit. So I got on the air and I said, "I got him at Second and Washington." I jumped out of my car and as I jumped out he tears away again. Now I'm ready to die of embarrassment. I have to get back on the air and say no I don't have him. So I got on the air and said, "Look, he's playing games with me now. He took off again." I said, "I'm still heading South on Second Street." He gets down to Lexington. He pulls over again. Well, this time I pulled the police car in front of him. . . . I go over to the car and I hear him lock the doors. I pull out my gun and I put it right in his window. I say, "Unlock that door." Well, he looked at the gun. He nearly liked to shit himself. He unlocked the door. I holster my gun. I go to grab his arms to pull him out and all of a sudden I realize Anne's got him. So we keep pulling him out of the car. Throw him on the trunk of his car and kept pounding him back down on the trunk. She's punching his head. I'm kicking him. Then I take out my blackjack. I jack him across the shoulder. Then I go to jack him in the head and I jack Anne's fingers. . . . The next thing they know is we're throwing him bodily into the wagon. And they said, "Did you search him?" We go to the wagon, drag him out again.

Now we're tearing through his pockets throwing everything on the ground. Pick him up bodily again, threw him in. . . . So I straightened it out with the sergeant. . . . I said, "What did you want me to do? Let any citizen on the street get stopped and pull away and that's the end of it?"

In this instance, a male suspect manages to convey a series of affronts to the officer's authority. These affronts become explicitly and insultingly sexual, turning the challenge from the claim that "no cop will stop me" to the more gender specific one, "no woman cop will stop me." Resistance ups the ante until the suspect backs down in the face of the officer's drawn revolver. The force to which the culprit was then subjected is normalized through all the accounts considered to this point—it is situationally justified as a means to reestablish and maintain immediate and symbolic control in a highly problematic encounter and it is excused as a natural, collective outburst following resolution of a dangerous, tension-filled incident. And finally, it is more implicitly justified as appropriate punishment, an account building upon standard police practices for abstract justification, to which I now turn.

Abstract Justifications

Police also justify the use of extreme force against certain categories of morally reprehensible persons. In this case, force is not presented as an instrumental means to regain control that has been symbolically or physically threatened. Instead, it is justified as an appropriate response to particularly heinous offenders. Categories of such offenders include: cop haters who have gained notoriety as persistent police antagonizers; cop killers or any person who has attempted seriously to harm a police officer (Westley, 1970:131); sexual deviants who prey on children and "moral women"; child abusers; and junkies and other "scum" who inhabit the street. The more morally reprehensible the act is judged, the more likely the police are to depict any violence directed toward its perpetrator as justifiable. Thus a man who exposes himself to children in a playground is less likely to experience police assault than one who rapes or sexually molests a child.

"Clean" criminals, such as high-level mafiosi, white-collar criminals, and professional burglars, are rarely subject to abstract force. Nor are perpetrators of violent and nonviolent street crimes who prey on adult males, prostitutes, and other categories of persons who belong on the street.[7] Similarly, the "psycho" or demented person is perceived as so mentally deranged that he is not responsible for his acts and hence does not merit abstract, punitive force (Van Maanen, 1978:233–34).

Police justify abstract force by invoking a higher moral purpose that legitimates the violation of commonly recognized standards. In one case, for example, a nun was raped by a seventeen-year-old male adolescent. When the police apprehended the suspect, he was severely beaten and his penis put in an electrical outlet to teach him a lesson. The story of the event was told to me by a police officer who, despite the fact that he rarely supported the use of extralegal force, depicted this treatment as legitimate. Indeed, when I asked if he would have participated had he been present, he responded, "I'm Catholic. I would have participated."

■ ■ ■ ■ EXCESSIVE FORCE AND PEER RESPONSES

Although police routinely excuse and justify many incidents where they or their co-workers have used extreme force against a citizen or suspect, this does not mean that on any and every occasion the officer using such force is exonerated. Indeed, the concept of normal force is useful because it suggests that there are specific circumstances under which police officers will not condone the use of force by themselves or colleagues as reasonable and acceptable. Thus, officer-recognized conceptions of normal force are subject to restrictions of the following kinds:

1. Police recognize and honor some rough equation between the behavior of the suspect and the harmfulness of the force to which it is subject. There are limits, therefore, to the degree of force that is acceptable in particular circumstances. In the following incident, for example, an officer reflects on a situation in which a "symbolic assailant" (Skolnick, 1975:45) was mistakenly subject to more force than he "deserved" and almost killed:

> One time Bill Johnson and I . . . had a particularly rude drunk one day. He was really rude and spit on you and he did all this stuff and we even had to cuff him lying down on the hard stretcher, like you would do an epileptic. . . . So we were really mad. We said let's just give him one or two shots . . . slamming on the brakes and having him roll. But we didn't use our heads . . . we heard the stretcher go nnnnnBam and then nothing. We heard nothing and we realized we had put this man in with his head to the front so when we slammed on the brakes his stretcher. . . . I guess it can roll four foot. Well, it was his head that had hit the front. . . . So, we went to Madison Street and parked. It's a really lonely area. And we unlocked the wagon and peeked in. We know he's in there. We were so scared and we look in and there's not a sound and we see blood coming in front of the wagon and think " . . .we killed this man. What am I gonna do? What am I gonna tell my family?" And to make a long story short, he was just knocked out. But boy was I scared. From then on we learned, feet first.

2. Similarly, even in cases where suspects are seen as deserving some violent punishment, this force should not be used randomly and without control. Thus, in the following incident, an officer who "snapped out" and began to beat a child abuser clearly regarded his partner's attempt to stop the beating as reasonable.

> . . . I knock on the door and a lady answers just completely hysterical. And I say, "Listen, I don't know what's going on in here," but then I hear this, just this screeching. You know. And I figure well I'm just going to find out what's going on so I just go past the lady and what's happening is that the husband had. . . . The kid was being potty trained and the way they were potty training this kid, this two-year-old boy, was that the boyfriend of this girl would pick up this kid and he would sit him down on top of the stove. It was their method of potty training. Well, first of all you think of your own kids. I mean afterwards you do. I mean I've never been this mad in my whole life. You see this little two-year-old boy seated on the top of the stove with rings around it being absolutely scalding hot. And he's saying "I'll teach you to go. . . ." It just triggered something. An uncontrollable. . . . It's just probably the most violent I ever got. Well you just grab that guy. You hit him ten, fifteen times . . . you don't know how many. You just get so mad. And I remember my partner eventually came in and grabbed me and said,

"Don't worry about it. We got him. We got him." And we cuffed him and we took him down. Yeah that was bad.

Learning these sorts of restrictions on the use of normal force and these informal practices of peer control are important processes in the socialization of newcomers. This socialization proceeds both through ongoing observation and experience and, on occasion, through explicit instruction. For example, one veteran officer advised a rookie, "The only reason to go in on a pursuit is not to get the perpetrator but to pull the cop who gets there first offa the guy before he kills him."

■ ■ ■ CONCLUSION

The organization of police work reflects a poignant moral dilemma: For a variety of reasons, society mandates to the police the right to use force but provides little direction as to its proper use in specific, "real life" situations. Thus, the police, as officers of the law, must be prepared to use force under circumstances in which its rationale is often morally, legally, and practically ambiguous. This fact explains some otherwise puzzling aspects of police training and socialization.

The police academy provides a semblance of socialization for its recruits by teaching formal rules for using force. . . . [T]he full socialization of a police officer takes place outside the academy as the officer moves from its idealizations to the practicalities of the street. . . .

. . . [J]ustifications and excuses . . . conventionalize but do not reform situations that are inherently charged and morally ambiguous. In this way they simultaneously preserve the self-image of police as agents of the conventional order, provide ways in which individual officers can resolve their personal doubts as to the moral status of their action and those of their colleagues, and reinforce the solidarity of the police community.

■ ■ ■ NOTES

1. Nonetheless masculine pronouns are generally used to refer to the police in this article, because the Metro P.D. remained dominated by men numerically, in style, and in tone. . . .

2. Some officers also substitute a large heavy duty flashlight for the nightstick. If used correctly, the flashlight can inflict more damage than the baton and is less likely to break when applied to the head or other parts of the body.

3. As the Metro City Police Commissioner commented in an interview: "In general, they [women] are physically weaker than males. . . . I believe they would be inclined to let their emotions all too frequently overrule their good judgment . . . there are periods in their life when they are psychologically unbalanced because of physical problems that are occurring within them."

4. The woman officer later explained that she did not obey the suspect's command because she saw no reflection of the partner in the suspect's glasses and therefore assumed he was lying.

5. The combat high is a state of controlled exhilaration in which the officer experiences a heightened awareness of the world around him. Officers report that perception, smell, and hearing seem acute; one seems to stand outside oneself, and the world appears extraordinarily vivid and clear. At the same time, officers insist that they are able to think rationally and instantly translate thoughts into action; when experienced, fear is not incapacitating but instead enhances the ability to act.

6. This police experience of fear and helplessness, leading to a violent outburst, may be analogized to a parent's reaction on seeing his child almost die in an accident. Imagine a scene in which a father is walking with his six-year-old son. Suddenly, the boy runs into the street to get a red ball on the pavement. The father watches a car slam on the brakes and miss the boy by two inches. He grabs his son and smacks him on the face before he takes him in his arms and holds him. . . .

7. The categories of persons who merit violence are not unique to the police. Prisoners, criminals, and hospital personnel appear to draw similar distinctions between morally unworthy persons; on the latter, see Sudnow (1967:105).

■ ■ ■ **REFERENCES**

Bittner, E. (1980). *The Functions of the Police in Modern Society.* Cambridge, MA: Oelgeschlager, Gunn & Hain.

Skolnick, J. (1975). *Justice Without Trial.* New York: John Wiley.

Sudnow, D. (1967). *Passing On: The Social Organization of Dying.* Englewood Cliffs, NJ: Prentice-Hall.

Van Maanen, J. (1978). "The Asshole." In P. K. Manning and J. Van Maanen (Eds.), *Policing: A View from the Street.* Santa Monica, CA: Goodyear.

Westley, W. A. (1970). *Violence and the Police: A Sociological Study of Law, Custom, and Morality.* Cambridge, MA: MIT Press.

PART III

Problems of Social Inequality

*W*hat huge disparities of income we have in our society! Some CEOs are paid millions of dollars a year, while other full-time workers earn just $10,000 a year. Some live in plush estates, with chauffeurs, maids, and groundskeepers at their beck and call. Others don't even have a home. They sleep under bridges, in cardboard boxes in back alleys, in shelters for the homeless, or, if they are lucky, on a friend's or relative's couch.

I have talked to many of these people. As a sociologist, I decided that I had to learn more about the homeless, what their lives are like, and how they ended up on the streets. To do so, I visited a dozen or so skid rows, traveling from one end of the country to the other, from Minneapolis to Atlanta and from Los Angeles to Manhattan. I also made a lot of stops in what have come to be called the "fly-over areas"—from Kansas and Missouri to Colorado and Texas. I interviewed homeless people in their tents in parks, as they rode streetcars, as they sunned on beaches, as they prepared their beds in back alleys, and as they ate meals in homeless shelters. As darkness was approaching, I sat with them in the middle of the sidewalk in rundown, threatening areas, with a tape recorder running and my mind flitting between what they were saying and what could be some approaching danger.

I ate with the homeless in the shelters. Some of the meals were good, most nondescript, and some horribly foul. I slept with them there, too. Some beds were clean, and some were so filthy you could see the dirt even in dim light. I slept peacefully in some shelters, but only fitfully in those in which I knew there had been killings. I saw violence on the streets.

I was treated with dignity in some shelters and inhumanely in others. In one, I was given good food, a clean bed, and some privacy. In another, I was ordered to take off all my clothing and to sit naked on my bed. When my number was called over an intercom, I had to carry a basket with my clothing to a counter, walking naked in front of the other homeless men, who were sitting on their beds, waiting for their number to be called. I was then ordered to take a group shower. From there, I had to walk nude to my bed. In the early morning, about 6, the overhead lights came on, accompanied by a blaring loudspeaker informing us that it was time to get up. As our number was called, each of us, still naked, had to parade once again before the others to retrieve our clothing and start our aimless day.

Being treated as though one has no dignity is one of the many negative consequences of being very poor in U.S. society. I'm sure that you can see how such treatment bruises the self-concept. "Of what value am I, since I'm treated like this?" goes the reasoning. This, in turn, leads to self-defeating behaviors. "If I'm of such little value, have such little worth in the eyes of others, then what difference does it make if I_____?" You can fill in the blank: don't care how I look, lie around and get drunk in public, urinate on the street, steal, get arrested, die.

It is almost impossible to maintain a good self-concept in the midst of continuous savage onslaughts, and the poor often are on the receiving end of interactions that challenge their sense of self-worth. Despite such debilitating erosions, some people in poverty, to my amazement, manage to maintain a sense of dignity and self-worth. In the midst of these obstacles, they keep themselves clean, maintain strong family relationships, and work toward goals to change their lives.

I don't know how they manage. I don't think I'm that strong.

As the barrage continues, however, most give up. Life is never going to be any different. Nothing will change. Tomorrow will be the same as today. Why struggle against the inevitable? Some people have abilities and opportunities, and they make it. Evidently, I don't have those abilities. I see no opportunities. I'm not worth much.

Despair sets in. Hopelessness replaces the vibrant goals that once drove life. Bitterness replaces hope. The future looks dark.

As eating becomes irregular, and as hopes fade, health deteriorates. Teeth go unbrushed, cavities unfilled. Gums rot. So do internal organs.

To say that the very poor receive inadequate health care is like saying that the sun also rises, that the wealthy eat well, or that politicians enjoy power. Of course they do. But just how unjust it is for people to live like this seems to be significant to only a few.

The consequences of social inequality, then, are pervasive. It is not just the external differences—the clothing, the car, the shopping, the food—but the social destinations to which these underlying forces propel people. It is differences in opportunities—for education, health care, nutrition, and enjoyment of life itself. It is death at an early age versus healthy living until old age. It is a sense of purpose in life, or despair that life still continues.

In short, poverty and wealth separate people into different worlds, and those worlds determine people's life chances. Social inequality means different social fates in life.

Race–ethnicity has similar effects. Because of our skin color, we experience one set of opportunities rather than another. One leads to greater chances for a good education and a more secure place in our economic system. One leads to better health, a sense of purpose, a feeling that one is being rewarded for achievements. Being male or female is another primary sorting device, one that also has major influences on our lives. Although there have been extensive changes in relations between the sexes—with some so startling, as in higher education, that some people have even begun to call for affirmative action for men—discrimination against women continues.

In this part of the book, we examine these areas of social inequality. We first turn our lens on extreme poverty. Based on his experiences working as a volunteer in a shelter for homeless women, Elliot Liebow analyzes the lives of the women who were living there. Raphael Ezekiel then reports on his participant observation study of groups whose avowed purpose is to promote racial–ethnic hatred as a way of life. Laura Miller then examines the situation of women in the military, focusing on the discrimination they face from male soldiers. In the selection that concludes this part, David Rosenhan's report on an experiment he conducted in mental hospitals takes us face to face with the surprising finding that psychiatrists cannot tell the sane from the insane.

The Lives of Homeless Women

Elliot Liebow

introduction ∎ ∎ ∎ ∎

The economic inequalities in the United States are remarkable. Some people make thousands of times more money each year than others do. No matter how hard they try, others can't even find a job. Some are so wealthy that they own several estates in resort areas, drive Rolls Royces, and fly to Paris for weekend shopping. Others can't afford even a beat-up car, and they have no home.

It is the homeless on which we focus in this selection. Elliot Liebow, who had been diagnosed with incurable cancer, retired from his research position with the federal government. He loved doing research, as he once told me, but he decided to spend his last days, which turned into years, doing things for others. Volunteering to work in a shelter for homeless women, he spent more and more time there. Many aspects of these women's lives impressed him, especially how they tried to maintain a sense of dignity in the midst of such demeaning circumstances. This is his account of those experiences. Liebow ended up doing more research, after all.

Thinking Critically

As you read this selection, ask yourself:

∎ What can be done to reduce homelessness?

This is a participant observer study of single, homeless women in emergency shelters in a small city just outside Washington, D.C. In participant observation, the researcher tries to participate as fully as possible in the lives of the people being studied. Of course, there are obvious and severe limits to how well a man with a home and family can put himself in the place of homeless women. One simply goes where they go, gets to know them over time as best one can, and tries very hard to see the world from their perspective.

It is often said that, in participant observation studies, the researcher is the research instrument. So is it here. Everything reported about the women in this study has been selected by me and filtered through me, so it is important that I tell you something about myself and my prejudices as well as how this study came about. Indeed, I feel obliged to tell you more than is seemly and more than you may want to know, but these are things that the women themselves knew about me and that had an important if unknown influence on my relationship with them.

In a real sense, I backed into this study, which took shape, more or less, as I went along. In 1984, I learned that I had cancer and a very limited life expectancy. I did not want to spend my last months on the 12th floor of a government office building, so at 58 I retired on disability from my job of 20-some years as an anthropologist with the National Institute of Mental Health.

I looked well, felt well, and had a lot of time on my hands, so I became a volunteer at a soup kitchen that had recently opened. I worked there one night a week. In the early part of the evening, I helped served food or just sat around with the men and women who had come there, usually eating with them. In case of trouble, I tried to keep the peace. Later I went upstairs to "the counselor's office," where I met with people who needed assistance in getting shelter for the night. For the next hour or so, I called around to the various shelters in the county or in downtown Washington, D.C., trying to locate and reserve sleeping space for the men and women who needed it.

I enjoyed the work and the people at the soup kitchen, but this was only one night a week, so I became a volunteer at The Refuge, an emergency shelter for homeless women. This, too, was one night a week, from 6:30 to 10:00, and involved sleeping overnight twice a month. I picked this shelter because I had visited there briefly the year before and liked the feel of it. Here, along with three other volunteers, my job was to help prepare the food (usually just heat the main dishes and make a salad); help serve the food; distribute towels, soap, and other sundries on request; socialize with the women; keep order; and keep a daily log that included the names of all the women present and their time of arrival.

Almost immediately, I found myself enjoying the company of the women. I was awed by the enormous effort that most of them made to secure the most elementary necessities and decencies of life that the rest of us take for granted. And I was especially struck by their sense of humor, so at odds with any self-pity—the ability to step back and laugh at oneself, however wryly. One evening, soon after I started working at the shelter, several of us remained at the table to talk after finishing dinner. Pauline turned to me and said, in a stage whisper, making sure that Hilda would hear her, "Hilda has a Ph.D."

Hilda laughed. "No," she said, "I don't have a Ph.D., but I do have a bachelor's degree in biology." She paused, then began again. "You know," she said, "all my life I wanted to be an MD and now, at the age of 54, I finally made it. I'm a Manic Depressive."

From *Tell Them Who I Am* by Elliot Liebow. 1993. Reprinted by permission.

Seduced by the courage and the humor of the women, and by the pleasure of their company, I started going to the shelter four and sometimes five days a week. (For the first two years, I also kept my one-night-a-week job with the soup kitchen.) Probably because it was something I was trained to do, or perhaps out of plain habit, I decided to take notes.

"Listen," I said at the dinner table one evening, after getting permission to do a study from the shelter director. "I want your permission to take notes. I want to go home at night and write down what I can remember about the things you say and do. Maybe I'll write a book about homeless women."

Most of the dozen or so women there nodded their heads or simply shrugged. All except Regina. Her acceptance was conditional. "Only if you promise not to publish before I do," she said. Believing that neither one of us, for different reasons, would ever publish anything in the future, I readily agreed.[1]

It is difficult to be precise about how I was perceived by the women. I am 6'1" and weigh about 175 pounds. I had a lot of white hair but was otherwise nondescript. I dressed casually, often in corduroy pants, shirt, and cardigan. The fact that I was Jewish did not seem to matter much one way or another so far as I could tell.

Most of the women probably liked having me around. Male companionship was generally in short supply and the women often made a fuss about the few male volunteers. I would guess that there were as many women who actively sought me out as there were women who avoided me. The fact that I had written a book that was available at the library (three or four women took the trouble to read it) enhanced my legitimacy in their eyes.[2]

Principally, I think, the women saw me as an important resource. I had money and a car, and by undertaking to write a book, I had made it my business to be with them. I routinely lent out $2, $5, $10, or even $20 on request to the handful who asked: I told them I had set aside a certain amount as a revolving fund and I could only keep lending money if they kept returning it. This worked fairly well.

There were a few women, of course, who would never be in a position to return the money, and this made for a problem. It would have been patronizing simply to make a gift of the money; they wanted to be borrowers, not beggars, and I was just as eager as they to avoid a demeaning panhandler/donor relationship. But I did not want them to be embarrassed or to avoid me simply because they couldn't repay a loan, nor did I want to shut them off from borrowing more. My solution was to reassure these women I had no immediate need for the money and could wait indefinitely for repayment.

Some of the women would perhaps characterize me as a friend, but I am not certain how deep or steadfast this sense of friendship might be. One day, Regina and I were talking about her upcoming trial about two months away. I had already agreed to accompany her to the courtroom and serve as an advisor, but Regina wanted further reassurance.

"You will be there, won't you?" she said.

As a way of noting the profundity that nothing in life is certain, I said, jokingly, "It's not up to me, it's up to The Man Upstairs."

"Well," she said, "if you die before the trial, you will ask one of your friends to help me, won't you?" I looked hard at her to see if she was joking, too. She wasn't. She was simply putting first things first.

One or two of the women did say something like "If you weren't married, would you give me a run for my money?" Neither "yes" nor "no" was a suitable response, but it usually sufficed for me to say (and mean), "I think you are a very nice person."

I tried to make myself available for driving people to Social Services, a job interview, a clinic or hospital, a cemetery, to someone's house, to another shelter, to help them move their belongings, or on other personal errands. With my consent, several women used my name as a personal reference for jobs or housing, and a few used my home as a mailing address for income tax refunds or other business.

Several of the women got to know my two daughters, both of whom came to The Refuge a few evenings each during the winters. One daughter was engaged to be married and her fiancé also came a few times. These visits helped strengthen my ties to those women who knew my daughters by face and name. They could ask me how my wife, Harriet, or Elisabeth and Jessica and Eric were doing, and my subsequent participation in discussions about family or child-rearing was much more personal and immediate as a result.

My association with the women was most intense during the winter of 1984–85, all of 1986, much of 1987, and the winter of 1987–88. Thereafter, I slackened off, partly for health reasons and partly because I had already collected more notes than I knew what to do with.[3] I continued to go to the shelters intermittently, and several of the women called me regularly at home. It was also at this time that I started playing around with the notes to see how I might eventually make sense of them.

In general, I have tried to avoid labeling any of the women as "mentally ill," "alcoholic," "drug addicted," or any other characterization that is commonly used to describe—or, worse, to explain—the homeless person. Judgments such as these are almost always made against a background of homelessness. If the same person were seen in another setting, the judgment might be altogether different. Like you, I know people who drink, people who do drugs, and bosses who have tantrums and treat their subordinates like dirt. They all have good jobs. Were they to become homeless, some of them would surely also become "alcoholics," "addicts," or "mentally ill." Similarly, if some of the homeless women who are now so labeled were to be magically transported to a more usual and acceptable setting, some of them—not all, of course—would shed their labels and take their places with the rest of us somewhere on the spectrum of normality.

The reader may be puzzled by the short shrift given here to mental illness. This was no oversight. I have no training as a mental health professional so it is not always clear to me who is mentally ill and who is not. There were always some women who acted crazy or whom most considered crazy, and the women themselves often agreed with the public at large that many homeless people are mentally ill.

From the beginning, however, I paid little attention to mental illness, partly because I had difficulty recognizing it, and partly for other reasons. Sometimes mental illness seemed to be "now-you-see-it, now-you-don't" phenomenon; some of the women were fine when their public assistance checks arrived, but became increasingly "symptomatic" as the month progressed and their money (security?) diminished, coming full circle when the next check arrived.[4] Others had good or bad days or weeks but with no obvious pattern or periodicity, although one woman linked her down period to her menstrual cycle. With a little patience on my part, almost all the women with mental or emotional problems were eventually and repeatedly accessible. Even on "bad" days, perhaps especially on "bad" days, these women sometimes said things that seemed to come, uncensored, from the depths of their emotional lives.

It seems to me that those women who may have been mentally ill (or alcoholic or drug addicted) by one or another standard were homeless for exactly the same proximal reason that everyone else was homeless: they had no place to live. Similarly, their greatest need of the moment was the same as everyone else's: to be assured of a safe, warm place to sleep at night, one or more hot meals a day, and the presence, if not the companionship, of fellow human beings. Given this perspective and my purposes, which and how many of the women were mentally ill was not a critical issue.

Whatever one's view of mental illness, it is probably true that the more one gets to know about a person, the easier it is to put oneself in that person's place or to understand his or her viewpoint, and the less reason one has for thinking of that person or treating that person as mentally ill.

This perspective—indeed, participant observation itself—raises the age-old problem of whether anyone can understand another or put oneself in another's place. Many thoughtful people believe that a sane person cannot know what it is to be crazy, that a white man cannot understand a black man, a Jew cannot see through the eyes of a Christian, a man through the eyes of a woman, and so forth in both directions. In an important sense, of course, and to a degree, this is certainly true; in another sense, and to a degree, it is surely false, because the logical extension of such a view is that no one can know another, that only John Jones can know John Jones, in which case social life would be impossible.

I do not mean that a man with a home and family can see and feel the world as homeless women see and feel it. I do mean, however, that it is reasonable and useful to try to do so. Trying to put oneself in the place of the other lies at the heart of the social contract and of social life itself . . .

In the early months, I sometimes tried to get Betty or one of the other women to see things as I saw them. One night Betty waited half an hour in back of the library for a bus that never came. She was convinced this was deliberate and personal abuse on the part of the Metro system. Metro was out to get her, she said. "But how did Metro know you were waiting for a bus at that time?" I asked. Betty shook her head in pity of me. "Well, Elliot, I was there on the street, right there in public, in the open! How could they not see me waiting for that damn bus?"

Fairly quickly, I learned not to argue with Betty but simply to relax and marvel at her end-of-the-month ingenuity. ("End-of-the-month" because that's when her public assistance money ran out and when she was most bitter at the way the world was treating her. At that time, a $10 or $20 loan could dramatically reduce or even eliminate her paranoid thoughts.) Once, when her food stamps had not come, even two days after Judy had received hers, Betty dryly observed that this was further proof that Richman County was trying to rid itself of homeless women. "They give Judy Tootie her food stamps so she'll eat herself to death [Judy weighed 300 pounds]. They won't give me mine so I'll starve to death." She got no argument from me. I had learned to go with the flow.

Sometimes I annoyed or even angered some of the women. When Louise told me that some of the women were following her around all day and harassing her, I asked her why they did these things. "You're just like the state's attorney," she said, "always asking for reasons. Whenever I tell him that someone assaulted me, he always asks me why they did it. People with criminal minds don't need a reason to do something. That's what makes them criminals."

. . . I think of Betty and Louise and many of the other women as friends. As a friend, I owe them friendship. Perhaps I also owe them something because I have so much and they have so little, but I do not feel under any special obligation to them as research subjects. Indeed, I do not think of them as "research subjects." Since they knew what I was trying to do and allowed me to do it, they could just as well be considered collaborators in what might fairly be seen as a cooperative enterprise.

■ ■ ■ NOTES

1. Let the record show that now, some seven-plus years later, I have her permission to go ahead.

2. *Tally's Corner: A Study of Negro Streetcorner Men.*

3. For the same reason, I stopped taking life histories. After the women had known me for a few months, I took about 20 life histories on tape, often at the request of the women themselves and over a period of two years or so. Some of these lasted several hours over two or three sessions and I found myself accumulating more information than I could handle.

4. Many schizophrenics are completely lucid for long periods of time, and their thoughts and behavior are completely indistinguishable from those of normals. Even Bleuler . . . asserted that there were certain very important cognitive processes . . . that were frequently identical among schizophrenics and normals. *"In many important respects, then, an insane person may be completely sane"* (emphasis added). Morris Rosenberg, "A Symbolic Interactionist View of Psychosis," *Journal of Health and Social Behavior,* 25, no. 3 (September 1984), p. 291.

READING 8

The Racist Mind

Raphael Ezekiel

introduction

Racism has declined considerably in the United States, so much so that it is difficult to recognize the past. There was a time when Klansmen rode through black neighborhoods, burning and killing with impunity. The mere accusation that a black man had raped a white woman was sufficient for the man to be lynched by an angry mob of whites. Ads for employment used to say, "No colored need apply." Blacks, if allowed at all, were confined to the balconies of movie theaters. There were separate schools, separate rest rooms, and separate drinking fountains.

Times have so changed that this description seems to be that of some mythical past. Yet, the racial–ethnic integration of today's society is far from complete. We can assume that the time will come when the urban ghetto, with all of its ills and the fears it brings to the middle class (both minority and white), as well as our almost all-black urban schools, will also become part of someone's mythical past.

Racism, though diminished, has not disappeared. There are still people who hate others because they look different from themselves. Racial hatred knows no color. It marks not only some whites, but also some blacks and some members of other minority groups. In this selection, Raphael Ezekiel reports on his observations and interviews with groups of white racists. No matter what your race–ethnicity, this thought-provoking selection should give you insight into hate-centered groups, as well as help you attain greater self-understanding.

Thinking Critically

As you read this selection, ask yourself:

- Who is attracted to the message of racial–ethnic hatred? Why? What can be done to reduce the appeal of hatred?

We do not know, the old joke says, who discovered water, but we do know that it was not a fish. Just so, in a society in which white folk predominate and are seldom challenged in everyday life, white Americans have little conscious awareness of being white or of what that might mean. Only challenge or crisis makes this categorization relevant. The militant white racist movement is composed of people who permanently feel in crisis.

The militant white racists look at a world in which white Americans and non-white Americans are treated differently in almost every interaction; they infer that race is a powerful biological construct that identifies essences. (They are unfamiliar with modern genetic research, which has found that "race" identifies only trivial aspects of human genetic variation.) They look at a world in which almost all positions of power are held by men who are white; they infer that whites (and men) have a nature that is superior. The *boss,* the person one must worry about, is white. Everyday experience tells the militant white racist that race is basic and that white is good.

Because most white Americans, at *some level,* share these perceptions, the potential exists at all times for the militant movement to expand its influence. The militant movement keeps these ideas fresh and strong, persistently reinjecting them into the social discourse, ensuring that people stay vulnerable to interested parties who wish to use racism to capture public allegiance.

We in the general European-American public share many beliefs with the militant white racists, but we are not identical to them—it is *not* that "we have met the enemy, and he is us." We whites believe many things; we believe most of them in a dull and muddled and jumbled fashion; many of our beliefs are contradictory. The militant movement takes one of the many jumbled belief sets in our heads and preserves it in sharpened, intense form, adding to it a sense that life is struggle, that the fundamental issue between humans is power, that the world divides into Good and Evil, and that Good and Evil must fight to the death. And that events usually have hidden causes.

Because the movement rests partly on beliefs that *are* a part of us white Americans, but a part that we do not acknowledge and do not deal with, it has enjoyed an extraordinarily long life; it is regenerated again and again, taking new forms as circumstances change. The situation is going to become worse. Our national economy is grinding through brutal transformation: An enormous number of people can have no confidence that their jobs, wage levels, health care, or pensions are safe. They face *erosion* of their positions. Their fears will become only more acute as the swelling populations of the underdeveloped nations try to save themselves through mass migration. These highly predictable changes are going to make white Americans more and more vulnerable to a movement whose ideas are already a part of their inner life.

• • •

For a decade I interviewed followers and leaders in the militant white racist movement, the white supremacist movement, and have observed some of their rallies and get-togethers. I dealt openly and honestly with these people, making it clear that I am Jewish, a leftist opposed to racism, a professor at the University of Michigan.

• • •

We drove through town toward the mountain, to a huge meadow at its foot. I saw little knots of men by small fires. We walked to a fire and met Dave Holland, a young leader who was organizing the rally, and two of his lieutenants. I walked across to four young men who leaned on a truck. They were hesitant and careful,

From *The Racist Mind* by Raphael Ezekiel. 1995. Reprinted by permission.

but soon got interested in talking. I talked at length with two of them. They were friends, trying to keep a North Carolina Klan alive after the arrest of its leader, worried about how to do that work without seeming to try to take over the group. Both were twenty-two years old; both came from blue-collar families. They believed in the Aryan Jesus, the Aryan Israelites.

Men were setting up their sleeping bags around the fires. People had driven in from a distance. It felt like a camping trip, a kids' gang.

Later I talked more with Venable [one of the main leaders] at the house, wrote some field notes in my motel room, and slept.

Saturday morning was cold with light rain. I had breakfasted with my former student, who wanted to join me in a brief morning reconnaissance. Raised in Chicago, Jewish, very thoughtful and very bright, Judy has lived in the South for some time, and I value her reactions. Back at the rally field we saw flags snapping in the wind: Masses of Reb flags lined the great stage that had been erected at the far edge of the meadow; flags flew from many of the dozens of vans and trucks that had by now accumulated—there were rattlesnake DON'T TREAD ON ME flags, Nazi battle flags with swastikas, and many more Reb flags.

We walked through the meadow. Additional vehicles arrived steadily. At four or five places, wooden booths set up beneath tents held books, buttons, and stickers for sale—WHITE BY BIRTH, SOUTHERN BY THE GRACE OF GOD, PRAISE GOD FOR AIDS. Judy chatted with an older woman who talked of her own childhood in Michigan's Upper Peninsula. I listened to the conversations; I looked at the mass of Confederate flags up at the speaker stand—the racists had taken over the handsome symbol. I listened to the lively country-western music coming over the loudspeaker. I started to be able to understand the words in the lyrics: Again and again the lyrics used the word "nigger." They had their own music, their own songs, and they were getting joy by being able to say "nigger" out loud.

I drove Judy back to the city. She talked about her work in nearby towns with country people. They are independent, she said; they are warm when they have accepted you; they are cautious, defensive, and secretive, afraid of being patronized by city people. This crowd at the rally ground had seemed familiar to her. My own mood was dark. I was getting a headache and feeling the strain: It is important for my goal to let a real sense of the stranger come into me, not to block it or distort it. At the same time I need to keep my own sense of myself. It would be less effort just to reject the stranger. But I would gain no understanding.

I thanked Judy and ate lunch. Wool socks made my feet warmer and I was happier. I returned to the rally field. The rain was lightening. Knots of men spread across the meadow.

[One of the men] stared at me. "I have no use for a Jew. Keep Hitler's dream alive: Kill a Jew."

He was trying to provoke me.

He said again that he had no use for a Jew.

I said, "Well, that's you."

I had already told him I was studying the movement; I now said, truthfully, that I would like to hear more about what he was saying—that this wasn't the time or place, but if it were, I would want to hear more about this.

He said, "If it were the time and the place, I would *show* you."

"That's you," I said in a level voice. I walked off.

I realize now, some years later and after much more interaction, that I must have been conspicuous since my first appearance. I had felt rather casual, strolling among the folk, nodding and saying "howdy" now and then. I was dressed in no particular manner. I had supposed I seemed out of place, but not especially noteworthy. I much misunderstood, I now can see the amount of fear in which these people live, and their belief that a Jewish power base was out to endanger them. There had undoubtedly been bits of gossip following me all morning and afternoon as I walked about. A strange few hours, harmless, deeply frightening, and deeply educational, followed.

As I experienced it, tentacles of hostility seemed to snake out from the encounter, seemed to spread through the meadow the rest of the afternoon. I was talking first with the North Carolina men, and someone called across from an enclosure, "He's a Jew!" As I walked about the meadow, I picked up pieces of conversation: "Jew," "Jewboy." There were periodic catcalls. As I passed near a row of parked vehicles, one of the Klansmen hidden in a van called over a speaker system in a metallic, loud, and nasty voice, *"Yeah,* just move your niggerized self along, Jewboy! Just *move along."* More catcalls; more frozen stares as I passed; more hard, hostile faces.

I talked then a long time with the men from North Carolina about Jews: What was the deal? I heard deep enmity. The Klan was profoundly anti-Semitic. I left that little group and continued to walk about; the catcalls followed, the nasty stares.

I stood near a tent, quietly. I was not willing to be driven away. More catcalls came. I understood: I would not be safe here if it were dark: If someone moved to hurt me, no one would stop him.

I had been defined. I was not "Rafe," not Raphael Ezekiel; I was not the individual my friends knew, my students knew, I knew. I was Alien, stripped of my particular history.

I was Jew.

It was incredibly lonesome.

I wandered quietly along the meadow, tasting the strange sense of isolation. People were stirring, thinking about getting ready for their parade. Venable arrived and we talked a moment; then he reached into the car for his robe and pulled it over his street clothes. Other old men followed suit. Soon men all over the meadow were pulling folded robes from the cabs of their trucks—robes of all designs, all manner of trim on the sleeves, one even reading KLAN BOAT SQUAD. Dressed now, the men— there may have been one or two women on the grounds—drove off, headed to a nearby schoolyard.

• • •

The ready pool of whites who will respond to the racist signal has posed an enticement. This population, always hungry for activity—or for the talk of activity—that promises dignity and meaning to lives that are working poorly in a highly competitive world, constitutes an alluring prize. The people are needy, and they respond quickly to the signal flag of race.

Much as I don't want to believe it, [the racist] movement brings a sense of meaning—at least for a while—to some of the discontented. To struggle in a cause that transcends the individual lends meaning to a life, no matter how ill-founded or narrowing the cause. For young men in the neo-Nazi group that I had studied in Detroit, membership was an alternative to atomization and drift; within the group they worked for a cause and took direct risks in the company of comrades. Similarly, many people derive a degree of self-confidence and dignity from the suggestion that they are engaged in a heroic struggle for the sake of a larger entity, the reborn family of Whites.

Having accepted a people particularly predisposed to racism as their base, the trap for the leaders is quite real. To animate this base, the leaders must put most of their energy into a particular kind of theater. The movement lives on demonstrations, rallies, and counterallies; on marches and countermarches; on rabid speeches at twilight; on cross-burnings with Gothic ritual by moonlight.

By their nature those actions guarantee failure and bear little relation to the issues of these lives. When interviewing the young neo-Nazis in Detroit, I have often found myself driving with them past the closed factories, the idled plants of our shrinking manufacturing base. The fewer and fewer plants that remain can demand better educated and more highly skilled workers. These fatherless Nazi youths, these high-school dropouts, will find little place in the emerging economy. Enacting the charade of white struggle only buys a wasteful time-out. The current economy has little use for overt racist drama; labor is surplus; a permanently underemployed white underclass is taking its place alongside the permanent black underclass. The struggle over race merely diverts youth from confronting the real issues of their lives. Not many seats are left on the train, and the train is leaving the station.

Stirred for a time by the emotions, but soon finding that nothing has changed in their lives, many waves of membership will pass through these movements. The symbols that are used by the movements touch them; the ape-beast, the Serpent, reflect deep human fears. But eventually the symbols lose their power, as the individual asks, *What is happening to my life?*

The weary cycle drains even the organizer. Butler [one of the leaders] ponders what it means to have accomplished nothing. Miles alludes to his own weariness. "What is he to do, though?" he asks. He has done this all his life. His wife is annoyed that he talks this way when he speaks with me. "You make him talk about things he doesn't think about normally," Dot charges.

• • •

I am concerned. At home, next to my typewriter, I keep a photo that was reproduced in *The New York Times* in 1980. The photo shows a ten-year-old boy and his eight-year-old brother. They are in coats and caps. A woman holding an infant stands in the background. Six-pointed stars are sewn to the coats of one of the boys and the woman. An officer of the SS snapped this photo of Selig Jacob and Zrilu Jacob minutes after they had arrived at Auschwitz, moments before they were marched into the gas chamber. In the photo, Selig's eyes are fixed. Zrilu's are puzzled, his mouth is twisted, he is near tears. The boys cannot tell what is happening. They are uncertain and frightened.

Their sister, who somehow survived Auschwitz, came upon the photo in an SS barracks the day after liberation.

This photo is my talisman; it reminds me why I study racism.

For four years I conducted interviews with black men and women on a terribly poor corner in Detroit. My respondents were all migrants from Alabama and Mississippi. Almost every one had stories of relatives or townspeople who had been tortured and killed by hooded men in the night.

The Klan, across time, has been a nesting ground for murder, whatever else it has been. Members of the Order did kill, as well as rob.

• • •

Organized white racism is about a mood—lonely resentment—and several ideas—white specialness, the biological significance of "race," and the primacy of power in human relations. These ideas and the feeling of being cheated (not unique to racists) are powerfully motivating in the absence of ideas that might lead to more positive action. People will find some way to make their lives meaningful, and if nothing richer is at hand, racism (or religious fanaticism or nationalism or gang membership) will do. The appeal of white racist ideologies reflects the absence of competing sets of thought, emotion, and experience, competing faiths that say "This is how the world is constructed" and "This is how you can become a person who matters and whose life matters."

Formal and informal education about racism tend to undervalue the importance of experience. You can't sell people a new idea backed only by your authority. You have to have respect for the lives the people have led to this point and begin with them there; their experiences have led them to their assumptions and conceptions. As you identify and legitimate those experiences, you can help people identify their own primary needs in society. Then they can begin to imagine other people as having parallel needs. You can begin to think together about what each of you needs in the world in order to get along, and you can begin to think together about what others need. Education about racism should be education about personal identity; we have to begin with our own lives. We must begin with respect for the lives of one another.

I've often encountered a related problem in courses I've taught. Students often want to say, "I am color blind; I don't see black and white." This is a way to say "I am a good girl/boy" in a subculture where racism is not chic. Students feel a push to declare their non-racism. The words used come from a misconception that racism is a thing out there in the environment that one could pick up or reject. The students don't understand. Racism is a way of perceiving the world and a way of thinking. To a certain degree it is part of everyone who lives in a racist society. Imagine growing up next to a cement factory, and imagine the cement dust inevitably becoming a part of your body. As we grow up within a society that is saturated in white racism, year after year we pass through interactions in which white racist conceptions are an unspoken subtext. We make lives in institutions in which this is true. We cannot live from day to day without absorbing a certain amount of white racism into our thoughts. (We similarly absorb homophobia and sexism.) It is foolish to say, "I am not racist." Part of one's mind (if one is white and perhaps if one is a person of color) has necessarily absorbed racist ways of thinking. It is important to discover the subtle ways our culture's racism has affected our thinking: to identify those habits of thought and learn how to keep them from influencing us. We can get tripped up by ideas we don't allow ourselves to acknowledge.

In one of his songs, Leadbelly tells us how to deal with the blues: When you wake up in the morning with the blues, you got to say "Good morning, blues," you got to sit down and talk with your blues, got to get to know them, got to talk it over. Whites (and maybe sometimes people of color) have to get well acquainted with the subtext of racism in our lives. Not in order to feel guilty, but in order to be sure the way we act more accurately reflects our intentions.

It doesn't matter whether or not you or I can call ourselves good folk. Our actions are what matter. Real people get hurt badly in our society by poverty and racism. We can alter the institutions that do the damage. We need to be fully conscious of our influences; we need to know ourselves. The militant racists let us see the racist parts of our souls with few filters; we should observe and learn.

Women in the Military

Laura L. Miller

introduction ▪ ▪ ▪ ▪ ▪

That we are immersed in rapid social change has become a taken-for-granted assumption of contemporary life. Not everyone, though, feels the pinch of change to the same degree. A change may affect one person's life profoundly, while for others that same change merely provides an interesting topic of conversation. Some change is so moderate that we can adjust to the new aspect of life with little difficulty. Other change upsets us because it challenges our assumptions about the way the world is or should be. Some people gain by change and like what is happening; others lose, and can't stand it. With perspectives so vastly different in our pluralistic society, some view the same change as long overdue, while others insist that it should never have come about in the first place.

Over the past several decades, relations between the sexes have changed considerably. If someone went into a coma in the 1950s and were to miraculously come to consciousness now, that person certainly would be bewildered by the vast technological changes that have taken place: televisions in every home, cell phones, videos, cameras without film, fax machines, satellites, missiles, the Internet. The changed relationships of the sexes would be similarly confusing. Many expectations of basic interaction have been fundamentally altered. That individual's deeply ingrained assumptions would be challenged in one situation after another.

As with other social change, not everyone has been touched in the same way. In this selection, we look at the integration of women in the military, where women now occupy positions from which they were excluded just a generation ago. As Laura Miller focuses on how men react to the presence of women in formerly all-male jobs, she notes that the men are using techniques of resistance more commonly associated with the protests of minorities.

Thinking Critically

As you read this selection, ask yourself:

- How can we reduce friction between men and women in the military? In other occupations?

The data presented here are taken from multiple stages of field research on active-duty Army soldiers from early 1992 to late 1994. I used a multimethod strategy to capture both large-scale attitudinal patterns and individual viewpoints. To collect the data, I traveled to eight stateside Army posts and two national training centers, where soldiers conduct war games on a simulated battlefield. I also lived with Army personnel for 10 days in Somalia during Operation Restore Hope, for seven days in Macedonia during Operation Able Sentry, and for six days in Haiti during Operation Uphold Democracy. . . .

Given the military context and the sensitive nature of some of the issues, [in my discussion groups and interviews] I relied on written notes rather than tape-recording. . . . I also collected large-scale survey data in order to analyze the relationships between soldiers' demographics and their attitudes on a wide array of issues. The ethnographic data were cross-validated by multiple stages of questionnaires totaling more than 4,100. . . .

In *Domination and the Arts of Resistance,* James C. Scott (1990) provides an extensive historical analysis explaining how powerless groups resist and subvert the efforts of those with power over them. His work demonstrates that people's fear of negative sanctions often drives them to resist in ways that cannot be traced to the initiator, or are lost in the anonymity of crowds. The greater the power exerted from above, the more fully masked the resistance from below. Scott provides numerous examples of the art of political disguise, including gossip, rumor, grumbling, folktales, possession by spirits, mass defiance, anonymous threats, symbolic inversion of the social order, and rituals of reversal such as carnival. Like much of the research on which he draws, Scott continues the Marxist tradition of dividing the world in two: those with economic power (the bourgeoisie, landlords, kings, the ruling class, employers) and those who depend on them or must serve them (the proletariat, peasants, serfs, slaves, workers). . . .

Scott's examples closely parallel behavior that I found in gender relations in the Army, except for one very significant anomaly: It is the structurally dominant group, Army men, who employ the strategies of resistance that are generally seen as the weapons of the weak. My research shows that some men devote a great deal of energy to resisting their women coworkers and commanders through methods such as sabotage, name-calling, foot-dragging, and spreading rumors. Women, paradoxically, do not appear to be using any of these strategies of the weak to gain power from men, according to either their accounts or men's.

What explains the use of weapons of the weak by the structurally dominant group but not by the subordinate minority? My investigation led me to social psychological studies of power. In this literature it is argued that people act according to perceptions of power based on their own experiences and knowledge, not according to some objective analysis of resources. . . . Frequently military men described themselves as unjustly constrained or controlled by military women. Furthermore, these men tend to believe that women's power is usually gained illegitimately and that women take advantage of their gender to promote their own careers. . . .

From Laura L. Miller, "Not Just Weapons of the Weak: Gender Harassment as a Form of Protest for Army Men." *Social Psychology Quarterly,* 60, 1 (Mar., 1997), pp. 32–51. Reprinted by permission.

For example, enlisted men may not enjoy the privileges of their sex as much as men at the higher command levels, particularly in relation to women officers; also, in this era of organizational downsizing, male career officers sometimes blame their limited opportunities on increased participation by women. Thus not all military men experience male privilege, and even some of the more privileged members are constrained within the organization. . . .

In this article I first describe men's resistance in the form of gender harassment. Then I examine who is likely to oppose expanded or even current roles for women soldiers, and why gender harassment is a product of this opposition. I conclude with the implications of this case for gender and other minority relations as well as for the study of power and resistance.

■ ■ ■ ■ GENDER HARASSMENT

Distinguishing Gender Harassment from Sexual Harassment

> Sexual harassment implies that you can only be harassed through sexual means. Women can also be harassed through the job in other ways. If your commander doesn't like you, you will encounter harassment, i.e., the shit details, made to work later than everyone else, constant field problems, low efficiency ratings, etc. It's more prejudice than harassment towards females in the Army. (black NCO [Non-Commissioned Officer] in administrative support)

Sexual harassment is not an analytically useful category because it may refer to situations as disparate as sexual assault, discrimination in promotion or assignment, sexual comments, and gender harassment. . . . In my analysis, I limit the term *sexual harassment* to unwanted sexual comments or advances.

Gender harassment refers to harassment that is not sexual, and is used to enforce traditional gender roles, or in response to the violation of those roles. This form of harassment also may aim to undermine women's attempts at gaining power or to describe that power as illegitimately obtained or exercised. Examples include men proclaiming "Women can't drive trucks" in the presence of female drivers or refusing to follow a superior's directives simply because that superior is a woman. Many Army women report that gender harassment on the job is more prevalent than sexual harassment.

Gender harassment also can be used against men who violate gender norms. For example, men who fail to live up to the "masculine ideal" by showing insecurity or hesitation during maneuvers may be called "fags" or "girls" by their comrades. . . . Because behavior that conflicts with one's gender role is stereotypically associated with homosexuality, both heterosexuality and traditional gender roles are enforced through gender harassment.

Because of the prevalence of gender harassment, workshops and policies that address only sexual harassment miss much of the picture. Women report that gender harassment can be just as disruptive in their lives as sexual harassment; it can interfere with their ability to do their work, with their private lives, and with their opportunities to receive some recognition and promotions. Gender harassment is often difficult to attribute to individuals, may not be recognized by command as a problem, and is often invisible in debates about harassment of women in the military. . . .

Gender harassment is hardly unique to military men and women; it is found in many studies of women in sex-atypical work. Examples of what I call gender harassment are scattered throughout studies of job climate, male coworkers' reactions to women, and subtle or covert sex discrimination:

> [We] also face another pervasive and sinister kind of harassment which is gender-based, but may have nothing to do with sex. It is a harassment aimed at us simply because we are women in a "man's" job, and its function is to discourage us from staying in our trades. (M. Martin 1988: 10)

Some Forms of Gender Harassment

Below are some illustrative examples of gender harassment.

Resistance to Authority.   Women who are officers or NCOs commonly complained of male subordinates, especially older enlisted men, who "just don't like answering to a woman." When given orders, they feign ignorance about what is expected of them, or engage in foot-dragging. This method is effective because the men do not risk the official reprimand warranted by an outright refusal to obey orders; yet they challenge women's authority by not complying completely. As one white NCO hypothesized, "Men are intimidated by women superiors and most try to undermine their work." Several women leaders reported having to "pull rank" more often than their male counterparts to get things done. . . .

Constant Scrutiny.   Hostile men use constant scrutiny to catch individual women making mistakes, and then use the mistakes to criticize the abilities of women in general. Because of this scrutiny women often feel obligated to work harder than those under less supervision. Women report that they experience such scrutiny as relentless harassment, and that it can make them feel self-conscious and extremely stressed.

Both enlisted and officer women report that as women they are subject to closer scrutiny than men. When women are singled out for observation by suspicious peers and superiors, they often feel they have to work harder than their coworkers just to be accepted as equal members of the unit. . . .

The behavior of a few women is often projected onto the entire gender, but the same is not true for men. To illustrate, some women soldiers serving in the early phases of operations in Haiti pointed out that if the three soldiers who committed suicide there had been women, a discussion would have ensued: People would have asked whether women could handle the stress of deployments or separation from their families. Yet because they were "just men," they were reported as *soldiers,* and the suicides were not interpreted as saying anything about men in general. . . .

Women leaders are rendered less flexible than men because of the constant scrutiny. Sometimes they believe that the people watching them are waiting for them to make mistakes or deviate from regulations; this is a disconcerting environment in

which to make decisions. As a result, some men as well as some women classify female superiors as unfair or "too hard." They prefer to serve under men, who have
more freedom to bend the rules in favor of their troops: "Women seem to feel they
have something to prove. They do, but should not abuse their soldiers [in the pro-
cess]" (white enlisted man in electronics).

   Scrutiny as a harassment strategy is particularly safe in the military because it
fits into the functioning of the organization. One cannot be punished for seeking out
and correcting errors, and it would be quite difficult to prove that women are being
watched more closely than men.

Gossip and Rumors.   Army women are often the subject of untrue gossip about
their sex lives. Repeatedly I heard that if a woman dates more than one man in the
Army, she is labeled a "slut." If she doesn't date, she is labeled a "dyke." Unlike
men, women who are promoted quickly or who receive coveted assignments are often rumored to have "slept their way to the top." At every post I visited, soldiers had
heard the rumor (which has never been verified) that a few women soldiers in the
Persian Gulf War made a fortune by setting up a tent and serving as prostitutes for
their male counterparts.

   Young Army women in particular feel that their personal lives are under intense scrutiny at all times, and that ridiculous lies can emerge from the rumor mill
for no apparent reason. One enlisted woman was shocked when her commander
took her aside one day and said, "Look, I know you're sleeping with all the guys in
your unit." She could not imagine why he said that to her; who would have started
such a rumor, or why; or why fellow soldiers—her friends—would have contributed
to spreading the stories. . . .

   Because rumors are usually untraceable, they cannot be addressed through a
formal complaint system. Scott discusses the power of such strategies:

> Gossip is perhaps the most familiar and elementary form of disguised popular aggres-
> sion. Though its use is hardly confined to attacks by subordinates on their superiors, it
> represents a relatively safe social sanction. Gossip, almost by definition, has no identifi-
> able author, but scores of eager retellers who can claim they are just passing on the
> news. Should the gossip—and here I have in mind malicious gossip—be challenged, ev-
> eryone can disavow responsibility for having originated it. . . .
>   The character of gossip that distinguishes it from rumor is that gossip consists typ-
> ically of stories that are designed to ruin the reputation of some identifiable person or
> persons. If the perpetrators remain anonymous, the victim is clearly specified. There is,
> arguably, something of a disguised democratic voice about gossip in the sense that it is
> propagated only to the extent that others find it in their interest to retell the story. If
> they don't, it disappears. (1990:142)

Sabotage.   I found evidence of sabotage, as a form of gender harassment, only in
work fields that are nontraditional for women. Because these nontraditional occupations can be strenuous and dangerous, the sabotage of equipment can be quite
threatening. . . .

   In one instance of sabotage from my research, two women new to an all-male
vehicle maintenance and repair unit arrived at work every morning to find that the

heavy, difficult-to-change track had been removed from their assigned vehicle. After a few weeks, during which they patiently replaced the track each day, the harassment ended. They had earned the men's respect by proving their skills and their willingness to work hard. The men's doubts were dispelled when they decided that the women's abilities had earned them a position in the unit, and that they would not use their gender to exempt themselves from dirty and difficult work.

Sabotage of equipment and tools was reported by women in mechanical fields, but I never heard of sabotage in the form of disappearing files, erased computer data, jammed typewriters, hidden medical supplies, or misplaced cooking utensils.

Indirect Threats.   Some soldiers reported that some of their fellow men would rape women who dared to enter infantry or armor units. The comments written on surveys include these remarks by a black enlisted man in the combat arms:

> The majority of men in the Army are sexist. I know, because I'm a man. Women in combat units would be harassed, if not raped. I say this because I've seen it and have nothing to hide. If you want the truth about issues, don't ask NCOs or officers. They'll tell you everything is all peaches and cream!! If you want the truth ask an E4 that's been in about 5 years. Women only have a fair shake as cooks or nurses. They'll be extremely harassed, if not molested, if they enter combat arms. I know, trust me.

Another infantryman echoed that assessment, although he proposed that male violence toward women is due to the conditions of deployments, not to sexism:

> In a situation where times are hard—less food, no showers, road marching, with 70–100 lbs ruck on your back, and [you] don't know when the next supply shipment will be in, the male soldiers will start thinking of sex and the female soldiers may be raped or something.

WHY GENDER HARASSMENT? PERCEPTIONS OF POWER
■ ■ ■ AND LIMITED FORMS OF PROTEST

Some men resort to gender harassment to protect changing gender norms, either because they personally prefer traditional norms or because they think that men and women are not capable of successfully working outside traditional roles. Many of these men believe that women's attempts to claim equality have resulted in favorable treatment for women who have been largely unwilling or unable to fully meet the demands of being a soldier. Gender harassment is an attempt to push women back into their more "natural" roles, restore the meritocratic order of the organization, and ensure that all soldiers on the battlefield can do their jobs and assist the wounded in times of war. Certainly these views are considered sexist by many, and potentially could cause problems for any soldier who expresses them openly in mixed company. Thus gender harassment is preferred as an often unattributable way to protest the expansion of women's roles and to attempt to balance scales that are perceived to be tilted in women's favor.

Hostile Proponents and Another
Version of Equality

"Women should be given totally equal treatment and standards. But I don't see it happening." This assertion by a male Army captain expresses the views of many Army men. Rather than championing women's rights, however, this officer is among the men who feel that women, not men, are the privileged and powerful group in the military. These men oppose expanding women's opportunities because they believe that women already enjoy too many advantages in the organization and have not yet met the requirements of the roles they already fill.

Some men believe that women use the term *equality* to advance their personal interests, and that they would object if true equality were offered:

> My opinion is that if women want the right to be in combat roles, they should have to register with selective service. Also, if women want to be treated and have the same rights as men, they should be treated equally all of the time and not just when it is convenient for them. (white enlisted man)

Interview data reveal that most of the men who favor opening combat roles to women on the same terms as men do so only because they are confident that women will fail in those roles. I term this group "hostile proponents" of women in combat. Such hostile proponents reason that the issue of women in the combat arms will not be put to rest until women have been given the opportunity to prove their incompetence. For example, a male driver agreed that women should be allowed to volunteer for combat roles—until he dropped off the female officer who was traveling with us. As soon as she left our group, he added that he thought women should be allowed into combat because they would see how hard the combat arms really are, and no one would have to listen any longer to their complaints about wanting to be included. This "treat women the same to watch them fail" attitude was expressed in writing by a white NCO in the combat arms:

> My feelings are that women just want a door open that is closed. If they want to be totally equal with us, shave their head in basic training [and] give them the same [physical training] test as men. Women in the infantry would ruin male bonding and get soldiers killed or hurt trying to cover for them in combat. Try an all female infantry basic training and [advanced individual training] with the exact same standards as males.

These hostile proponents have found that they can voice their objections by appropriating the language of the feminist activists. Arguments that women should stay home and raise children can be denounced as sexist; agreeing with activists that women and men are "equal" and should be expected to be treated equally cannot. When women are kept out of certain occupations, feminists can continue to argue that women, given the chance, could perform as well as men. Hostile proponents believe that admitting women is a better strategy for reducing the credibility of such arguments because, they insist, the reality will prove the arguments false.

One resistant male soldier provided the formula "(Equal pay = equal job = equal responsibility = equal risk) = equal opportunity" to stress that equality should be sought across the board, not only in pay or opportunity. He was one of the many men who believed that the differential policies actually work in women's favor, disrupt the meritocratic order, and are likely to imperil soldiers in times of war.

A few combat soldiers in my survey were motivated by self-interest to support admitting women to their Military Occupational Specialties (MOSs). One such man, a black NCO, wrote:

> If women are allowed in combat they should be made to shave their heads like men, or let men grow their hair like women. And if women are allowed, field duty would become better for men, because of [women's] needs. So therefore, I'm for them in combat. Yes, let them in.

Men's Perceptions of Women's Privileges

Why do some Army men perceive themselves, and not women, to be the disadvantaged gender in the military? Although other respondents offer counterarguments to these men's opinions, I focus here on the viewpoint of men who regard themselves as underdogs. In this section I demonstrate how a structurally dominant group can perceive itself to be a disadvantaged group, and therefore resort to the types of resistance strategies that Scott attributes to the weak. The unifying theme of these examples is the belief that most military women do not take the same risks or work as hard as do military men, and yet are promoted more quickly than men because of their gender.

Easier Physical Training Standards.   Both men and women reported that women's physical training requirements are not only different from men's, but easier for most women to meet than men's are for most men. Although this training is supposed to maintain physical fitness, most soldiers interpret it as a measure of strength. That the women's requirements are easier than the men's is seen by many as proof that women are less well qualified for physically strenuous work:

> I can't be adamant enough. There is no place for women in the infantry. Women do not belong in combat units. If you haven't been there, then you wouldn't understand. As far as equal rights, some women say they are as physically strong as a man. Then why are the [physical training] standards different? (white NCO in the combat arms)

Thus some soldiers argue that only one standard should exist for men and for women, and that such a standard should reflect the requirements of the job. A white lieutenant in intelligence and communications explained his view:

> The standards are never the same for men and women. The [Army Physical Fitness Test] is a perfect example. [W]hat most junior leaders feel (that I have discussed the topic with) . . . there should be no difference for either sex. [The Department of the Army] has established minimum standards and they should apply across the board, regardless of sex. Which means the female standards would have to go out the window. A man who can only do 18 pushups is unfit for service, so it should be [the same] for females. If a female can meet the same standards as me, I will gladly serve with, for, or over her. But

if she can't I will also gladly chapter her out of the Army as unfit for service. I've seen action in Grenada and Iraq and know there are females who could've done my job. Few, but some. However my wife, who went to Saudi, is 104 lbs., 5'4" and couldn't carry my 201 lbs. across the living room, much less the desert if I was wounded. Whose standards should apply?

In deployments and field exercises, the differences are most apparent. Some commanders find them difficult to know how to handle:

> The topic about women in combat MOS's has finally cleared up with me, I have completed [platoon leadership training], and found that the women on my patrol team could not perform their squad duties. For example, being a 60-gunner, or radio operator I was patrol leader. I assigned the females on my team the 60 and the radio. After about 2 miles of patrolling, the females could not do their jobs. I was accused of being sexist, but when it came down to it, men had to take those assigned jobs in my squad from these women. I'm sure that there are some females that could "keep up" or "hang" with the men, but the fact is that women are not physically strong enough. (white enlisted man in the combat arms)

Pregnancy as an Advantage.   Some men find it unfair that women have an honorable option out of the service, deployments, or single barracks that men do not have: pregnancy. A white enlisted man in intelligence and communications wrote:

> There seems to be a trend that females in the Army take advantage of free medical and have kids while serving. The 9 months of pregnancy limits them to no physical labor and is bad on morale. They are still a soldier, but they are only working at about 30% of their potential, forcing men or non-pregnant women to compensate.

A white lieutenant in the medical field noted, "I am currently in a unit with female soldiers, about 60–75% are pregnant or on some type of profile." "Profile" is a standing in which soldiers' physical abilities are limited; therefore they are exempt from physically strenuous tasks, including daily physical training. Pregnant women are among the most common sources of resentment and thus are targets of harassment. Pregnancy then, is another way in which some men feel that women are receiving equal pay and promotion, but are not doing equal work and not taking equal risks and responsibilities.

Better Educational Opportunities.   Many men feel that restrictions on women's roles are unfair not because they limit women, but because they appear to give women opportunities to receive more schooling than men, thus improving their chances for promotion. A white enlisted man wrote, "Most women are in rear units and have the chance to go to school and complete correspondence courses." A black NCO viewed these opportunities as tipping the balance in women's favor in competitions for promotion: "Of most of the units that I've served, the female soldier is more apt to attend schools, i.e., military and civilian. This constant trend allows them better opportunities for career progression."

Some men feel that with this extra training, women will be more qualified than men, with the result that "Most women are promoted above their peers" (white

NCO). One white enlisted man expressed the view that it is wasteful to allow women to take coveted slots in combat-related training to help their careers when they are currently restricted from performing those tasks in the event of a real war:

> Each person male or female will perform according to his or her gifts. We cannot make that determination. Congress needs to get off its lazy butt and make a decision one way or the other. Until that time, it remains a waste of time and taxpayer's money to send women to combat related schools (jump schools and air assault, etc.) just for the sake of being "stylish" and to appease those women who whine about discrimination when they're not allowed to do something a male soldier does.

Exemption from Combat Arms as a Way to Faster Promotion, Better Assignments, and "Cushy" Jobs. In some units there is a hierarchy of assignments, which is sometimes disrupted by the way women are integrated. The lowest jobs are often the "grunt work"—hard, mindless labor. Some men protested to me that when women are assigned to such a unit, they are spared the grunt work and placed (often by male superiors) ahead of men for more desirable assignments. Not only are they excused from doing what men have to do; they also delay men's progress into better positions and sometimes have authority over the men they have bumped. A white lieutenant cited an example of the problems created because a man in a signal MOS can be assigned to a combat unit and required to do grunt work, but a woman is always assigned elsewhere:

> Currently, females in combat support roles (e.g., signal, chemical, [military police], medical services) can not hold a designated position in Combat Units. For example, females are allowed to serve in the signal corps, but they are not allowed to serve as a signal [platoon leader] in a combat arms unit. There is too much animosity towards females in a specific branch if they can't hold the same positions that their male counterparts [do]. The females are seen as getting the "cushy" jobs and interesting jobs as the males have to fulfill the combat roles. If a female can not hold a position in their designated specialty, they should not be allowed in that specific specialty.

These men view women not only as obtaining easier work, but as jumping up the hierarchy without earning it. As a white lieutenant explains, this can breed resentment:

> Chemical corps: females should not be allowed in this branch if they cannot serve in all positions. For example, they get sent to this division, but cannot serve in the infantry, armor, or forward artillery units. This leaves very few slots for them to fill. [The Army] does not manage this very [well] at all. As a new lieutenant, we must put in our time at the battalion staff level, first, then we are awarded a platoon at the chem company. (One company per division). [The Department of the Army] sends us more females than we have slots for, so they wind up being platoon leaders at the company ahead of the males who have put in their time at the battalions. A lot of hard feelings about this. They (females) should not be branched chemical or some of the other combat support branches.

Men complained that women are not required to do the heaviest or dirtiest part of any job, and that they can get away with it without reprimand because of their sex. Although men may find it humorous when Beetle Bailey shirks his assignments, they may become resentful when women have an unfair advantage based on their sex. One black enlisted man wrote: "Today all you hear in the Army is that we are equal, but men do all the hard and heavy work whether it's combat or not."

According to some men, women's current behavior is proof that most are unable or unwilling to do the work required of soldiers in the combat arms. Thus they resist putting their lives on the line with such soldiers: "I feel women are useless to the Army, most do not do their part when it comes to real work! Most won't change a tire, or pick up a box if it weighs more than 5 lbs. I would not go to war with women in or out of a combat role." Some of these conclusions are based on experience in the States:

> When given the same opportunity, most [women] look for excuses not to do the work. You in your position can not see it. However, I am exposed to it daily. The majority of females I know are not soldiers. They are employed. Anything strenuous is avoided with a passion. I would hate to serve with them during combat! I would end up doing my job and 2/3 of theirs just to stay alive. (black NCO in administrative work)
>
> I feel as if women in the military are ordered to do less work, get out of doing things such as field problems, and when it comes to doing heavy work, they just stand around and watch the work until it is completed. This is part of the reason I feel they could not handle a combat role because of a weaker physical and mental capability under such a stressful situation. I say this because it is proved in an everyday day of work. (black enlisted man in a technical field)

Women's gender identity traditionally has been tied to "delicacy," while men's identity has been tied to the ability to be tough and strong. So men may try to avoid work in general, but avoiding heavy labor in particular would make them look weak, cast doubt on their masculinity, and draw ridicule from other men about their "femininity." Thus many men resent that women can avoid a great deal of dirty, heavy work and still succeed in the military, while men's lives are considerably tougher. Although men tend to lay most of the blame for "getting by" on women, this behavior could not persist unless the leaders allowed it.

Paternalism Allowing Women to Get Away with More.   Both men and women may try to bend the rules, but when women succeed because of their gender, male coworkers may hold it against them. Several times women told me how they could avoid certain duties by complaining of cramps to particular male commanders. At the first mention of anything "menstrual" their commander would grimace and wave them away. (This did not work with women superiors, who sent them to sick call if they thought the cramps were serious.) Two women told me that they could hide off-limits items such as candy by placing tampons or underwear on top of the contents of their lockers or drawers. During inspections, their male commander took one look at their belongings, saw the personal items, and moved on, apparently too embarrassed to examine the rest of the contents.

As another example, one man wrote on his survey.

> I don't think women can withstand not being able to take showers for as long as men. When I was in the Gulf, we were ordered to use the water that we had only for drinking. But after one week the women were using our drinking water to take bird baths. This made me very upset.

This problem is framed as a matter of women's behavior, not the command's enforcement of rules.

Male commanders enforce rules differently for women, for several reasons. In the case of the water, the leader may have made this exception for women because he perceived them as more fragile than men, or felt that some sort of chivalry was appropriate. Padavic and Reskin (1990) call such behavior "paternalism," which they measured in their study of blue-collar workers according to whether women "had been relieved of some hard assignments, whether male coworkers had given them special treatment because of their sex, and whether their supervisors had favored them because of their sex" (p. 618).

Men in command positions sometimes fear disciplining women or pushing them to excel. These men worry that they will be accused of harassing women soldiers because of their gender, or of being insensitive to women's needs or limitations. Also, some are too embarrassed about women's underwear or hygiene to perform the ritual invasion of privacy men must undergo. As a result, even when sensitivity to women is intended, women receive privileges that men do not; this situation breeds disdain for women soldiers among some of the men.

In the military, some believe that male leaders' unwillingness to push women to excel creates a weakness among the troops that could have grave consequences during a war:

> The more fundamental question is whether women should be in the military at all. They have served well, but are victims of a male dominated system which has always demanded less of them than they would (hopefully) of themselves. If every soldier in the U.S. Army today had been trained at the same low level of expectation that female soldiers routinely are, the U.S. Army today would either be dead or in Prisoner of War camps. (an "other race" major)

Quotas, Sex, and Other Paths to the Top. As noted earlier, some men believe that women can "sleep their way" to the top, and that quotas allow women to receive undeserved promotions and assignments because of their minority status. Some men also believe that women can and do challenge poor performance reviews by claiming discrimination, and that they can use false harassment claims to punish or remove men they do not like. The perception is that women usually are believed over men in harassment cases; as a result, men's careers are ruined by the whims of ambitious or vengeful women.

Most of these perceptions reinforce the view that women want the prestige and promotions that come with serving in the combat arms, but do not intend to make the same efforts as men: "They want equal rights, but don't want to do what it takes to become equal" (white enlisted man in administration).

Limited Forms of Protest

When I asked men who opposed women in combat roles what they thought would happen in the future, they all asserted that integration was inevitable. They concluded that women eventually would "have their way" despite any reasonable objections. Perhaps because women's gains have been made gradually over the years, men perceive this progression not as a series of slow, incremental change toward one goal but as a string of victories for women over men.

One white major said, "As minorities, women have advantages." White men were likely to have a similar attitude about race; for example, they tended to think that nonwhite soldiers unfairly charge racial discrimination to challenge negative performance reviews. One white NCO spoke for many of his comrades in defining himself as a member of the oppressed minority: "I feel that the white enlisted male has more prejudice against him than any other sector in the military." He specified not only his gender but also his race and rank as contributing to his position.

Scott analyzes both the micro interactional forms of resistance by subjugated people and the outward rebellion of the powerless that occurs when "an entire category of people suddenly finds its public voice no longer stifled" (1990:210). I found the reverse among military men: a category of people who have assumed and enjoyed gender privilege, and who rebel because their public voice has been deemed sexist and has been silenced.

Because of the nature of the military organization, many forms of protest are not realistic options for men who contend that they are disadvantaged. Army men cannot strike, circulate petitions, organize rallies or demonstrations, walk out during the workday, or quit collectively in response to a policy change. (Before quitting they would have to meet their enlistment obligations or complete time-consuming formal exit procedures and paperwork.) Boycotts and "client preference" arguments are generally irrelevant here. Thus men who are silent in mixed-sex environments may be channeling their frustrations into underground grumbling.

I experienced firsthand evidence of men's perception that they must hide their opinions. Often the men who eventually voiced their objections to working with women were not initially forthright. When asked about gender issues, they first told me what they imagined I wanted to hear, or recited the "party line" that would keep them out of trouble should any statements be attributed to them. After calculating my opinion on the basis of my status as a young civilian woman conducting research on military women, they hesitated at my opening questions and then said reluctantly that they thought women should and could serve in any military roles. Then, when I raised an opposing argument (such as "So you don't see any problem with close contact between men and women serving in tanks together?"), their true feelings burst forth.

In mixed-sex groups (particularly groups of officers), some of the men squirmed, rolled their eyes, or shook their heads, but did not speak up during discussions about gender. After I dismissed the group, I privately asked those men to stay behind, and asked them why they were silent but seemingly dissatisfied. They revealed that they refrained from participating because they believed that organizational constraints prohibited them from stating their true opinions, particularly in the presence of officer women. In this way I learned which arguments were considered legitimate in the organization (at least when women were present) and which would be censured. The opportunity to write anonymous comments on the formal questionnaires may have been particularly appreciated by soldiers who felt their views were controversial. Men were concerned that they would be held accountable for any statements that could be considered sexist; they feared an official reprimand and negative consequences for their career.

These soldiers' perceptions are evidence that the Army has made some headway in controlling men's willingness to make openly sexist statements. (Soldiers' self-censorship about gender contrasted sharply with their comments about allowing open gays and lesbians to serve in the military; men did not hesitate to make loud, violent threats against any gays they might discover.) Many of these men resent the inability to speak their minds. They believe that even if they could speak candidly, their concerns would not be addressed formally because they think women have the advantage in gender-based disputes. Therefore they express their resentment in ways that the institution cannot control.

Male soldiers interpret the "suppression" of some arguments against women as proof that those arguments are valid and that women have no legitimate counterargument. Thus some men are angry because they perceive women as having gained their power in the military illegitimately or as having taken advantage of that power. Others simply object to changing gender norms and increasing participation of women in non-traditional roles. This tension is exacerbated by the perceived prohibition against expressing their dissatisfaction. Therefore many men hold their tongues in public, but complain among themselves and retaliate with gender harassment. Although grumbling is certainly a part of military culture, the resistance strategies I found directed against women are rarely employed for similar complaints against male leaders or fellow soldiers in general.

■ ■ ■ ■ IMPLICATIONS OF GENDER HARASSMENT

The Army's formal sexual harassment [policies] in the 1990s have taught many men the definitions and the possible consequences of this behavior.

Yet improvements in controlling sexual harassment do not necessarily mean that women are now working in a supportive or even a tolerant environment. Although women can be hurt by public sexist comments that express doubts about their abilities, it is also debilitating when such comments are forced underground, where they cannot be challenged. In addition, because many men perceive themselves as unable to safely voice their concerns about women as coworkers, some men feel that gender harassment is a justified means of registering their complaints.

As previously disadvantaged groups gain some power in legislating discriminatory behavior, their opponents may come to rely on forms of resistance that are difficult to regulate. These implications go beyond gender and affect areas such as race, ethnicity, and sexual orientation. Even as minorities enjoy increased success in controlling overt harassment, they must recognize that people will seek other ways to express hostility. When minority groups call for equality, they should be prepared to be informed about inequities that favor them, and to learn how the language of equality might be used against them.

Underlying the cases in the resistance literature is the assumption that the reader is sympathetic to the oppressed groups; groups claiming oppression in fact are oppressed and are justified in their resistance. Resistance, then, has been treated as something constructive, which preserves human dignity and may lead to the overthrow of an unjust system. Thus nobody has asked how to eliminate the "hidden transcript" and dismantle underground forms of resistance. In the traditional dichotomous framework of resistance studies, that question would have been asked only by oppressors seeking compliance—seeking to use their power for manipulation or indoctrination.

But what do we say when the resisting group is not entirely powerless and does not wish to relinquish one of the realms in which it holds power? The powerful can appropriate for themselves the language and framework used to explain dominance and resistance. They can portray themselves as victims, as "silenced," when *they* suddenly are required to monitor their behavior in the presence of others. Is the attempt to regulate racist, sexist, and homophobic speech and behavior equivalent to the past suppression of minority groups' voices? Are we to be sympathetic when previously powerful groups develop underground resistance because their behavior is suppressed?

In this paper I have sought to demonstrate that in order to effectively examine power dynamics, studies of resistance must supplement cultural and structural analyses. Future work must recognize the importance of perceptions of power because such perceptions do not necessarily correspond to objective measures of power. These perceptions, however, strongly influence people's attitudes and behavior. In the military, soldiers' experience of gender varies according to rank, age, race, and occupational specialty.

Resistance studies also must move beyond seeing the world in terms of only two classes: the oppressors and the oppressed. This dichotomy cannot fully explain the dynamics of a world in which multiple hierarchies can make people simultaneously powerful and powerless relative to others. Future research must account for people's multiple statuses which result in a much more varied distribution of power than a dichotomous model would allow. The behavior of some military men toward women soldiers demonstrates that researchers must look for "weapons of the weak" in the hands of people at all levels of both perceived and structurally measured power.

■ ■ ■ REFERENCES

Martin, M. (Ed.). (1988). *Hard Hatted Women: Stories of Struggle and Success in the Trades.* Seattle: Seal Press.

Padavic, I., and B. F. Reskin. (1990). "Men's Behavior and Women's Interest in Blue-Collar Jobs." *Social Problems, 37:* 613–628.

Scott, J. G. (1990). *Domination and the Arts of Resistance: Hidden Transcripts.* New Haven: Yale University Press.

On Being Sane in Insane Places

David L. Rosenhan

introduction

People who violate explicit rules written into law find themselves enmeshed in a formal system that involves passing judgment on their fitness to remain in society. The result can be the loss of their freedom and being watched over by guards. People who violate implicit rules (the background assumptions that we all carry around with us about what "normal" people are like) can also find themselves caught up in a formal system that involves passing judgment on their fitness to remain in society. If found, let's say, "guilty of insanity," they, too, are institutionalized—placed in the care of keepers who oversee almost all aspects of their lives.

Institutionalizing people who violate implicit rules is based on this taken-for-granted background assumption: We *are* able to tell the sane from the insane. If we cannot, the practice of institutionalizing the "insane" would be insane! In that case, we would have to question psychiatry as a mechanism of social control. But what kind of question is this? Even most of us non–psychiatrists can tell the difference between who is sane and who is not, can't we? In a fascinating experiment, Rosenhan put to the test whether even psychiatrists can differentiate between the sane and the insane. As detailed in this account, the results contain a few surprises.

Thinking Critically

As you read this selection, ask yourself:

- With their vast experience, why did the medical personnel, both psychiatrists and psychiatric nurses, not recognize that the pseudopatients in this experiment were sane?

If sanity and insanity exist . . . how shall we know them? The question is neither capricious nor itself insane. However much we may be personally convinced that we can tell the normal from the abnormal, the evidence is simply not compelling. It is commonplace, for example, to read about murder trials wherein eminent psychiatrists for the defense are contradicted by equally eminent psychiatrists for the prosecution on the matter of the defendant's sanity. More generally, there are a great deal of conflicting data on the reliability, utility, and meaning of such terms as "sanity," "insanity," "mental illness," and "schizophrenia."[1] Finally, as early as 1934, Benedict suggested that normality and abnormality are not universal.[2] What is viewed as normal in one culture may be seen as quite aberrant in another. Thus, notions of normality and abnormality may not be quite as accurate as people believe they are.

To raise questions regarding normality and abnormality is in no way to question the fact that some behaviors are deviant or odd. Murder is deviant. So, too, are hallucinations. Nor does raising such questions deny the existence of the personal anguish that is often associated with "mental illness." Anxiety and depression exist. Psychological suffering exists. But normality and abnormality, sanity and insanity, and the diagnoses that flow from them may be less substantive than many believe them to be.

At its heart, the question of whether the sane can be distinguished from the insane (and whether degrees of insanity can be distinguished from each other) is a simple matter: Do the salient characteristics that lead to diagnoses reside in the patients themselves or in the environments and contexts in which observers find them? From Bleuler, through Kretschmer, through the formulators of the recently revised *Diagnostic and Statistical Manual* of the American Psychiatric Association, the belief has been strong that patients present symptoms, that those symptoms can be categorized, and, implicitly, that the sane are distinguishable from the insane. More recently, however, this belief has been questioned. Based in part on theoretical and anthropological considerations, but also on philosophical, legal, and therapeutic ones, the view has grown that psychological categorization of mental illness is useless at best and downright harmful, misleading, and pejorative at worst. Psychiatric diagnoses, in this view, are in the minds of the observers and are not valid summaries of characteristics displayed by the observed.[3,4,5]

Gains can be made in deciding which of these is more nearly accurate by getting normal people (that is, people who do not have, and have never suffered, symptoms of serious psychiatric disorders) admitted to psychiatric hospitals and then determining whether they were discovered to be sane and, if so, how. If the sanity of such pseudopatients were always detected, there would be *prima facie* evidence that a sane individual can be distinguished from the insane context in which he is found. Normality (and presumably abnormality) is distinct enough that it can be recognized wherever it occurs, for it is carried within the person. If, on the other hand, the sanity of the pseudopatients were never discovered, serious difficulties would arise for those who support traditional modes of psychiatric diagnosis. Given that the hospital staff was not incompetent, that the pseudopatient had been behaving as sanely as he had been outside of the hospital, and that it had never been previously suggested that he belonged in a psychiatric hospital, such an unlikely outcome

From David L. Rosenhan, "On Being Sane in Insane Places." *Science, 179,* pp. 250–258. January 19. Copyright 1973, AAAS. Reprinted by permission.

would support the view that psychiatric diagnosis betrays little about the patient but much about the environment in which an observer finds him.

This article describes such an experiment. Eight sane people gained secret admission to twelve different hospitals.[6] Their diagnostic experiences constitute the data of the first part of this article; the remainder is devoted to a description of their experiences in psychiatric institutions. Too few psychiatrists and psychologists, even those who have worked in such hospitals, know what the experience is like. They rarely talk about it with former patients, perhaps because they distrust information coming from the previously insane. Those who have worked in psychiatric hospitals are likely to have adapted so thoroughly to the settings that they are insensitive to the impact of that experience. And while there have been occasional reports of researchers who submitted themselves to psychiatric hospitalization,[7] these researchers have commonly remained in the hospitals for short periods of time, often with the knowledge of the hospital staff. It is difficult to know the extent to which they were treated like patients or like research colleagues. Nevertheless, their reports about the inside of the psychiatric hospital have been valuable. This article extends those efforts.

■ ■ ■ PSEUDOPATIENTS AND THEIR SETTINGS

The eight pseudopatients were a varied group. One was a psychology graduate student in his twenties. The remaining seven were older and "established." Among them were three psychologists, a pediatrician, a psychiatrist, a painter, and a housewife. Three pseudopatients were women, five were men. All of them employed pseudonyms, lest their alleged diagnoses embarrass them later. Those who were in mental health professions alleged another occupation in order to avoid the special attentions that might be accorded by staff, as a matter of courtesy or caution, to ailing colleagues.[8] With the exception of myself (I was the first pseudopatient and my presence was known to the hospital administrator and chief psychologist and, so far as I can tell, to them alone), the presence of pseudopatients and the nature of the research program were not known to the hospital staffs.[9]

The settings were similarly varied. In order to generalize the findings, admission into a variety of hospitals was sought. The twelve hospitals in the sample were located in five different states on the East and West coasts. Some were old and shabby; some were quite new. Some were research-oriented, others not. Some had good staff–patient ratios; others were quite understaffed. Only one was a strictly private hospital. All of the others were supported by state or federal funds, or in one instance, by university funds.

After calling the hospital for an appointment, the pseudopatient arrived at the admissions office complaining that he had been hearing voices. Asked what the voices said, he replied that they were often unclear, but as far as he could tell they said "empty," "hollow," and "thud." The voices were unfamiliar and were of the same sex as the pseudopatient. The choice of these symptoms was occasioned by their apparent similarity to existential symptoms. Such symptoms are alleged to arise from painful concerns about the perceived meaninglessness of one's life. It is as if the hallucinating person were saying, "My life is empty and hollow." The choice of these symptoms was also determined by the *absence* of a single report of existential psychoses in the literature.

Beyond alleging the symptoms and falsifying name, vocation, and employment, no further alterations of person, history, or circumstances were made. The significant events of the pseudopatient's life history were presented as they had actually occurred. Relationships with parents and siblings, with spouse and children, with people at work and in school, consistent with the aforementioned exceptions, were described as they were or had been. Frustrations and upsets were described along with joys and satisfactions. These facts are important to remember. If anything, they strongly biased the subsequent results in favor of detecting sanity, since none of their histories or current behaviors were seriously pathological in any way.

Immediately upon admission to the psychiatric ward, the pseudopatient ceased simulating *any* symptoms of abnormality. In some cases, there was a brief period of mild nervousness and anxiety, since none of the pseudopatients really believed that they would be admitted so easily. Indeed, their shared fear was that they would be immediately exposed as frauds and greatly embarrassed. Moreover, many of them had never visited a psychiatric ward; even those who had, nevertheless had some genuine fears about what might happen to them. Their nervousness, then, was quite appropriate to the novelty of the hospital setting, and it abated rapidly.

Apart from that short-lived nervousness, the pseudopatient behaved on the ward as he "normally" behaved. The pseudopatient spoke to patients and staff as he might ordinarily. Because there is uncommonly little to do on a psychiatric ward, he attempted to engage others in conversation. When asked by staff how he was feeling, he indicated that he was fine, that he no longer experienced symptoms. He responded to instructions from attendants, to calls for medication (which was not swallowed), and to dining-hall instructions. Beyond such activities as were available to him on the admissions ward, he spent his time writing down his observations about the ward, its patients, and the staff. Initially these notes were written "secretly," but as it soon became clear that no one much cared, they were subsequently written on standard tablets of paper in such public places as the dayroom. No secret was made of these activities.

The pseudopatient, very much as a true psychiatric patient, entered a hospital with no foreknowledge of when he would be discharged. Each was told that he would have to get out by his own devices, essentially by convincing the staff that he was sane. The psychological stresses associated with hospitalization were considerable, and all but one of the pseudopatients desired to be discharged almost immediately after being admitted. They were, therefore, motivated not only to behave sanely, but to be paragons of cooperation. That their behavior was in no way disruptive is confirmed by nursing reports, which have been obtained on most of the patients. These reports uniformly indicate that the patients were "friendly," "cooperative," and "exhibited no abnormal indications."

Despite their public "show" of sanity, the pseudopatients were never detected. Admitted, except in one case, with a diagnosis of schizophrenia,[10] each was discharged with a diagnosis of schizophrenia "in remission." The label "in remission" should in no way be dismissed as a formality, for at no time during any hospitalization had any question been raised about any pseudopatient's simulation. Nor are there any indications in the hospital records that the pseudopatient's status was suspect. Rather, the evidence is strong that, once labeled schizophrenic, the pseudopatient was stuck with that label. If the pseudopatient was to be discharged, he must naturally be "in remission"; but he was not sane, nor, in the institution's view, had he ever been sane.

The uniform failure to recognize sanity cannot be attributed to the quality of the hospitals, for, although there were considerable variations among them, several are considered excellent. Nor can it be alleged that there was simply not enough time to observe the pseudopatients. Length of hospitalization ranged from seven to fifty-two days, with an average of nineteen days. The pseudopatients were not, in fact, carefully observed, but this failure clearly speaks more to traditions within psychiatric hospitals than to lack of opportunity.

Finally, it cannot be said that the failure to recognize the pseudopatients' sanity was due to the fact that they were not behaving sanely. While there was clearly some tension present in all of them, their daily visitors could detect no serious behavioral consequences—nor, indeed, could other patients. It was quite common for the patients to "detect" the pseudopatients' sanity. During the first three hospitalizations, when accurate counts were kept, 35 of a total of 118 patients on the admissions ward voiced their suspicions, some vigorously. "You're not crazy. You're a journalist, or a professor [referring to the continual note-taking]. You're checking up on the hospital." While most of the patients were reassured by the pseudopatient's insistence that he had been sick before he came in but was fine now, some continued to believe that the pseudopatient was sane throughout his hospitalization.[11] The fact that the patients often recognized normality when staff did not raises important questions.

Failure to detect sanity during the course of hospitalization may be due to the fact that physicians operate with a strong bias toward what statisticians call the type 2 error.[5] This is to say that physicians are more inclined to call a healthy person sick (a false positive, type 2) than a sick person healthy (a false negative, type 1). The reasons for this are not hard to find: It is clearly more dangerous to misdiagnose illness than health. Better to err on the side of caution, to suspect illness even among the healthy.

But what holds for medicine does not hold equally well for psychiatry. Medical illnesses, while unfortunate, are not commonly pejorative. Psychiatric diagnoses, on the contrary, carry with them personal, legal, and social stigmas.[12] It was therefore important to see whether the tendency toward diagnosing the sane insane could be reversed. The following experiment was arranged at a research and teaching hospital whose staff had heard these findings but doubted that such an error could occur in their hospital. The staff was informed that at some time during the following three months, one or more pseudopatients would attempt to be admitted into the psychiatric hospital. Each staff member was asked to rate each patient who presented himself at admissions or on the ward according to the likelihood that the patient was a pseudopatient. A 10-point scale was used, with a 1 and 2 reflecting high confidence that the patient was a pseudopatient.

Judgments were obtained on 193 patients who were admitted for psychiatric treatment. All staff who had had sustained contact with or primary responsibility for the patient—attendants, nurses, psychiatrists, physicians, and psychologists— were asked to make judgments. Forty-one patients were alleged, with high confidence, to be pseudopatients by at least one member of the staff. Twenty-three were considered suspect by at least one psychiatrist. Nineteen were suspected by one psychiatrist and one other staff member. Actually, no genuine pseudopatient (at least from my group) presented himself during this period.

The experiment is instructive. It indicates that the tendency to designate sane people as insane can be reversed when the stakes (in this case, prestige and diagnostic acumen) are high. But what can be said of the nineteen people who were suspected of being "sane" by one psychiatrist and another staff member? Were these people truly "sane," or was it rather the case that in the course of avoiding the type 2 error the staff tended to make more errors of the first sort—calling the crazy "sane"? There is no way of knowing. But one thing is certain: Any diagnostic process that lends itself so readily to massive errors of this sort cannot be a very reliable one.

■ ■ ■ THE STICKINESS OF PSYCHODIAGNOSTIC LABELS

Beyond the tendency to call the healthy sick—a tendency that accounts better for diagnostic behavior on admission than it does for such behavior after a lengthy period of exposure—the data speak to the massive role of labeling in psychiatric assessment. Having once been labeled schizophrenic, there is nothing the pseudopatient can do to overcome the tag. The tag profoundly colors others' perceptions of him and his behavior.

From one viewpoint, these data are hardly surprising, for it has long been known that elements are given meaning by the context in which they occur. Gestalt psychology made this point vigorously, and Asch[13] demonstrated that there are "central" personality traits (such as "warm" versus "cold") which are so powerful that they markedly color the meaning of other information in forming an impression of a given personality.[14] "Insane," "schizophrenic," "manic-depressive," and "crazy" are probably among the most powerful of such central traits. Once a person is designated abnormal, all of his other behaviors and characteristics are colored by that label. Indeed, that label is so powerful that many of the pseudopatients' normal behaviors were overlooked entirely or profoundly misinterpreted. Some examples may clarify this issue.

Earlier I indicated that there were no changes in the pseudopatient's personal history and current status beyond those of name, employment, and, where necessary, vocation. Otherwise, a veridical description of personal history and circumstances was offered. Those circumstances were not psychotic. How were they made consonant with the diagnosis of psychosis? Or were those diagnoses modified in such a way as to bring them into accord with the circumstances of the pseudopatient's life, as described by him?

As far as I can determine, diagnoses were in no way affected by the relative health of the circumstances of a pseudopatient's life. Rather, the reverse occurred: The perception of his circumstances was shaped entirely by the diagnosis. A clear example of such translation is found in the case of a pseudopatient who had had a close relationship with his mother but was rather remote from his father during his early childhood. During adolescence and beyond, however, his father became a close friend, while his relationship with his mother cooled. His present relationship with his wife was characteristically close and warm. Apart from occasional angry exchanges, friction was minimal. The children had rarely been spanked. Surely there is nothing especially pathological about such a history. Indeed, many readers may see a similar pattern in their own experiences, with no markedly deleterious consequences. Observe, however, how such a history was translated in the psychopathological context, this from the case summary prepared after the patient was discharged.

> This white 39-year-old male . . . manifests a long history of considerable ambivalence in close relationships, which begins in early childhood. A warm relationship with his mother cools during adolescence. A distant relationship to his father is described as becoming very intense. Affective stability is absent. His attempts to control emotionality with his wife and children are punctuated by angry outbursts and, in the case of the children, spankings. And while he says that he has several good friends, one senses considerable ambivalence embedded in those relationships also. . . .

The facts of the case were unintentionally distorted by the staff to achieve consistency with a popular theory of the dynamics of schizophrenic reaction.[15] Nothing of an ambivalent nature had been described in relations with parents, spouse, or friends. To the extent that ambivalence could be inferred, it was probably not greater than is found in all human relationships. It is true the pseudopatient's relationships with his parents changed over time, but in the ordinary context that would hardly be remarkable—indeed, it might very well be expected. Clearly, the meaning ascribed to his verbalizations (that is, ambivalence, affective instability) was determined by the diagnosis: schizophrenia. An entirely different meaning would have been ascribed if it were known that the man was "normal."

All pseudopatients took extensive notes publicly. Under ordinary circumstances, such behavior would have raised questions in the minds of observers, as, in fact, it did among patients. Indeed, it seemed so certain that the notes would elicit suspicion that elaborate precautions were taken to remove them from the ward each day. But the precautions proved needless. The closest any staff member came to questioning these notes occurred when one pseudopatient asked his physician what kind of medication he was receiving and began to write down the response. "You needn't write it," he was told gently. "If you have trouble remembering, just ask me again."

If no questions were asked of the pseudopatients, how was their writing interpreted? Nursing records for three patients indicate that the writing was seen as an aspect of their pathological behavior. "Patient engages in writing behavior" was the daily nursing comment on one of the pseudopatients who was never questioned about his writing. Given that the patient is in the hospital, he must be psychologically disturbed. And given that he is disturbed, continuous writing must be a behavioral manifestation of that disturbance, perhaps a subset of the compulsive behaviors that are sometimes correlated with schizophrenia.

One tacit characteristic of psychiatric diagnosis is that it locates the sources of aberration within the individual and only rarely within the complex of stimuli that surrounds him. Consequently, behaviors that are stimulated by the environment are commonly misattributed to the patient's disorder. For example, one kindly nurse found a pseudopatient pacing the long hospital corridors. "Nervous, Mr. X?" she asked. "No, bored," he said.

The notes kept by pseudopatients are full of patient behaviors that were misinterpreted by well-intentioned staff. Often enough, a patient would go "berserk" because he had, wittingly or unwittingly, been mistreated by, say, an attendant. A nurse coming upon the scene would rarely inquire even cursorily into the environmental stimuli of the patient's behavior. Rather, she assumed that his upset derived from his pathology, not from his present interactions with other staff members. Occasionally, the staff might assume that the patient's family (especially when they had recently visited) or other patients had stimulated the outburst. But never were the staff found to assume that one of themselves or the structure of the hospital had anything to do with a patient's behavior. One psychiatrist pointed to a group of patients who were sitting outside the cafeteria entrance half an hour before lunchtime. To a group of young residents, he indicated that such behavior was characteristic of the oral-acquisitive nature of the syndrome. It seemed not to occur to him that there were very few things to anticipate in the psychiatric hospital besides eating.

A psychiatric label has a life and an influence of its own. Once the impression has been formed that the patient is schizophrenic, the expectation is that he will continue to be schizophrenic. When a sufficient amount of time has passed, during which the patient has done nothing bizarre, he is considered to be in remission and available for discharge. But the label endures beyond discharge, with the unconfirmed expectation that he will behave as a schizophrenic again. Such labels, conferred by mental health professionals, are as influential on the patient as they are on his relatives and friends, and it should not surprise anyone that the diagnosis acts on all of them as a self-fulfilling prophecy. Eventually, the patient himself accepts the diagnosis, with all of its surplus meanings and expectations, and behaves accordingly.[15]

The inferences to be made from these matters are quite simple. Much as Zigler and Phillips have demonstrated that there is enormous overlap in the symptoms presented by patients who have been variously diagnosed,[16] so there is enormous overlap in the behaviors of the sane and the insane. The sane are not "sane" all of the time. We lose our tempers "for no good reason." We are occasionally depressed or anxious, again for no good reason. And we may find it difficult to get along with one or another person—again for no reason that we can specify. Similarly, the insane are not always insane. Indeed, it was the impression of the pseudopatients while living with them that they were sane for long periods of time—that the bizarre behaviors upon which their diagnoses were allegedly predicated constituted only a small fraction of their total behavior. If it makes no sense to label ourselves permanently depressed on the basis of an occasional depression, then it takes better evidence than is presently available to label all patients insane or schizophrenic on the basis of bizarre behaviors or cognitions. It seems more useful, as Mischel[17] has pointed out, to limit our discussions to *behaviors,* the stimuli that provoke them, and their correlates.

It is not known why powerful impressions of personality traits, such as "crazy" or "insane," arise. Conceivably, when the origins of and stimuli that give rise to a behavior are remote or unknown, or when the behavior strikes us as immutable, trait labels regarding the *behavior* arise. When, on the other hand, the origins and stimuli are known and available, discourse is limited to the behavior itself. Thus, I may hallucinate because I am sleeping, or I may hallucinate because I have ingested a peculiar drug. These are termed sleep-induced hallucinations, or dreams, and drug-induced hallucinations, respectively. But when the stimuli to my hallucinations are unknown, that is called craziness, or schizophrenia—as if that inference were somehow as illuminating as the others. . . .

■ ■ ■ THE CONSEQUENCES OF LABELING AND DEPERSONALIZATION

Whenever the ratio of what is known to what needs to be known approaches zero, we tend to invent "knowledge" and assume that we understand more than we actually do. We seem unable to acknowledge that we simply don't know. The needs for diagnosis and remediation of behavioral and emotional problems are enormous. But rather than acknowledge that we are just embarking on understanding, we continue to label patients "schizophrenic," "manic-depressive," and "insane," as if in those words we had captured the essence of understanding. The facts of the matter are that we have known for a long time that diagnoses are often not useful or reliable, but we have nevertheless continued to use them. We now know that we cannot distinguish insanity from sanity. It is depressing to consider how that information will be used.

Not merely depressing, but frightening. How many people, one wonders, are sane but not recognized as such in our psychiatric institutions? How many have been needlessly stripped of their privileges of citizenship, from the right to vote and drive to that of handling their own accounts? How many have feigned insanity in order to avoid the criminal consequences of their behavior, and, conversely, how many would rather stand trial than live interminably in a psychiatric hospital—but are wrongly thought to be mentally ill? How many have been stigmatized by well-intentioned, but nevertheless erroneous, diagnoses? On the last point, recall again that a "type 2 error" in psychiatric diagnosis does not have the same consequences it does in medical diagnosis. A diagnosis of cancer that has been found to be in error is cause for celebration. But psychiatric diagnoses are rarely found to be in error. The label sticks, a mark of inadequacy forever.

■ ■ ■ **NOTES**

1. P. Ash, *J. Abnorm. Soc. Psychol. 44,* 272 (1949); A. T. Beck, *Amer. J. Psychiat. 119,* 210 (1962); A. T. Boisen, *Psychiatry 2,* 233 (1938); N. Kreitman, *J. Ment. Sci. 107,* 876 (1961); N. Kreitman, P. Sainsbury, J. Morrisey, J. Towers, J. Scrivener, *ibid.,* p. 887; H. O. Schmitt and C. P. Fonda, *J. Abnorm. Soc. Psychol. 52,* 262 (1956); W. Seeman, *J. Nerv. Ment. Dis. 118,* 541 (1953). For an analysis of these artifacts and summaries of the disputes, see J. Zubin, *Annu. Rev. Psychol. 18,* 373 (1967); L. Phillips and J. G. Draguns, *ibid. 22,* 447 (1971).

2. R. Benedict. *J. Gen. Psychol. 10,* 59 (1934).

3. See in this regard H. Becker, *Outsiders: Studies in the Sociology of Deviance* (New York: Free Press, 1963); B. M. Braginsky, D. D. Braginsky, K. Ring, *Methods of Madness: The Mental Hospital as a Last Resort* (New York: Holt, Rinehart & Winston, 1969); G. M. Crocetti and P. V. Lemkau, *Amer. Sociol. Rev. 30,* 577 (1965); E. Goffman, *Behavior in Public Places* (New York: Free Press, 1964); R. D. Laing, *The Divided Self: A Study of Sanity and Madness* (Chicago: Quadrangle, 1960); D. L. Phillips, *Amer. Sociol. Rev. 28,* 963 (1963): T. R. Sarbin, *Psychol. Today 6,* 18 (1972); E. Schur, *Amer J. Sociol. 75,* 309 (1969); T. Szasz, *Law, Liberty and Psychiatry* (New York: Macmillan, 1963); *The Myth of Mental Illness: Foundations of a Theory of Mental Illness* (New York: Hoeber Harper, 1963). For a critique of some of these views, see W. R. Cove, *Amer. Sociol. Rev. 35,* 873 (1970).

4. E. Coffman. *Asylums* (Garden City, NY: Doubleday, 1961).

5. T. J. Scheff, *Being Mentally Ill: A Sociological Theory* (Chicago: Aldine, 1966).

6. Data from a ninth pseudopatient are not incorporated in this report because, although his sanity went undetected, he falsified aspects of his personal history, including his marital status and parental relationships. His experimental behaviors therefore were not identical to those of the other pseudopatients.

7. A. Barry, *Bellevue Is a State of Mind* (New York: Harcourt Brace Jovanovich, 1971); I. Belknap, *Human Problems of a State Mental Hospital* (New York: McGraw-Hill, 1956); W. Caudill, F. C. Redlich, H. R. Gilmore, E. B. Brody, *Amer J. Orthopsychiat. 22,* 314 (1952); A. R. Goldman, R. H. Bohr, T. A. Steinberg, *Prof. Psychol. 1,* 427 (1970); unauthored, *Roche Report 1* (No. 13), 8 (1971).

8. Beyond the personal difficulties that the pseudopatient is likely to experience in the hospital, there are legal and social ones that, combined, require considerable attention before entry. For example, once admitted to a psychiatric institution, it is difficult, if not impossible, to be discharged on short notice, state law to the contrary notwithstanding. I was not sensitive to these difficulties at the outset of the project, nor to the personal and situational emergencies that can arise, but later a writ of habeas corpus was prepared for each of the entering pseudopatients and an attorney was kept "on call" during every hospitalization. I am grateful to John Kaplan and Robert Bartels for legal advice and assistance in these matters.

9. However distasteful such concealment is, it was a necessary first step to examining these questions. Without concealment, there would have been no way to know how valid these experiences were; nor was there any way of knowing whether whatever detections occurred were a tribute to the diagnostic acumen of the staff or to the hospital's rumor network. Obviously, since my concerns are general ones that cut across individual hospitals and staffs, I have respected their anonymity and have eliminated clues that might lead to their identification.

10. Interestingly, of the twelve admissions, eleven were diagnosed as schizophrenic and one, with the identical symptomatology, as manic-depressive psychosis. This diagnosis has a more favorable prognosis, and it was given by the only private hospital in our sample. On the relations between social class and psychiatric diagnosis, see A. B. Hollingshead and F. C. Redlich, *Social Class and Mental Illness: A Community Study* (New York: Wiley, 1958).

11. It is possible, of course, that patients have quite broad latitudes in diagnosis and therefore are inclined to call many people sane, even those whose behavior is patently aberrant. However, although we have no hard data on this matter, it was our distinct impression that this was not the case. In many instances, patients not only singled us out for attention, but came to imitate our behaviors and styles.

12. J. Cumming and E. Cumming, *Community Ment. Health 1,* 135 (1965); A. Farina and K. Ring. J. *Abnorm. Psychol. 70,* 47 (1965); H. E. Freeman and O. G. Simmons, *The Mental Patient Comes Home* (New York: Wiley, 1963); W. J. Johannsen, *Mental Hygiene 53,* 218 (1969); A. S. Linsky, *Soc. Psychiat. 5,* 166 (1970).

13. S. E. Asch, *J. Abnorm. Soc. Psychol. 41,* 258 (1946); *Social Psychology* (New York: Prentice-Hall, 1952).

14. See also, I. N. Mensh and J. Wishner, *J. Personality 16,* 188 (1947); J. Wishner, *Psychol. Rev. 67,* 96 (1960); J. S. Bruner and R. Tagiuri, in *Handbook of Social Psychology,* G. Lindzey, ed. (Cambridge, MA: Addison-Wesley, 1954), vol. 2, pp. 634–54; J. S. Bruner, D. Shapiro, R. Tagiuri, in *Person Perception and Interpersonal Behavior,* R. Tagiuri and L. Petrullo, eds. (Stanford, CA: Stanford Univ. Press, 1958), pp. 277–88.

15. For an example of a similar self-fulfilling prophecy, in this instance dealing with the "central" trait of intelligence, see R. Rosenthal and L. Jacobson, *Pygmalion in the Classroom* (New York: Holt, Rinehart & Winston, 1968).

16. E. Zigler and L. Phillips, J. *Abnorm. Soc. Psychol. 63,* 69 (1961). See also R. K. Freudenberg and J. P. Robertson, *A.M.A. Arch. Neurol. Psychiatr. 76,* 14 (1956).

17. W. Mischel, *Personality and Assessment* (New York: Wiley, 1968).

PART
IV Social Change and Megaproblems

As you read the selections in this book, it should have become increasingly apparent how our welfare depends on social structure. If the elements of society are put together one way, we experience a certain type of life; if they are put together another way, we experience quite different circumstances. This overarching thing called society, which we have such a difficult time defining and grasping, holds the key to our welfare in life.

Beyond society itself lie social forces that affect our social structure. These broad social forces are usually difficult to perceive because, as discussed earlier, our eyes are ordinarily focused on our personal experiences, not on the factors that bring our experiences into being. Consider the selection by Celia Falicov which opens this last part of the book. Imagine that a family in Mexico has decided to take its chances and migrate to the United States, regardless of what the laws are. What do they perceive? Their current poverty, a possible life of abundance, and some of the obstacles that stand in the way of their dream. Out of their vision entirely are the global connections that have led to their predicament, that which has prompted their decision to uproot themselves. Such matters as balances of trade, technological developments, and global markets are invisible to them. After they migrate, these factors will still remain outside their field of vision. What they will perceive will be the wrenching changes to which they must adjust—the new customs, the changed gender roles, the bewildering attitudes of their children, the nostalgia for the security of their old way of life.

It is similarly the case with the legal structure within which we live our lives. We are aware that it exists. We all know that police officers patrol our society and that we had better keep an eye out when we speed. Most of us know about April 15 and that "something" will happen if we fail to declare our income. And we all know that 18 and 21 are magical ages, opening new worlds of voting and legal drinking. We are familiar with these smaller parts of the legal structure, as well as laws against vandalism, stealing, burglary, rape, murder, and a few other such acts.

Lying outside our perception, though, are the social forces that have led to our legal structure. This goes unquestioned. Why, for example, are there laws against loitering or being a vagrant? As William Chambliss analyzes the laws against vagrancy, he changes our angle of vision, making visible such things as relations among property ownership, industrialization, and the need of workers. The broader question is how the economic elite continue today to influence our laws, which, in turn, help to set the stage on which we live our lives.

A good part of the social structure that surrounds us was established a long time ago, as with laws against vagrancy. The past sets the stage for things that we don't even think about, much less that lie below our level of awareness if we do think about them. The answer to why some people go hungry, for example, seems so obvious that it is hardly worth asking. This is how it used to seem to Frances Lappé, too. When she began to do research on this topic, she gained a new perception, one that continued to develop as it turned into a lifetime of learning. Her selection (with Joseph Collins) turns our eyes onto past events with which few of us are familiar. Yet those events, a part of colonialism, a form of the more powerful nations exploiting weaker nations, continue to have direct effects on the present.

Thanks to headline-seeking activists and the quieter activities of countless groups of concerned people, we are all familiar with the environment. We all know at least something about global warming, water shortages, plant extinction, and rain forests. Few of us, however, are very concerned about such matters. Almost all of us go about our lives with a blasé attitude, convinced that somehow everything will fall into place. Perhaps a few spotted owls will die, or some darting snails will no longer dart about, but so what? Those big animals will make it, and if a few of them don't, well, it won't be the first time some larger animals went out of existence. We'll muddle through. We always have.

The problem with such thinking is that we haven't always muddled through. Researchers have uncovered remarkable instances in which human groups didn't see the writing on the wall. They continued on their course blindly until they destroyed the very environment on which their existence depended. The selection by Jared Diamond can serve as a significant lesson to us.

Of course, all our efforts to preserve the environment and, if successful, assure a healthy world for coming generations can turn out to be fruitless because of war, the final topic of this book. Nuclear holocaust could destroy us all, but other than this, it looks as though we'll muddle through war and terrorism. This is most likely, granted that we are the world's primary war power to be reckoned with. The selection that closes this book looks at a specific social problem within this broader problem of war. Mike Wessels turns our focus on children who are forced to become soldiers. He recounts how they become child-killers, what their life as soldiers is like, and then examines how they can be reintegrated into their societies.

Migration and Marginalization

Celia Jaes Falicov

introduction ■ ■ ■ ■

The social institution called the family is on the receiving end of social change. Consider economic changes. If the economy is robust, family members can find employment easily, and they have an easier time providing food, clothing, housing, education, medical care, and recreation. If the economy is stale, jobs are harder to come by, and these things are more difficult to provide. If the economy goes into a serious tailspin, leading to a depression, there simply are no jobs to be had. Many families can't pay their mortgages or their rent, and they lose their homes. They can't afford regular meals. Other social changes such as those in education (greater demand for more educated workers in the face of rapidly rising costs of higher education) and medicine (greater demand for more advanced technological diagnoses and treatments in the face of escalating medical costs) also affect the welfare of families.

In this selection, the focus is placed on immigrant Latino families. To understand the broad-scale social forces that underlie the experiences of these families, it is important to understand that the Latinos who migrate to the United States don't wake up one day in Mexico or Guatemala and suddenly say to one another, "Isn't it getting tiring to live here with all of our friends, the people and places that anchor our family memories, our fiestas, our language, and our history? Wouldn't it be fun to rip these ties out of our lives and move to a strange land with customs we don't understand and a language we can't speak? We don't have any money, but let's borrow some and hire someone to sneak us across the border. All those stories we've heard about being abandoned by the coyotes (illegal guides) and about the gangs waiting on the other side of the border who rob the men and rape the women—they couldn't possibly be true. What do you say?" And the family gleefully replies, "Let's do it. This sounds like fun."

These migrants feel *forced* to uproot themselves. Global economic changes have left them in poverty in their villages, with little land, crops that pay next to nothing, and no jobs available. On the other side of the border is a country that is a major player in the global economy, one that has employers who don't ask questions about the legal residence of people who will take any work offered them and who do not demand costly medical and unemployment benefits. In this selection, Celia Falicov examines the costs of the decision to migrate.

Thinking Critically

As you read this selection, ask yourself:

■ What would life be like for me if my family decided to migrate to Latvia or to some other place where none of us knows the language or way of life?

Latino immigrants, like many other immigrants, experience some degree of loss, grief and mourning. These experiences have been compared with the processes of grief and mourning precipitated by the death of loved ones (Shuval 1982; Warheit et al. 1985; Grinberg and Grinberg 1989; Volkan and Zintl 1993). Here I will argue, however, that migration loss has special characteristics that distinguish it from other kinds of losses. Compared with the clear-cut, inescapable fact of death, migration loss is both larger and smaller. It is larger because migration brings with it losses of all kinds. Gone are family members and friends who stay behind, gone is the native language, the customs, and rituals, and gone is the land itself. The ripples of these losses touch the extended kin back home and reach into the future generations born in the new land.

Yet migration loss is also smaller than death, because despite the grief and mourning occasioned by physical, cultural, and social separation, the losses are not absolutely clear, complete, and irretrievable. Everything is still alive but is just not immediately reachable or present. Unlike the finality of death, after migration it is always possible to fantasize the eventual return or a forthcoming reunion. Furthermore, immigrants seldom migrate toward a social vacuum. A relative, friend, or acquaintance usually waits on the other side to help with work and housing and to provide guidelines for the new life. A social community and ethnic neighborhood reproduce in pockets of remembrance, the sights, sounds, smells, and tastes of ones country. All of these elements create a mix of emotions—sadness and elation, loss and restitution, absence and presence—that makes grieving incomplete, postponed, ambiguous.

In this paper, I attempt to integrate concepts from family systems theory (ambiguous loss, boundary ambiguity, relational resilience) with concepts drawn from studies on migration, race, and ethnicity (familism, biculturalism, double consciousness) to deepen our understanding of the risks and resiliences that accompany migration loss for Latinos. I propose that an inclusive, "both/and" approach rather than an "either/or" approach, to the dilemmas of cultural and family continuity and change increases family resilience in the face of multiple migration losses. As we will see, however, risks arise when the experience of ambiguous loss becomes unbearable and thwarts attempts at integrating continuity with change.

From "Ambiguous Loss" by Celia Jaes Falicov from *Latinos: Remaking America*, Marcelo Suarez-Orozco and Mariela Paez, eds., pp. 274–288. 2002. Reprinted with permission from the University of California Press.

Although Latinos share many similarities in the aspects of family coping with loss that are addressed in this paper, each family has a particular "ecological niche" created by combinations of nationality, ethnicity, class, education, religion, and occupation and by its individual history. Other variables that mediate the experience of migration are the degree of choice (voluntary or forced migration), proximity and accessibility to the country of origin, gender, age and generation, family form, and the degree and level of social acceptance encountered in the new environment (Falicov 1995, 1998).

■ ■ ■ AMBIGUOUS LOSS AND MIGRATION

The concept of ambiguous loss proposed by Pauline Boss (1991, 1999) describes situations in which loss is unclear, incomplete, or partial. Basing her thesis on stress theory, Boss describes two types of ambiguous loss. In one, people are physically absent but psychologically present (the family with a soldier missing in action, the noncustodial parent in divorce, the migrating relative). In the second, family members are physically present but psychologically absent (the family living with an Alzheimer's victim, the parent or spouse who is emotionally unavailable because of stress or depression).

Migration represents what Boss (1999) calls a "crossover" in that it has elements of both types of ambiguous loss. Beloved people and places are left behind, but they remain keenly present in the psyche of the immigrant. At the same time, homesickness and the stresses of adaptation may leave some family members emotionally unavailable to others. The very decision to migrate has at its core two ambiguous poles. Intense frustration with economic or political conditions compels the immigrant to move, but love of family and surroundings pull in another direction.

Dealing with Ambiguous Loss

Many internal conflicts, moods, and behaviors of immigrants can be more easily understood when seen through the lens of "ambiguous loss."

Visits to the country of origin close the gap between the immigrant and that which is psychologically present but physically absent. Phone calls, money remittances, gifts, messages, and trips back home contribute to transnational lifestyles (Rouse 1992)—and to a psychologically complex experience of presence and absence.

Leaving family members behind has pragmatic and economic justifications, but it may also ensure a powerful psychological link. It may symbolize that migration is provisional and experimental rather than permanent. Leaving a young child with the immigrant's own parents may also assuage the immigrant's guilt about leaving and offer an emotional exchange for the help of shared parenting.

Encouraging relatives and friends to migrate eases the wrenching homesickness of migration. It is a way of saying "hello again" to some of the many to whom one has bid good-byes. It also means that social networks dismantled by migration may stand a chance of being partially reconstructed in the host country.

Latino immigrants also reconstruct urban landscapes of open markets and ethnic neighborhoods that provide experiences with familiar foods, music, and language. *Recreating cultural spaces* in this manner reestablishes links with the lost land, while helping to transform the receiving cultures into more syntonic spaces (Ainslie 1998).

The long-lasting dream of returning home reinforces the gap between physical absence and psychological presence. A family may remain in a provisional limbo, unable to make settlement decisions or take full advantage of existing opportunities, paralyzed by a sort of frozen grief.

Family polarizations ensue when ambiguities overwhelm, as it were, the immigrant family's psyche. Spouses may come to represent each side of the conflict between leaving and staying, one idealizing and the other denigrating the country of origin or the "new" culture (Sluzki 1979). When such polarizations exist, they hint powerfully at denied or suppressed grief that may result in symptoms: depression or other emotional blocks to adaptation in adults, psychosomatic illness and selective mutism in children (Sluzki 1979, 1983; Grinberg and Grinberg 1989; Falicov 1998).

Generational legacies evolve when immigrant parents pass on their doubts, nostalgia, and sense of ambiguities to their children, who are sometimes recruited to one side or the other of the polarizations. Immigrant children may experience ambiguous loss themselves, but exposure to their parents' mixed emotions may significantly increase their stress.

The migration story itself can provide meaning and narrative coherence (Cohler 1991) to all life events. Experiences of success or of failure, the wife's new-found assertiveness, the ungrateful adult child—all can be readily explained: "It is because we came here." The question that will remain perennially unanswered is "How much is it migration, or is it just life challenges that would have appeared anywhere?" (Troya and Rosenberg 1999).

The construction of bicultural identities may result. The flow of people and information in a two-home, two-country lifestyle may give rise to a sense of "fitting in" in more than one place. Equally possible is the sense of not belonging in either place.

These behaviors of immigrants demonstrate the ambiguous, conflictual nature of migration losses. Yet they carry with them certain dynamic responses or "solutions" that demonstrate that people can learn to live with the ambiguity of never putting final closure to their loss. The adaptation depends on the contextual stresses that families encounter. Some are so excruciatingly oppressive that they prompt the family to repatriate. Under better circumstances, mixed feelings may be counter-acted in part by building on family ties, social supports, and cultural strengths. Concepts from family systems theory and from acculturation studies can help us understand how ambiguous losses come to be tolerated and integrated in ways that strengthen families' resilience and empower their activism against social marginal-ization and injustice.

Dual Visions of Continuity and Change

From a family systems viewpoint, for a family to be successful in coping with family transitions, flexible attitudes toward change and flexible efforts to preserve continu-ity need to coexist (Hansen and Johnson 1979; Melitto 1985; Falicov 1993). Most immigrant families manage to maintain contacts with their culture of origin and to reinvent old family themes while carving out new lives. New acculturation theories reflect this dynamic balance of continuity and change, rather than the traditional "either/or" linear theory of abandoning one culture to embrace the other. Terms such as *binationalisim, bilingualisim, biculturalisim,* and *cultural bifocality* (see Lev-itt, this volume) describe dual visions, wars of maintaining familiar cultural prac-tices while making new spaces manageable, and ways of alternating language or cultural codes according to the requirements of the social context at hand (LaFram-boise, Coleman, and Gerton 1993; Rouse 1992). Although there are compelling ad-aptational reasons for acquiring new language and cultural practices, there are equally compelling reasons for retaining cultural themes in the face of change, among them the attempt to preserve a sense of family coherence.

■ ■ ■ RELATIONAL RESILIENCE IN THE FACE OF LOSS

The concept of a "family sense of coherence" developed by Antonovsky and Sourani (1988), refers to the human struggle to perceive life as comprehensible, manageable, and meaningful. This striving for a sense of coherence (and hopefulness) is one of the key ingredients of *relational resilience,* those processes by which families cope and attempt to surmount persistent stress (Walsh 1998).

In this section, I explore immigrant families' attempts to restore meaning and purpose in life in the midst of multiple ambiguous losses. The aspects of relational resilience addressed in this discussion are family connectedness, family rituals, awareness of social marginalization, and belief or spiritual systems.

Family Connectedness

Latinos' ethnic narratives almost invariably stress familism: inclusiveness and inter-dependence. In family systems terms, family connectedness—the obligation to care and support one another—is a defining feature of extended family life. This cultural tendency toward family connectedness seems to withstand migration and to persist in some form for at least one or two or more generations (Suárez-Orozco and Suárez-Orozco 1995; Sabogal et al. 1987). For immigrant families, familism may be manifest in the persistence of long-distance attachments and loyalties in the face of arduous social or economic conditions. In attempts to migrate as a unit and live close to one another, and in the desire to reunify when individuals have taken up the journey alone. The family members and the ideologies of these richly joined systems make their presence felt at a psychological and a physical level.

The Psychological Presence of Extended Familism. When extended family members are far away, *la familia* may become the emotional container that holds both dreams not yet realized and lost meanings that are no longer recoverable. At the most concrete level, immigrants send remittances back home in exchange for collective care-taking of remaining family members (children and/or elders), thus reinforcing a traditional system of emotional and economic interdependence. At a more abstract level, the idea itself of three-generational family can trigger other large existential meanings, such as one's lost national identity. A study of young adults (Troya and Rosenberg 1999) who had migrated to Mexico as children with parents seeking political refuge from South America demonstrates the powerful psychological presence of absent relatives. When asked for their spontaneous images formed in response to the words *patria* ("fatherland") and *tierra* ("land"), they associated these with the street or house where the grandmother or the aunt lived, reflecting (or perhaps creating anew) deep intergenerational bonds between country and family—a psychological familism.

Other studies show that as families acculturate (Rueschenberg and Buriel 1989; Sabogal et al. 1987; Suárez-Orozco and Suárez-Orozco 1995) they learn how to behave externally in a dominant culture that values assertiveness, independence, and achievement. Yet they do not abandon internally the connectedness and interpersonal controls of many collectivistic family systems.

The Physical Presence of Extended Family. When extended family members are physically present, they play a significant role in shoring up the immigrant family. Their familism drives a concern for one another's lives, a pulling together to weather crises, a sociocentric child rearing (Harwood, Miller, and Irizarry 1995), and a closeness among adult siblings (Chavez 1985).

Multigenerational dwellings, particularly the presence of grandmothers, can be influential in terms of transfers of knowledge, cultural exposures, nurturance, and instrumental help embedded in established sociocultural practices (Garcia-Coll et al. 1996) or even as a buffer against parental neglect or abuse (Gomez 1999). However, family life is not always as rosy as it seems. The description of Latino family connectedness is sometimes taken to such extremes that stereotypical images of picturesque family life dominate while tensions and disconnectedness among extended family members simmer below, ignored or discounted. Perhaps what matters, regardless of the particular positive or negative tone of the interactions, is the sense of being part of a family group, and that in itself affords a sense of continuity in the face of ruptured attachments and the disruptions of relocation.

Cultural Family Rituals

Another interesting avenue to study family resilience in the face of ambiguous losses is through the transmission of family rituals that reaffirm family and cultural identity. Family systems theorists have long known about the power of rituals to restore continuity with a family's heritage while reinforcing family bonds and community pride (Bennett, Wolin, and McAvity 1988; Imber-Black, Roberts, and Whiting 1988). A good example is a clinical case of mine.

A poor, working-class, Mexican-immigrant mother was very distressed over her daughter's refusal to have a *quinceañera* party. The intensity of the mother's emotion surprised me, because the party's ritual affirmation of the girl's virginity and future availability for dating hardly applied—everybody knew the girl was sexually involved with an older boyfriend. But for the mother, the *quinceañera* was the most unforgettable (*"inolvidable,"* she said) event in a woman's life and a memory that all parents dream of bestowing upon a daughter ever since the time of her birth. To abandon this valued ritual that lends coherence to a woman's life—even when its original contents had shifted or faded—represented too much cultural discontinuity for this mother.

The enactment of life cycle rituals in the midst of cultural transformation can be construed as reflecting dual lifestyles, as being both ethnic and modern at the same time. Studies of immigrant families should include a close look at the persistence and the evolving new shapes of traditional family rituals—from routine family interactions (dinners or prayers) to celebrations of birthdays, holidays, and rites of passage or any gathering where a sense of family and national belonging is reaffirmed. Such study could help its understand not only the stable and shifting meanings of rituals but also their functions as metaphors for continuity and change.

Awareness of Social Marginalization

Although the notion of "dual vision" characterizes the incorporation of culture in the inner workings of many immigrant families, it also captures the nature of their interaction with larger external and institutional systems of the host country. The concept of "double consciousness," first described by Du Bois (1903) for African Americans, is useful here because it encompasses a perception of who one really is as a person within one's own group *and* a perception of who one is in the attributions of the larger society's story regarding the same group. Racial, ethnic, and class discriminations plague the individual stories of many Latino and Latina immigrant adults and children. One case of mine illustrates the painful awareness a Mexican family had of the gross, racist preconceptions of Latino immigrants by whites.

This family, a married couple with six children who had arrived from Oaxaca seven years ago, consulted me because a white, upper-class neighbor had accused their nine-year-old son of "molesting" their four-year-old daughter. As the Mexican boy's story unfolded, I learned that several children had been playing together in the fields when the little girl said she needed to urinate. The boy quickly pulled her panties down and held her in the upright position, but the girl ran crying home. Racism was undoubtedly part of the reaction to the boy's behavior. I recounted to the parents the alternative explanation to the "molestation," but the father responded, "I thank you but we want you to tell [the white family that you think] our son is cured and this will never happen again." When asked why should I do this, he said, "Because, when they look at us, they think 'These Mexicans are good people, *le hacen la lucha* [they struggle hard],' but if something goes wrong they suddenly see in us the faces of rapists and abusers. I promise you I will keep an eye on this boy, but please do not question their story. *No vale la pena* [It is not worth it]. It could cost us everything we worked for."

Here again is the ambiguity of gains, losses, and dual visions of immigrants. Striving for the dream of stability in a new land is riddled with pressures to subscribe to the dominant culture's story, which negatively judges dark-skinned, poor immigrants and deprives them of legal resources to fight unfair accusations. The social climate of structural exclusion and psychological violence suffered by immigrants and their children is not only detrimental to their participation in the opportunity structure but it also affects the immigrant children's sense of self, through a process of what Carola Suárez-Orozco (2000) aptly calls "social mirroring."

Indeed, most immigrants and their children are aware of the hostilities and prejudice with which they are regarded. From a psychological viewpoint, this awareness may be debilitating when internalized or denied, but it may be empowering when it helps stimulate strategic activism for social justice. Educators who stress the need for minority families' democratic participation in schools emphasize that awareness of one's own marginal status is the first step toward empowerment (Trueba 1999). Thus awareness of social injustices may create a measure of family resilience against assaults on identity.

Long-Held Beliefs and Spiritual Systems

People's *belief system*, or the meaning they make of their lives and experience, is a narrative construct that helps us understand a family's ability to deal with adversity (Walsh 1998; Wright, Watson, and Bell 1996). A family's tolerance for loss and ambiguity is related to its culture's tolerance for ambiguity; fatalistic and optimistic stances are likewise embedded in culturally based systems of meaning (Boss 1999).

Some Latino cultural narratives and spiritual beliefs promote acceptance of life's adversities, tempering the need to find answers and definitive solutions to losses (Falicov 1998). Roman Catholic beliefs value acceptance of suffering, destiny, and God's will. A belief that little in life is under one's control is also related to conditions of poverty and decreased agency (Garza and Ames 1972; Comas-Díaz 1989). These beliefs should not be misconstrued as passivity, however, but as a way of marshaling one's initiative to solve what can be solved while accepting what cannot be changed—a sort of mastery of the possible.

Like other cultural and ritual practices, the old religion often takes new forms and functions in the new land. Church participation may actually help inscribe various Latino groups in dual, evolving transnational spaces. As Peggy Levitt so cogently describes in this volume, immigrants' church attendance can allow a double membership that crosses border arenas in the homeland while it grounds them lo-cally through host country participation and even civic engagement. This balance of continuity and change may be at the core of resilient adaptations to ambiguous loss. Yet these dual visions are not always obtainable, nor is it always possible to make positive meaning out of the experience of migration. In the next sections, I describe situations where attempts to restore a sense of family coherence fail in the face of in-tense loss and irreparable ambiguity.

■ ■ ■ WHEN AMBIGUOUS LOSS BECOMES UNBEARABLE

Many circumstances surrounding migration can lead to overwhelmingly problem-atic physical and emotional disconnections among family members. Two of these circumstances are addressed here: (1) the overlap of the consequences of migration with the impact of other life cycle transitions at any point in the life of an immigrant and (2) the short- and long-term effects of migration separations and reunifications among all family members. Both situations can be understood better by utilizing the concept of boundary ambiguity.

Boundary Ambiguity

Ambiguous loss may become problematic when it generates confusion about who is in and who is out of the family. Boss (1991) labeled this phenomenon "boundary ambiguity," a concept that is increasingly being used in family research to describe effects of family membership loss over time (Boss, Greenberg, and Pearce-McCall 1990) and that may be very helpful in illuminating migration losses. This construct encompasses the rules and definitions of family subsystems (parental, marital, sib-ling and other subgroups) and how they are perceived by each family group.

When Ambiguous Loss Is Compounded
by Life Cycle Transitions

When nonambiguous, irretrievable losses—such as the death of a relative back home—occur in the life of an immigrant family the uncertain, provisional, and am-biguous quality of the old good-byes accentuates that loss and creates confusion about where one belongs and exactly who constitutes one's family.

A thirty-six-year-old woman consulted me for depression after her father died suddenly in Argentina. Overwhelmed by sadness and guilt at not having made the effort to see him more often and by the unbearable loneliness of not being able to participate in communal grieving, this woman asked to have a separation from her Anglo-American husband. He was the one who had brought her to this country, and she felt him to be a much less loving man than her father. Asked about her adoring father's reaction to her leaving her country twelve years ago to get married, she promptly said, "Everybody told me that for him that day was like *el velorio del angelito* [the wake of his little angel]." Now she was experiencing a great deal of confusion about where she belonged. Her husband and children, who hardly knew her father, provided little comfort. She needed the support of her family of origin, but her own shared history with them had been truncated long ago. This case illustrates the rippling effects of ambiguous loss for the immigrant, for their children, and for the family of origin left behind. This woman's eight-year-old daughter was having behavior and school difficulties that paralleled the mother's depression.

Calling Two Women "Mami"

In addition to separations between extended and nuclear family. Latino immigrants increasingly experience separations between parents and children. A father or a mother frequently migrates first, leaving children behind and planning for later reunification. Such separations complicate experiences of loss, raise issues of inclusion/exclusion, and set the stage for boundary ambiguity.

When a father or a mother migrates first, leaving the family to be reunited later, the confusion may be mild and temporary or intense and prolonged. If sufficient time passes a family in which the father migrated first may reorganize into a single-parent household, with mother as head and substitutes performing the parental functions of the absent parent. Subsequent reunification is often stressful because family boundaries need to change yet again to allow for reentry of the absent member.

Increasingly today, mothers recruited for work make the journey north alone, leaving the children with other women in the family or social network. It is only after several years that these mothers are joined by their children, who often travel unaccompanied. Sociologist Pierrette Hondagneu-Sotelo's incisive analysis (this volume) of the changing labor demands driving these emergent transnational family forms, and of the possible new meanings of family and motherhood, provides a historical, economic, and social context for these complex and often traumatic separations and equally traumatic reunifications between mothers and children. Children are left behind with grandparents or other relatives so that an immigrant parent can face the dangers of illegal passage and the economic hardships of getting established in the new country without the added worry of haying youngsters under their wing. Over time, the costs of these arrangements are significant.

The adjustments to parting and the adjustments at the time of a subsequent reunion place not only mother and child but also all the subsystems of a three-generational family (including siblings who stayed in the sending culture and those born in the receiving country) at risk for developing boundary ambiguities and concomitant individual and relational problems. Psychotherapists and social workers often encounter an immigrant child who calls two women "Mami." We know very little about the meaning of this behavior. Does it point to an attempt to deal with ambiguous loss by accepting two mothers, one here and one there? Could it represent a fluid definition of family that reflects multiple attachments and wherein

"Mami" is just a generic term for significant others? Of more concern, does it signify boundary ambiguity, the beginning of divided loyalties, and confusion about who is the real mother? What makes for a successful separation and reunion? What are the consequences of separation at different ages and for various lengths of time? What transforms ambiguous loss into conflict-laden boundary ambiguity?

A recent international furor over the fate of one young Cuban immigrant highlights an extreme case of boundary ambiguity. Custody of Elián González, a six-year-old Cuban shipwreck survivor was fiercely contested by his deceased mother's relatives in Miami and by his father and grandmothers in Cuba, each side of the family (the immigrants and the nonimmigrants) claiming the right to decide where Elián belonged (Cooper Ramo 2000). At the political level, the boundary ambiguity could not be resolved because it represented the long-standing tensions between Little Havana in Miami and Havana in Cuba. Yet the symbolism of belonging goes beyond the political. At the level of migration loss, the dispute struck deep in the hearts of immigrants who have remained in perpetual mourning for the total loss of the Cuba they once knew. It is tempting to speculate that it is precisely the prohibition to visit that makes it impossible for these immigrants to lead satisfactory dual lives, recharging their emotional batteries and becoming binational or bicultural. Their ambiguous losses instead solidify into a rigid migration narrative confined to an idealization of the island's past, recreated exclusively in the space of Little Havana. The conflict over Elián González's future was magnified by these historical factors, but it illustrates what may happen in families that polarize over their efforts to keep a child close to both sides of their existential predicament.

Clinicians encounter many families from Mexico, Central America, and the Caribbean who have undergone separation and reunion with children of all ages. After a period of time following reunification, mothers often request professional help with behavior problems and defiance of their authority. Many social and psychological factors contribute to mother–child disconnections and to the development of conflict. From a family systems viewpoint, we can speculate on the family interactions that may contribute to—or help prevent—pernicious family boundary ambiguities. One factor seems to be each family member's positive or negative perceptions of the decision to migrate—that is, how much approval or disapproval there is among the adults (the biological mother and the caretaker, for example) about the decision to separate temporarily. A related outcome is the quality of the relationship between the migrating parent(s) and the temporary caretakers and whether they all try to be cooperative and inclusive at long distance.

Ongoing studies will help us learn more about how to help families strengthen their resilience in the face of the many individual and relational risks inherent in these separations, yet the separations themselves, especially if prolonged, may pose nearly insurmountable obstacles to family cohesion. Studies of the nature of the ruptured attachments among family members, the loss of shared histories, and the effects of persistent economic stress on family life may yield greater understanding of the problematic "costs of transnationalism" for immigrant families.

■ ■ ■ **REFERENCES**

Ainslie, R. C. 1998. Cultural mourning, immigration, and engagement: Vignettes from the Mexican experience. In M. M. Suárez-Orozco (ed.), *Crossings*. Cambridge, MA: Harvard University Press, pp. 285–305.

Antonovsky, A., and Sourani, T. 1988. Family sense of coherence and family adaptation. *Journal of Marriage and the Family*, 50:79–92.

Bennett, L. A., Wolin, S. J., and McAvity, K. J. 1988. Family identity, ritual, and myth: A cultural perspective on life cycle transitions. In C. J. Falicov (ed.), *Family transitions: Continuity and change over the life cycle*. New York: Guilford Press.

Boss, P. 1991. Ambiguous loss. In F. Walsh and M. McGoldrick (eds.), *Living Beyond Loss: Death in the family*. New York: Norton.

Boss, P. 1999. *Ambiguous Loss: Learning to live with unresolved grief*. Cambridge, MA: Harvard University Press.

Boss, P., Greenberg. J. R., and Pearce-McCall, D. 1990. Measurement of boundary ambiguity in families. *Minnesota Agricultural Experiment Station Bulletin* 593:1–25.

Chavez, L. R. 1985. Households, migration, and labor market participation: The adaptation of Mexicans to life in the United States. *Urban Anthropology* 14:301–346.

Cohler, B. 1991. The life story and the study of resilience and response to adversity. *Journal of Narrative and Life History* 1:169–200.

Comas-Díaz, L. 1989. Culturally relevant issues and treatment implications for Hispanics. In D. R. Koslow and E. Salett (eds.), *Crossing cultures in mental health*. Washington, DC: Society for International Education, Training, and Research.

Cooper Ramo, J. 2000. A big battle over a little boy. *Time*, January 17.

Du Bois, W. E. B. 1903. *The souls of black folk*. Chicago: McClurg.

Falicov, C. J. 1993. Continuity and change: Lessons from immigrant families. *American Family Therapy Association Newsletter*, Spring:30–36.

Falicov, C. J. 1995. Training to think culturally: A multidimensional comparative framework. *Family Process*, 34:373–388.

Falicov, C. J. 1998. *Latino families in therapy: A guide to multicultural practice*. New York: Guilford Press.

García-Coll, C., Lamberty, G., Jenkins, R., McAdoo, H. P., Crnic, K., Wasik, B. H., and Vásquez García, H. 1996. An integrative model for the study of developmental competencies in minority children. *Child Development* 67:1891–1914.

Garza, R. T., and Ames, R. E. 1972. A comparison of Anglo and Mexican-American college students on locus of control. *Journal of Consulting and Clinical Psychology*, 42:919–922.

Gomez, M. Y. 1999. The grandmother as an enlightened witness in the Hispanic culture. *Psycheline* 3(2):15–22.

Grinberg, L., and Grinberg, R. 1989. P*sychoanalytic perspectives on migration and exile*. New Haven, CT: Yale University Press.

Harwood, R. L., Miller, J. G., and Irizarry, N. L. 1995. *Culture and attachment: Perceptions of the child in context*. New York: Guilford Press.

LaFramboise, T., Coleman. H. L., and Gerton, J. 1993. Psychological impact of biculturalism: Evidence and theory. *Psychological Bulletin* 114(3):395–412.

Melitto, R. 1985. Adaptation in family systems: A development perspective. *Family Process* 24(1):89–100.

Rouse, R. 1992. Making sense of settlement: Class transformation, cultural struggle and transnationalism among Mexican immigrants in the United States. In N. G. Schiller, L. Basch and C. Blanc-Szanton (eds.), *Towards a transnational perspective on migration*. New York: New York Academy of Sciences.

Rueschenberg, E., and Buriel, R. 1989. Mexican American family functioning and acculturation: A family systems perspective. *Hispanic Journal of Behavioral Sciences* 11(3):232–244.

Sabogal, F., Marín, G., Otero-Sabogal, R., Marín, B. V., and Perez-Stable, P. 1987. Hispanic familism and acculturation: What changes and what doesn't. *Hispanic Journal of Behavioral Sciences* 9(4):397–412.

Shuval, J. T. 1982. Migration and stress. In L. Goldberger and S. Breznitz (eds.), *Handbook of stress: Theoretical and clinical aspects*, 2nd ed. New York: Free Press, pp. 641–657.

Sluzki, C. E. 1979. Migration and family conflict. *Family Process* 18(1):79–92.

Sluzki, C. E. 1983. The sounds of silence. In C. J. Falicov (ed.), *Cultural perspectives in family therapy*. Rockville, MD: Aspen, pp. 68–77.

Suárez-Orozco, C. E. 2000. Identities under siege: Immigration stress and social mirroring among the children of immigrants. In A. Robben and M. Suárez-Orozco (eds.), *Culture under siege: Violence and trauma in interdisciplinary perspective*. Cambridge: Cambridge University Press.

Suárez-Orozco, M. M., and Suárez-Orozco, C. E. 1995. *Transformations: Immigration, family life and achievement motivation among Latino adolescents*. Stanford, CA: Stanford University Press.

Troya, E., and Rosenberg, F. 1999. "Nos fueron a México: ¿Qué nos paso a los jóvenes exiliados consureños?" *Sistemas Familiares* 15(3):79–92.

Trueba, E. T. 1999. *Latinos Unidos: From cultural diversity to the politics of solidarity*. Lanham, MD: Rowman & Littlefield.

Volkan, V. D., and Zintl, E. 1993. *Living beyond loss: The lessons of grief*. New York: Charles Scribner's Sons.

Walsh, F. 1998. *Strengthening family resilience*. New York: Guilford Press.

Warheit, G., Vega, W., Auth, J., and Meinhardt, K. 1985. Mexican-American immigration and mental health: A comparative analysis of psychosocial stress and dysfunction. In W. Vega and M. Miranda (eds.), *Stress and Hispanic mental health*. Rockville, MD: National Institutes of Health, pp. 76–109.

Wright, L. M., Watson, W. L., and Bell, J. M. 1996. *Beliefs: The heart of healing in families and illness*. New York: Basic Books.

A Sociological Analysis of the Law of Vagrancy

William J. Chambliss

introduction ▪ ▪ ▪ ▪

Underlying many social problems is the legal institution. As societies change, so do laws. The changed laws make a direct impact on our lives, changing the conditions under which we live, the circumstances to which we must adjust. These are simple statements, understood by all, but they represent profound conditions that affect our lives.

Laws change because of *politics*, which can be defined as the manipulation of power. Because laws are the result of a political process, to understand them we need to consider the interest groups that promoted specific laws. Who wanted the power of the police to enforce particular needs and views? Who benefits from the legal change? To understand the legal system, we can and should ask these questions of all laws, for law is not the impartial managing of a society.

Contrary to the ideologies we learn, the law is not some attempt to achieve justice for all. Legal change, rather, is bound up in both broad historical events and in specific behind-the-scenes relationships. Some of these factors become visible in this selection by William Chambliss, who examines the law of vagrancy.

Thinking Critically

As you read this selection, ask yourself:

- Why do we have our particular laws; that is, why were they passed, and who benefits from them?

*W*ith the outstanding exception of Jerome Hall's (1935) analysis of theft, there has been a severe shortage of sociologically relevant analyses of the relationship between particular laws and the social setting in which these laws emerge, are interpreted, and take form.[1] The paucity of such studies is somewhat surprising in view of widespread agreement that such studies are not only desirable but absolutely essential to the development of a mature sociology of law.[2] A fruitful method of establishing the direction and pattern of this mutual influence is to systematically analyze particular legal categories, to observe the changes which take place in the categories and to explain how these changes are themselves related to and stimulate changes in the society. This paper is an attempt to provide such an analysis of the law of vagrancy in Anglo-American law.

LEGAL INNOVATION: THE EMERGENCE OF THE LAW OF VAGRANCY IN ENGLAND

There is general agreement among legal scholars that the first full-fledged vagrancy statute was passed in England in 1349. As is generally the case with legislative innovations, however, this statute was preceded by earlier laws which established a climate favorable to such change. The most significant forerunner to the 1349 vagrancy statute was in 1274 when it was provided:

> Because that abbies and houses of religion have been overcharged and sore grieved, by the resort of great men and other, so that their goods have not been sufficient for themselves, whereby they have been greatly hindered and impoverished, that they cannot maintain themselves, nor such charity as they have been accustomed to do; it is provided, that none shall come to eat or lodge in any house of religion, or any other's foundation than of his own, at the costs of the house, unless he be required by the governor of the house before his coming hither. (3 Ed. 1. c. 1)[3]

Unlike the vagrancy statutes this statute does not intend to curtail the movement of persons from one place to another, but is solely designed to provide the religious houses with some financial relief from the burden of providing food and shelter to travelers. The philosophy that the religious houses were to give alms to the poor and to the sick and feeble was, however, to undergo drastic change in the next fifty years. The result of this changed attitude was the establishment of the first vagrancy statute in 1349 which made it a crime to give alms to any who were unemployed while being of sound mind and body. To wit:

> Because that many valiant beggars, as long as they may live of begging, do refuse to labor, giving themselves to idleness and vice, and sometimes to theft and other abominations; it is ordained, that none, upon pain of imprisonment shall, under the colour of pity or alms, give anything to such which may labour, or presume to favour them towards their desires; so that thereby they may be compelled to labour for their necessary living. (35 Ed. 1. c. 1)

It was further provided by this statute that:

> ... every man and woman, of what condition he be, free or bond, able in body, and within the age of threescore years, not living in merchandize nor exercising any craft,

From William J. Chambliss, "A Sociological Analysis of the Law of Vagrancy." *Social Problems, 12,* Summer 1964, pp. 67–77. Reprinted by permission.

nor having of his own whereon to live, nor proper land whereon to occupy himself, and not serving any other, if he in convenient service (his estate considered) be required to serve, shall be bounded to serve him which shall him require. . . . And if any refuse, he shall on conviction by two true men, . . . be committed to gaol till he find surety to serve. (35 Ed. 1. c. 1)

And if any workman or servant, of what estate or condition he be, retained in any man's service, do depart from the said service without reasonable cause or license, before the term agreed on, he shall have pain of imprisonment (23 Ed. 3).

There was also in this statute the stipulation that the workers should receive a standard wage. In 1351 this statute was strengthened by the stipulation:

An none shall go out of the town where he dwelled in winter, to serve the summer, if he may serve in the same town. (25 Ed. 3)

By 1360 the punishment for these acts became imprisonment for fifteen days and if they "do not justify themselves by the end of that time, to be sent to gaol till they do" (34 Ed. 3).

A change in official policy so drastic as this did not, of course, occur simply as a matter of whim. The vagrancy statutes emerged as a result of changes in other parts of the social structure. The prime mover for this legislative innovation was the Black Death which struck England about 1348. Among the many disastrous consequences this had upon the social structure was the fact that it decimated the labor force. It is estimated that by the time the pestilence had run its course at least 50 percent of the population of England had died from the plague. This decimation of the labor force would necessitate rather drastic innovations in any society but its impact was heightened in England where, at this time, the economy was highly dependent upon a ready supply of cheap labor.

Even before the pestilence, however, the availability of an adequate supply of cheap labor was becoming a problem for the landowners. The crusades and various wars had made money necessary to the lords and, as a result, the lords frequently agreed to sell the serfs their freedom in order to obtain the needed funds. The serfs, for their part, were desirous of obtaining their freedom (by "fair means" or "foul") because the larger towns which were becoming more industrialized during this period could offer the serf greater personal freedom as well as a higher standard of living. This process is nicely summarized by Fredrick Bradshaw:

By the middle of the 14th century the outward uniformity of the manorial system had become in practice considerably varied . . . for the peasant had begun to drift to the towns and it was unlikely that the old village life in its unpleasant aspects should not be resented. Moreover the constant wars against France and Scotland were fought mainly with mercenaries after Henry III's time and most villages contributed to the new armies. The bolder serfs either joined the armies or fled to the towns, and even in the villages the free men who held by villein tenure were as eager to commute their services as the serfs were to escape. Only the amount of 'free' labor available enabled the lord to work his demense in many places. (Bradshaw 1927: 54)

And he says regarding the effect of the Black Death:

. . . in 1348 the Black Death reached England and the vast mortality that ensued destroyed that reserve of labour which alone had made the manorial system even nominally possible. (Bradshaw 1927: 54)

The immediate result of these events was of course no surprise: Wages for the "free" man rose considerably and this increased, on the one hand, the landowners problems and, on the other hand, the plight of the unfree tenant. For although wages increased for the personally free laborers, it of course did not necessarily add to the standard of living of the serf; if anything it made his position worse because the landowner would be hard pressed to pay for the personally free labor which he needed and would thus find it more and more difficult to maintain the standard of living for the serf which he had heretofore supplied. Thus the serf had no alternative but flight if he chose to better his position. Furthermore, flight generally meant both freedom and better conditions since the possibility of work in the new weaving industry was great and the chance of being caught small (Bradshaw 1927: 57).

It was under these conditions that we find the first vagrancy statutes emerging. There is little question but that these statutes were designed for one express purpose: to force laborers (whether personally free or unfree) to accept employment at a low wage in order to ensure the landowner an adequate supply of labor at a price he could afford to pay. Caleb Foote concurs with this interpretation when he notes:

> The anti-migratory policy behind vagrancy legislation began as an essential complement of the wage stabilization legislation which accompanied the break-up of feudalism and the depopulation caused by the Black Death. By the Statutes of Labourers in 1349–1351, every able-bodied person without other means of support was required to work for wages fixed at the level preceding the Black Death; it was unlawful to accept more, or to refuse an offer to work, or to flee from one county to another to avoid offers of work or to seek higher wages, or go give alms to able-bodied beggars who refused to work. (Foote 1956: 615)

In short, as Foote says in another place, this was an "attempt to make the vagrancy statutes a substitute for serfdom" (1956: 615). This same conclusion is equally apparent from the wording of the statute where it is stated:

> Because great part of the people, and especially of workmen and servants, later died in pestilence; many seeing the necessity of masters, and great scarcity of servants, will not serve without excessive wages, and some rather willing to beg in idleness than by labour to get their living: it is ordained, that every man and woman, of what condition he be, free or bond, able in body and within the age of threescore years, not living in merchandize, (etc.) be required to serve. (3 Ed. 1. c. 1) (35 Ed. 1. c. 1)

The innovation in the law, then, was a direct result of the aforementioned changes which had occurred in the social setting. In this case these changes were located for the most part in the economic institution of the society. The vagrancy laws were designed to alleviate a condition defined by the lawmakers as undesirable. The solution was to attempt to force a reversal, as it were, of a social process which was well under-way; that is, to curtail mobility of laborers in such a way that labor would not become a commodity for which the landowners would have to compete.

■ ■ ■ STATUTORY DORMANCY: A LEGAL VESTIGE

In time, of course, the curtailment of the geographical mobility of laborers was no longer requisite. One might well expect that when the function served by the statute was no longer an important one for the society, the statutes would be eliminated from the law. In fact, this has not occurred. The vagrancy statutes have remained in effect since 1349. Furthermore, as we shall see in some detail later, they were taken over by the colonies and have remained in effect in the United States as well.

The substance of the vagrancy statutes changed very little for some time after the first ones in 1349–1351 although there was a tendency to make punishments harsher than originally. For example, in 1360 it was provided that violators of the statute should be imprisoned for fifteen days (34 Ed. 3), and in 1388, the punishment was to put the offender in the stocks and to keep him there until "he find surety to return to his service" (12 R. 2). That there was still, at this time, the intention of providing the landowner with labor is apparent from the fact that this statute provides:

> . . . and he or she which use to labour at the plough and cart, or other labour and ser-vice of husbandry, till they be of the age of 12 years, from thence-forth shall abide at the same labour without being put to any mistery or handicraft: and any covenant of ap-prenticeship to the contrary shall be void. (12 R. 2)

The next alteration in the statutes occurs in 1495 and is restricted to an in-crease in punishment. Here it is provided that vagrants shall be "set in stocks, there to remain by the space of three days and three nights, and there to have none other sustenance but bread and water; and after the said three days and nights, to be had our and set at large, and then to be commanded to avoid the town" (11 H. & C. 2).

The tendency to increase the severity of punishment during this period seems to be the result of a general tendency to make finer distinctions in the criminal law. During this period the vagrancy statutes appear to have been fairly inconsequential in either their effect as a control mechanism or as a generally enforced statute.[4] The processes of social change in the culture generally and the trend away from serfdom and into a "free" economy obviated the utility of these statutes. The result was not unexpected. The judiciary did not apply the law and the legislators did not take it upon themselves to change the law. In short, we have here a period of dormancy in which the statute is neither applied nor altered significantly.

■ ■ ■ A SHIFT IN FOCAL CONCERN

Following the squelching of the Peasants' Revolt in 1381, the services of the serfs to the lords ". . . tended to become less and less exacted, although in certain forms they lingered on till the seventeenth century . . . By the sixteenth century few knew that there were any bondmen in England . . . and in 1575 Queen Elizabeth listened to the prayers of almost the last serfs in England . . . and granted them manumission" (Bradshaw 1927: 61).

In view of this change we would expect corresponding changes in the vagrancy laws. Beginning with the lessening of punishment in the statute of 1503 we find these changes. However, instead of remaining dormant (or becoming more so) or being negated altogether, the vagrancy statutes experienced a shift in focal concern. With this shift the statutes served a new and equally important function for the social order of England. The first statute which indicates this change was in 1530. In this statute it was stated:

> If any person, being whole and mighty in body, and able to labour, be taken in begging, or be vagrant and can give no reckoning how he lawfully gets his living; and all other idle persons going about, some of them using divers and subtle crafty and unlawful games and plays, and some of them feigning themselves to have knowledge of . . . crafty sciences shall be punished as provided. (22 H. 8. c. 12 1530)

What is most significant about this statute is the shift from an earlier concern with laborers to a concern with criminal activities. To be sure, the stipulation of persons "being whole and mighty in body, and able to labour, be taken in begging, or be vagrant" sounds very much like the concerns of the earlier statutes. Some important differences are apparent however when the rest of the statute includes those who ". . . can give no reckoning how he lawfully gets his living"; "some of them using divers subtil and unlawful games and plays." This is the first statute which specifically focuses upon these kinds of criteria for adjudging someone a vagrant.

It is significant that in this statute the severity of punishment is increased so as to be greater not only than provided by the 1503 statute but the punishment is more severe than that which had been provided by any of the pre-1503 statutes as well. For someone who is merely idle and gives no reckoning of how he makes his living the offender shall be:

> . . . had to the next market town, or other place where they [the constables] shall think most convenient, and there to be tied to the end of a cart naked, and to be beaten with whips throughout the same market town or other place, till his body be bloody by reason of such whipping. (22 H. 8 c. 12)

But, for those who use "divers and subtil crafty and unlawful games and plays," etc., the punishment is "whipping at two days together in manner aforesaid" (22 H. 8. c. 12). For the second offense, such persons are:

> . . . scourged two days, and the third day to be put upon the pillory from nine of the clock till eleven before noon of the same day and to have one of his ears cut off. (22 H. 8. c. 12)

And if he offend the third time "to have like punishment with whipping, standing on the pillory and to have his other ear cut off" (22 H. 8. c. 12).

This statute (1) makes a distinction between types of offenders and applies the more severe punishment to those who are clearly engaged in "criminal" activities, (2) mentions a specific concern with categories of "unlawful" behavior, and (3) applies a type of punishment (cutting off the ear) which is generally reserved for offenders who are defined as likely to be a fairly serious criminal.

Only five years later do we find for the first time that the punishment of death is applied to the crime of vagrancy. We also note a change in terminology in the statute:

> and if any ruffians . . . after having been once apprehended . . . shall wander, loiter, or idle use themselves and play the vagabonds . . . shall be eft-soons not only whipped again, but shall have the gristle of his right ear clean cut off. And if he shall again offend, he shall be committed to gaol till the next sessions; and being there convicted upon indictment, he shall have judgment to suffer pains and execution of death, as a felon, as an enemy of the commonwealth. (27 H. 8. c. 25)

It is significant that the statute now makes persons who repeat the crime of vagrancy a felon. During this period then, the focal concern of the vagrancy statutes becomes a concern for the control of felons and is no longer primarily concerned with the movement of laborers.

These statutory changes were a direct response to changes taking place in England's social structure during this period. We have already pointed out that feudalism was decaying rapidly. Concomitant with the breakup of feudalism was an increased emphasis upon commerce and industry. The commercial emphasis in England at the turn of the sixteenth century is of particular importance in the development of vagrancy laws. With commercialism came considerable traffic bearing valuable items. Where there were 169 important merchants in the middle of the fourteenth century there were three thousand merchants engaged in foreign trade alone at the beginning of the sixteenth century (Hall 1935: 21). England became highly dependent upon commerce for its economic support. Italians conducted a great deal of the commerce of England during this early period and were held in low repute by the populace. As a result, they were subject to attacks by citizens and, more important, were frequently robbed of their goods while transporting them. "The general insecurity of the times made any transportation hazardous. The special risks to which the alien merchant was subjected gave rise to the royal practice of issuing formally executed covenants of safe conduct through the realm" (Hall 1935: 23).

Such a situation not only called for the enforcement of existing laws but also called for the creation of new laws which would facilitate the control of persons preying upon merchants transporting goods. The vagrancy statutes were revived in order to fulfill just such a purpose. Persons who had committed no serious felony but who were suspected of being capable of doing so could be apprehended and incapacitated through the application of vagrancy laws once these laws were refocused so as to include ". . . any ruffians . . . [who] shall wander, loiter, or idle use themselves and play the vagabonds . . ." (27 H. 8. c. 25).

The new focal concern is continued in 1547 and in fact is made more general so as to include:

> Whoever man or woman, being not lame, impotent, or so aged or diseased that he or she cannot work, not having whereon to live, shall be lurking in any house, or loitering or idle wandering by the highway side, or in streets, cities, towns, or villages, not applying themselves to some honest labour, and so continuing for three days; or running away from their work; every such person shall be taken for a vagabond. And . . . upon conviction of two witnesses . . . the same loiterer [shall] be marked with a hot iron in

the breast with the letter V, and adjudged him to the person bringing him, to be his slave for two years. . . . (1 Ed. 6. c. 3)

Should the vagabond run away, upon conviction, he was to be branded by a hot iron with the letter S on the forehead and to be thenceforth declared a slave forever. And in 1571 there is modification of the punishment to be inflicted, whereby the offender is to be "branded on the chest with the letter V" (for vagabond). And, if he is convicted the second time, the brand is to be made on the forehead. It is worth noting here that this method of punishment, which first appeared in 1530 and is repeated here with somewhat more force, is also an indication of a change in the type of person to whom the law is intended to apply. For it is likely that nothing so permanent as branding would be applied to someone who was wandering but looking for work, or at worst merely idle and not particularly dangerous per se. On the other hand, it could well be applied to someone who was likely to be engaged in other criminal activities in connection with being "vagrant."

By 1571 in the statute of 14 El. C. 5 the shift in focal concern is fully developed:

> All rogues, vagabonds, and sturdy beggars shall . . . be committed to the common gaol . . . he shall be grievously whipped, and burnt thro' the gristle of the right ear with a hot iron of the compass of an inch about; . . . And for the second offense, he shall he adjudged a felon, unless some person will take him for two years in to his service. And for the third offense, he shall be adjudged guilty of felony without benefit of clergy.

And there is included a long list of persons who fall within the statute: "proctors, procurators, idle persons going about using subtil, crafty and unlawful games or plays; and some of them feigning themselves to have knowledge of . . . absurd sciences . . . and all fencers, bearwards, common players in interludes, and minstrels . . . all juglers, pedlars, tinkers, petty chapmen . . . and all counterfeiters of licenses, passports and users of the same." The major significance of this statute is that it includes all the previously defined offenders and adds some more. Significantly, those added are more clearly criminal types, counterfeiters, for example. It is also significant that there is the following qualification of this statute: "Provided also, that this act shall not extend to cookers, or harvest folks, that travel for harvest work, corn or hay."

That the changes in this statute were seen as significant is indicated by the following statement which appears in the statute of 1571:

> And whereas by reason of this act, the common gaols of every shire are like to be greatly pestered with more number of prisoners than heretofore hath been, for that the said vagabonds and other lewd persons before recited shall upon their apprehension be committed to the said gaols; it is enacted . . . (14 Ed. C. 5)

And a provision is made for giving more money for maintaining the gaols. This seems to add credence to the notion that this statute was seen as being significantly more general than those previously.

It is also of importance to note that this is the first time the term "rogue" has been used to refer to persons included in the vagrancy statutes. It seems, a priori, that a "rogue" is a different social type than is a "vagrant" or a "vagabond"; the latter terms implying something more equivalent to the idea of a "tramp" whereas the former (rogue) seems to imply a more disorderly and potentially dangerous person.

The emphasis upon the criminalistic aspect of vagrants continues in Chapter 17 of the same statute:

> Whereas divers licentious persons wander up and down in all parts of the realm, to countenance their wicked behavior; and do continually assemble themselves armed in the highways, and elsewhere in troops, to the great terror of her majesty's true subjects, the impeachment of her laws, and the disturbance of the peace and tranquility of the realm; and whereas many outrages are daily committed by these dissolute persons, and more are likely to ensue if speedy remedy be not provided.

With minor variations (e.g., offering a reward for the capture of a vagrant) the statutes remain essentially of this nature until 1743. In 1743 there was once more an expansion of the types of persons included such that "all persons going about as patent gatherers, or gatherers of alms, under pretense of loss by fire or other casualty; or going about as collectors for prisons, gaols, or hospitals; all persons playing of betting at any unlawful games; and all persons who run away and leave their wives or children . . . all persons wandering abroad, and lodging in alehouses, barns, outhouses, or in the open air, not giving good account of themselves," were types of offenders added to those already included.

By 1743 the vagrancy statutes had apparently been sufficiently reconstructed by the shifts of concern so as to be once more a useful instrument in the creation of social solidarity. This function has apparently continued down to the present day in England and the changes from 1743 to the present have been all in the direction of clarifying or expanding the categories covered but little has been introduced to change either the meaning or the impact of this branch of the law.

We can summarize this shift in focal concern by quoting from the Earl of Halsbury. He has noted that in the vagrancy statutes:

> . . . elaborate provision is made for the relief and incidental control of destitute wayfarers. These latter, however, form but a small portion of the offenders aimed at by what are known as the Vagrancy Laws, . . . many offenders who are in no ordinary sense of the word vagrants, have been brought under the laws relating to vagrancy, and the great number of the offenses coming within the operation of these laws have little or no relation to the subject of poor relief, but are more properly directed towards the prevention of crime, the preservation of good order, and the promotion of social economy. (Earl of Halsbury: 606–607)

Before leaving this section it is perhaps pertinent to make a qualifying remark. We have emphasized throughout this section how the vagrancy statutes underwent a shift in focal concern as the social setting changed. The shift in focal concern is not meant to imply that the later focus of the statutes represents a completely new law.

It will be recalled that even in the first vagrancy statute there was reference to those who "do refuse labor, giving themselves to idleness and vice and sometimes to theft and other abominations." Thus the possibility of criminal activities resulting from persons who refuse to labor was recognized even in the earliest statute. The fact remains, however, that the major emphasis in this statute and in the statutes which followed the first one was always upon the "refusal to labor" or "begging." The "criminalistic" aspect of such persons was relatively unimportant. Later, as we have shown, the criminalistic potential becomes of paramount importance. The thread runs back to the earliest statute but the reason for the statutes' existence as well as the focal concern of the statutes is quite different in 1743 than it was in 1349.

■ ■ ■ VAGRANCY LAWS IN THE UNITED STATES

In general, the vagrancy laws of England, as they stood in the middle eighteenth century, were simply adopted by the states. There were some exceptions to this general trend. For example, Maryland restricted the application of vagrancy laws to "free" Negroes. In addition, for all states the vagrancy laws were even more explicitly concerned with the control of criminals and undesirables than had been the case in England. New York, for example, explicitly defines prostitutes as being a category of vagrants during this period. These exceptions do not, however, change the general picture significantly and it is quite appropriate to consider the U.S. vagrancy laws as following from England's of the middle eighteenth century with relatively minor changes. The control of criminals and undesirables was the raison de'être of the vagrancy laws in the United States. This is as true today as it was in 1750. As Foote's analysis of the application of vagrancy statutes in the Philadelphia court shows, these laws are presently applied indiscriminately to persons considered a "nuisance." Foote (1956: 613) suggests that ". . . the chief significance of this branch of the criminal law lies in its quantitative impact and administrative usefulness."[5] Thus it appears that in America the trend begun in England in the sixteenth, seventeenth, and eighteenth centuries has been carried to its logical extreme and the laws are now used principally as a mechanism for "clearing the streets" of the derelicts who inhabit the "skid roads" and "Bowerys" of our large urban areas.

Since the 1800s there has been an abundant source of prospects to which the vagrancy laws have been applied. These have been primarily those persons deemed by the police and the courts to be either actively involved in criminal activities or at least peripherally involved. In this context, then, the statutes have changed very little. The functions served by the statutes in England of the late eighteenth century are still being served today in both England and the United States. The locale has changed somewhat and it appears that the present-day application of vagrancy statutes is focused upon the arrest and confinement of the "down-and-outers" who inhabit certain sections of our larger cities but the impact has remained constant. The lack of change in the vagrancy statutes, then, can be seen as a reflection of the society's perception of a continuing need to control some of its "suspicious" or "undesirable" members.[6]

A word of caution is in order lest we leave the impression that this administrative purpose is the sole function of vagrancy laws in the U.S. today. Although it is our contention that this is generally true it is worth remembering that during certain periods of our recent history, and to some extent today, these laws have also been used to control the movement of workers. This was particularly the case during the depression years and California is of course infamous for its use of vagrancy laws to restrict the admission of migrants from other states.[7] The vagrancy statutes, because of their history, still contain germs within them which make such effects possible. Their main purpose, however, is clearly no longer the control of laborers but rather the control of the undesirable, the criminal, and the "nuisance."

■ ■ ■ DISCUSSION

The foregoing analysis of the vagrancy laws has demonstrated that these laws were a legislative innovation which reflected the socially perceived necessity of providing an abundance of cheap labor to landowners during a period when serfdom was breaking down and when the pool of available labor was depleted. With the eventual breakup of feudalism the need for such laws eventually disappeared and the increased dependence of the economy upon industry and commerce rendered the former use of the vagrancy statutes unnecessary. As a result, for a substantial period the vagrancy statutes were dormant, undergoing only minor changes and, presumably, being applied infrequently. Finally, the vagrancy laws were subjected to considerable alteration through a shift in the focal concern of the statutes. Whereas in their inception the laws focused upon the "idle" and "those refusing to labor" after the turn of the sixteenth century and emphasis came to be upon "rogues," "vagabonds," and others who were suspected of being engaged in criminal activities. During this period, the focus was particularly upon "roadmen" who preyed upon citizens who transported goods from one place to another. The increased importance of commerce to England during this period made it necessary that some protection be given persons engaged in this enterprise and the vagrancy statutes provided one source for such protection by refocusing the acts to be included under these statutes.

Comparing the results of this analysis with the findings of Hall's study of theft we see a good deal of correspondence. Of major importance is the fact that both analyses demonstrate the truth of Hall's assertion that "[t]he functioning of courts is significantly related to concomitant cultural needs, and this applies to the law of procedure as well as to substantive law" (1935: xii).

Our analysis of the vagrancy laws also indicates that when changed social conditions create a perceived need for legal changes that these alterations will be effected through the revision and refocusing of existing statutes. This process was demonstrated in Hall's analysis of theft as well as in our analysis of vagrancy. In the case of vagrancy, the laws were dormant when the focal concern of the laws was shifted so as to provide control over potential criminals. In the case of theft the laws were reinterpreted (interestingly, by the courts and not by the legislature) so as to include persons who were transporting goods for a merchant but who absconded with the contents of the packages transported.

It also seems probable that when the social conditions change and previously useful laws are no longer useful there will be long periods when these laws will remain dormant. It is less likely that they will be officially negated. During this period of dormancy it is the judiciary which has principal responsibility for not applying the statutes. It is possible that one finds statutes being negated only when the judiciary stubbornly applies laws which do not have substantial public support. An example of such laws in contemporary times would be the "Blue Laws." Most states still have laws prohibiting the sale of retail goods on Sunday yet these laws are rarely applied. The laws are very likely to remain but to be dormant unless a recalcitrant judge or a vocal minority of the population insist that the laws be applied. When this happens we can anticipate that the statutes will be negated.[8] Should there arise a perceived need to curtail retail selling under some special circumstances, then it is likely that these laws will undergo a shift in focal concern much like the shift which characterized the vagrancy laws. Lacking such application the laws will simply remain dormant except for rare instances where they will be negated.

This analysis of the vagrancy statutes (and Hall's analysis of theft as well) has demonstrated the importance of "vested interest" groups in the emergence and/or alteration of laws. The vagrancy laws emerged in order to provide the powerful landowners with a ready supply of cheap labor. When this was no longer seen as necessary and particularly when the landowners were no longer dependent upon cheap labor nor were they a powerful interest group in the society the laws became dormant. Finally a new interest group emerged and was seen as being of great importance to the society and the laws were then altered so as to afford some protection to this group. These findings are thus in agreement with Weber's contention that "status groups" determine the content of the law (Rheinstein 1954). The findings are inconsistent, on the other hand, with the perception of the law as simply a reflection of "public opinion" as is sometimes found in the literature (Friedman 1959). We should be cautious in concluding, however, that either of these positions are necessarily correct. The careful analysis of other laws, and especially of laws which do not focus so specifically upon the "criminal," are necessary before this question can be finally answered.

In conclusion, it is hoped that future analyses of changes within the legal structure will be able to benefit from this study by virtue of (1) the data provided and (2) the utilization of a set of concepts (innovation, dormancy, concern, and negation) which have proved useful in the analysis of the vagrancy law. Such analyses should provide us with more substantial grounds for rejecting or accepting as generally valid the description of some of the processes which appear to characterize changes in the legal system.

■ ■ ■ ■ NOTES

1. See also Alfred R. Lindesmith (1959).
2. See, for example, Arnold Rose (1962) and Gilbert Geis (1960).

3. For a more complete listing of most of the statutes dealt with in this report the reader is referred to Richard Burn (1973), *The History of the Poor Laws.* Citations of English statutes should be read as follows: 3 Ed. 1. c. 1. refers to the third act of Edward the first, chapter one, etc.

4. As evidenced for this note the expectation that ". . . the common gaols of every shire are likely to be greatly pestered with more numbers of prisoners than heretofore. . ." when the statutes were changed by the statute of 14 Ed. c. 5 (1571).

5. Also see in this connection, Irwin Deutscher (1955).

6. It is on this point that the vagrancy statutes have been subject to criticism. See, for example, Lacey, Forrest W. (1952), "Vagrancy and Other Crimes of Personal Condition," *Harvard Law Review* 66: 1203.

7. See, for example, *Edwards vs. California* 314 S: 160 (1941).

8. Negation, in this instance, is most likely to come about by the repeal of the statute. More generally, however, negation may occur in several ways including the declaration of a statute as unconstitutional. This latter mechanism has been used even for laws which have been "on the books" for long periods of time. Repeal is probably the most common, although not the only, procedure by which a law is negated.

■ ■ ■ **REFERENCES**

Bradshaw, Fredrick. 1927. *A Social History of England,* 3rd edition. London: W. B. Clive, University Tutorial Press.

Burn, Richard. 1973. *The History of Poor Laws.* New York: August M. Kelly.

Deutscher, Irwin. 1955. "The Petty Offender." *Federal Probation, XIX,* June, 1955.

Earl of Halsbury. 1912. *The Laws of England. New* York: Butterworth & Co., Bell Yard, Temple Bar.

Foote, Caleb. 1956. "Vagrancy-Type Law and Its Administration." *University of Pennsylvania Law Review* 104: 503–650.

Friedman, N. 1959. *Law in a Changing Society.* Berkeley: University of California Press.

Geis, Gilbert L. 1960. "Sociology, Criminology, and Criminal Law." *Social Problems* 7, 1: 40–47.

Hall, Jerome. 1935. *Theft, Law and Society.* Boston: Little, Brown.

Lacey, Forrest W "Vagrancy and Other Crimes of Personal Condition." *Harvard Law Review* 66: 1203.

Lindesmith, Alfred R. 1959. "Federal Law and Drug Addiction." *Social Problems* 7, 1: 48.

Rheinstein, Max. 1954. Max *Weber on Law in Economy and Society.* Cambridge, MA: Harvard University Press.

Rose, Arnold. 1962. "Some Suggestions for Research in the Sociology of Law." *Social Problems* 9, 3:281–283.

Why Can't People Feed Themselves?

Frances Moore Lappé and Joseph Collins

introduction ■ ■ ■ ■

Global hunger breaks into the news from time to time, making us feel sorry for "those people." As the topic recedes from the news, so it recedes from our consciousness. Why don't people have enough food to eat? Are there too many people in the world? Is there not enough land for the billions of people who now inhabit this little, tired globe? Are people who go hungry ignorant of how to produce food? Are they lazy? Why don't they work harder to feed their families? Could we be dealing with broader issues, social forces that underlie global hunger?

In some preceding selections we focused on how people struggle with problems that they face. As we examined consequences of social problems for people's lives, the threads that connect the social problem to the broader social forces to which it is related were sometimes obscured. In this selection, however, it is precisely those broader forces that are the focus of the analysis. As Lappé and Collins answer the question of why some people can't feed themselves, they break stereotypes that would blame the people who go hungry. Their analysis of how colonialism worked and its lingering effects can open your mind to a different reality.

Thinking Critically

As you read this selection, ask yourself:

■ Why are some nations so wealthy and dominant in the world while others are so poor and weak?

Question: *You have said that the hunger problem is not the result of overpopulation. But you have not yet answered the most basic and simple question of all: Why can't people feed themselves? As Senator Daniel P. Moynihan put it bluntly, when addressing himself to the Third World, "Food growing is the first thing you do when you come down out of the trees. The question is, how come the United States can grow food and you can't?"*

Our Response: In the very first speech I, Frances, ever gave after writing Diet for a Small Planet, *I tried to take my audience along the path that I had taken in attempting to understand why so many are hungry in this world. Here is the gist of that talk that was, in truth, a turning point in my life:*

> When I started I saw a world divided into two parts: a *minority* of nations that had "taken off" through their agricultural and industrial revolutions to reach a level of unparalleled material abundance and a *majority* that remained behind in a primitive, traditional, undeveloped state. This lagging behind of the majority of the world's peoples must be due, I thought, to some internal deficiency or even to several of them. It seemed obvious that the underdeveloped countries must be deficient in natural resources—particularly good land and climate—and in cultural development, including modern attitudes conducive to work and progress.
>
> But when looking for the historical roots of the predicament, I learned that my picture of these two separate worlds was quite false. My "two separate worlds" were really just different sides of the same coin. One side was on top largely because the other side was on the bottom. Could this be true? How were these separate worlds related?
>
> Colonialism appeared to me to be the link. Colonialism destroyed the cultural patterns of production and exchange by which traditional societies in "underdeveloped" countries previously had met the needs of the people. Many precolonial social structures, while dominated by exploitative elites, had evolved a system of mutual obligations among the classes that helped to ensure at least a minimal diet for all. A friend of mine once said: "Precolonial village existence in subsistence agriculture was a limited life indeed, but it's certainly not Calcutta." The misery of starvation in the streets of Calcutta can only be understood as the end-point of a long historical process—one that has destroyed a traditional social system.
>
> "Underdeveloped," instead of being an adjective that evokes the picture of a static society, became for me a verb (to "underdevelop") meaning the *process* by which the minority of the world has transformed—indeed often robbed and degraded—the majority.

That was in 1972. I clearly recall my thoughts on my return home. I had stated publicly for the first time a world view that had taken me years of study to grasp. The sense of relief was tremendous. For me the breakthrough lay in realizing that today's "hunger crisis" could not be described in static, descriptive terms. Hunger and underdevelopment must always be thought of as a *process.*

To answer the question "why hunger?" it is counterproductive to simply *describe* the conditions in an underdeveloped country today. For these conditions, whether they are the degree of malnutrition, the levels of agricultural production, or even the country's ecological endowment, are not static factors—they are not "givens." They are rather the *results* of an ongoing historical process. As we dug ever deeper into that historical process for the preparation of this book, we began to discover the existence of scarcity-creating mechanisms that we had only vaguely intuited before.

We have gotten great satisfaction from probing into the past since we recognized it is the only way to approach a solution to hunger today. We have come to see that it is the *force* creating the condition, not the condition itself, that must be the target of change. Otherwise we might change the condition today, only to find tomorrow that it has been recreated—with a vengeance.

Asking the question "Why can't people feed themselves?" carries a sense of bewilderment that there are so many people in the world not able to feed themselves adequately. What astonished us, however, is that there are not *more* people in the world who are hungry—considering the weight of the centuries of effort by the few to undermine the capacity of the majority to feed themselves. No, we are not crying "conspiracy!" If these forces were entirely conspiratorial, they would be easier to detect and many more people would by now have risen up to resist. We are talking about something more subtle and insidious; a heritage of a colonial order in which people with the advantage of considerable power sought their own self-interest, often arrogantly believing they were acting in the interest of the people whose lives they were destroying.

■ ■ ■ ■ THE COLONIAL MIND

The colonizer viewed agriculture in the subjugated lands as primitive and backward. Yet such a view contrasts sharply with documents from the colonial period now coming to light. For example, A. J. Voelker, a British agricultural scientist assigned to India during the 1890s, wrote:

> Nowhere would one find better instances of keeping land scrupulously clean from weeds, of ingenuity in device of water-raising appliances, of knowledge of soils and their capabilities, as well as of the exact time to sow and reap, as one would find in Indian agriculture. It is wonderful, too, how much is known of rotation, the system of "mixed crops" and of fallowing. . . . I, at least, have never seen a more perfect picture of cultivation."[1]

None the less, viewing the agriculture of the vanquished as primitive and backward reinforced the colonizer's rationale for destroying it. To the colonizers of Africa, Asia, and Latin America, agriculture became merely a means to extract wealth—much as gold from a mine—on behalf of the colonizing power. Agriculture was no longer seen as a source of food for the local population, nor even as their livelihood. Indeed the English economist John Stuart Mill reasoned that colonies should not be thought of as civilizations or countries at all but as "agricultural establishments" whose sole purpose was to supply the "larger community to which they belong." The colonized society's agriculture was only a subdivision of the agricultural system of the metropolitan country. As Mill acknowledged, "Our West India colonies, for example, cannot be regarded as countries. . . . The West Indies are the place where England *finds it convenient* to carry on the production of sugar, coffee and a few other tropical commodities."[2]

Prior to European intervention, Africans practiced a diversified agriculture that included the introduction of new food plants of Asian or American origin. But colonial rule simplified this diversified production to single cash crops—often to the exclusion of staple foods—and in the process sowed the seeds of famine.[3] Rice farming once had been common in Gambia. But with colonial rule so much of the best land was taken over by peanuts (grown for the European market) that rice had to be imported to counter the mounting prospect of famine. Northern Ghana, once famous for its yams and other foodstuffs, was forced to concentrate solely on cocoa. Most of the Gold Coast thus became dependent on cocoa. Liberia was turned into a virtual plantation subsidiary of Firestone Tire and Rubber. Food production in Dahomey and southeast Nigeria was all but abandoned in favor of palm oil; Tanganyika (now Tanzania) was forced to focus on sisal and Uganda on cotton.

The same happened in Indochina. About the time of the American Civil War the French decided that the Mekong Delta in Vietnam would be ideal for producing rice for export. Through a production system based on enriching the large landowners, Vietnam became the world's third largest exporter of rice by the 1930s; yet many landless Vietnamese went hungry.[4]

Rather than helping the peasants, colonialism's public works programs only reinforced export crop production. British irrigation works built in nineteenth-century India did help increase production, but the expansion was for spring export crops at the expense of millets and legumes grown in the fall as the basic local food crops.

Because people living on the land do not easily go against their natural and adaptive drive to grow food for themselves, colonial powers had to force the production of cash crops. The first strategy was to use "physical or economic force to get the local population to grow cash crops instead of food on their own plots and then turn them over to the colonizer for export. The second strategy was the direct takeover of the land by large-scale plantations growing crops for export.

■ ■ ■ FORCED PEASANT PRODUCTION

As Walter Rodney recounts in *How Europe Underdeveloped Africa,* cash crops were often grown literally under threat of guns and whips.[5] One visitor to the Shale commented in 1928: "Cotton is an artificial crop and one the value of which is not entirely clear to the natives . . ." He wryly noted the "enforced enthusiasm with which the natives . . . have thrown themselves into . . . planting cotton."[6] The forced cultivation of cotton was a major grievance leading to the Maji Maji wars in Tanzania (then Tanganyika) and behind the nationalist revolt in Angola as late as 1960.[7]

Although raw force was used, taxation was the preferred colonial technique to force Africans to grow cash crops. The colonial administrations simply levied taxes on cattle, land, houses, and even the people themselves. Since the tax had to be paid in the coin of the realm, the peasants had either to grow crops to sell or to work on the plantations or in the mines of the Europeans.[8] Taxation was both an effective tool to "stimulate" cash cropping and a source of revenue that the colonial bureaucracy needed to enforce the system. To expand their production of export crops to pay the mounting taxes, peasant producers were forced to neglect the farming of food crops. In 1830, the Dutch administration in Java made the peasants an offer they could not refuse; if they would grow government-owned export crops on one fifth of their land, the Dutch would remit their land taxes.[9] If they refused and thus could not pay the taxes, they lost their land.

Marketing boards emerged in Africa in the 1930s as another technique for getting the profit from cash crop production by native producers into the hands of the colonial government and international firms. Purchases by the marketing boards were well below the world market price. Peanuts bought by the boards from peasant cultivators in West Africa were sold in Britain for more than *seven times* what the peasants received.[10]

The marketing board concept was born with the "cocoa hold-up" in the Gold Coast in 1937. Small cocoa farmers refused to sell to the large cocoa concerns like United Africa Company (a subsidiary of the Anglo-Dutch firm, Unilever—which we know as Lever Brothers) and Cadbury until they got a higher price. When the British government stepped in and agreed to buy the cocoa directly in place of the big business concern, the smallholders must have thought they had scored at least a minor victory. But had they really? The following year the British formally set up the West African Cocoa Control Board. Theoretically, its purpose was to pay the peasants a reasonable price for their crops. In practice, however, the board, as sole purchaser, was able to hold down the prices paid the peasants for their crops when the world prices were rising. Rodney sums up the real "victory":

> None of the benefits went to Africans, but rather to the British government itself and to the private companies.... Big companies like the United African Company and John Holt were given . . . quotas to fulfill on behalf of the boards. As agents of the government, they were no longer exposed to direct attack, and their profits were secure.[11]

These marketing boards, set up for most export crops, were actually controlled by the companies. The chairman of the Cocoa Board was none other than John Cadbury of Cadbury Brothers (ever had a Cadbury chocolate bar?) who was part of a buying pool exploiting West African cocoa farmers.

The marketing boards funneled part of the profits from the exploitation of peasant producers indirectly into the royal treasury. While the Cocoa Board sold to the British Food Ministry at low prices, the ministry upped the price for British manufacturers, thus netting a profit as high as 11 million pounds in some years.[12]

These marketing boards of Africa were only the institutionalized rendition of what is the essence of colonialism—the extraction of wealth. While profits continued to accrue to foreign interests and local elites, prices received by those actually growing the commodities remained low.

■ ■ ■ PLANTATIONS

A second approach was direct takeover of the land either by the colonizing government or by private foreign interests. Previously self-provisioning farmers were forced to cultivate the plantation fields through either enslavement or economic coercion.

After the conquest of the Kandyan Kingdom (in present day Sri Lanka), in 1815, the British designated all the vast central part of the island as crown land. When it was determined that coffee, a profitable export crop, could be grown there, the Kandyan lands were sold off to British investors and planters at a mere five shillings per acre, the government even defraying the cost of surveying and road building.[13]

Java is also a prime example of a colonial government seizing territory and then putting it into private foreign hands. In 1870, the Dutch declared all uncultivated land—called waste land—property of the state for lease to Dutch plantation enterprises. In addition, the Agrarian Land Law of 1870 authorized foreign companies to lease village-owned land. The peasants, in chronic need of ready cash for taxes and foreign consumer goods, were only too willing to lease their land to the foreign companies for very modest sums and under terms dictated by the firms. Where land was still held communally, the village headman was tempted by high cash commissions offered by plantation companies. He would lease the village land even more cheaply than would the individual peasant or, as was frequently the case, sellout the entire village to the company.[14]

The introduction of the plantation meant the divorce of agriculture from nourishment, as the notion of food value was lost to the overriding claim of "market value" in international trade. Crops such as sugar, tobacco, and coffee were selected, not on the basis of how well they feed people, but for their high price value relative to their weight and bulk so that profit margins could be maintained even after the costs of shipping to Europe.

■ ■ ■ SUPPRESSING PEASANT FARMING

The stagnation and impoverishment of the peasant food-producing sector was not the mere by-product of benign neglect, that is, the unintended consequence of an overemphasis on export production. Plantations—just like modern "agro-industrial complexes"—needed an abundant and readily available supply of low-wage agricultural workers. Colonial administrations thus devised a variety of tactics, all to undercut self-provisioning agriculture and thus make rural populations dependent on plantation wages. Government services and even the most minimal infrastructure (access to water, roads, seeds, credit, pest and disease control information, and so on) were systematically denied. Plantations usurped most of the good land, either making much of the rural population landless or pushing them onto marginal soils. (Yet the plantations have often held much of their land idle simply to prevent the peasants from using it—even to this day. Del Monte owns 57,000 acres of Guatemala but plants 9000. The rest lies idle except for a few thousand head of grazing cattle.)[15]

In some cases a colonial administration would go even further to guarantee itself a labor supply. In at least twelve countries in the eastern and southern parts of Africa the exploitation of mineral wealth (gold, diamonds, and copper) and the establishment of cash-crop plantations demanded a continuous supply of low-cost labor. To assure this labor supply, colonial administrations simply expropriated the land of the African communities by violence and drove the people into small reserves.[16] With neither adequate land for their traditional slash-and-burn methods nor access to the means—tools, water, and fertilizer—to make continuous farming of such limited areas viable, the indigenous population could scarcely meet subsistence needs, much less produce surplus to sell in order to cover the colonial taxes. Hundreds of thousands of Africans were forced to become the cheap labor source so "needed" by the colonial plantations. Only by laboring on plantations and in the mines could they hope to pay the colonial taxes.

The tax scheme to produce reserves of cheap plantation and mining labor was particularly effective when the Great Depression hit and the bottom dropped out of cash crop economies. In 1929 the cotton market collapsed, leaving peasant cotton producers, such as those in Upper Volta, unable to pay their colonial taxes. More and more young people, in some years as many as 80,000, were thus forced to migrate to the Gold Coast to compete with each other for low-wage jobs on cocoa plantations.[17]

The forced migration of Africa's most able-bodied workers—stripping village food farming of needed hands—was a recurring feature of colonialism. As late as 1973 the Portuguese "exported" 400,000 Mozambican peasants to work in South Africa in exchange for gold deposited in the Lisbon treasury.

The many techniques of colonialism to undercut self-provisioning agriculture in order to ensure a cheap labor supply are no better illustrated than by the story of how, in the mid-nineteenth century, sugar plantation owners in British Guiana coped with the double blow of the emancipation of slaves and the crash in the world sugar market. The story is graphically recounted by Alan Adamson in *Sugar Without Slaves*.[18]

Would the ex-slaves be allowed to take over the plantation land and grow the food they needed? The planters, many ruined by the sugar slump, were determined they would not. The planter-dominated government devised several schemes for thwarting food self-sufficiency. The price of crown land was kept artificially high, and the purchase of land in parcels smaller than 100 acres was outlawed—two measures guaranteeing that newly organized ex-slave cooperatives could not hope to gain access to much land. The government also prohibited cultivation on as much as 400,000 acres—on the grounds of "uncertain property titles." Moreover, although many planters held part of their land out of sugar production due to the depressed world price, they would not allow any alternative production on them. They feared that once the ex-slaves started growing food it would be difficult to return them to sugar production when world market prices began to recover. In addition, the government taxed peasant production, then turned around and used the funds to subsidize the immigration of laborers from India and Malaysia to replace the freed slaves, thereby making sugar production again profitable for the planters. Finally, the government neglected the infrastructure for subsistence agriculture and denied credit for small farmers.

Perhaps the most insidious tactic to "lure" the peasant away from food production—and the one with profound historical consequences—was a policy of keeping the price of imported food low through the removal of tariffs and subsidies.

The policy was double-edged: first, peasants were told they need not grow food because they could always buy it cheaply with their plantation wages; second, cheap food imports destroyed the market for domestic food and thereby impoverished local food producers.

Adamson relates how both the Governor of British Guiana and the Secretary for the Colonies Earl Grey favored low duties on imports in order to erode local food production and thereby release labor for the plantations. In 1851 the governor rushed through a reduction of the duty on cereals in order to "divert" labor to the sugar estates. As Adamson comments, "Without realizing it, he [the governor] had put his finger on the most mordant feature of monoculture: . . . its convulsive need to destroy any other sector of the economy which might compete for 'its' labor."[19]

Many colonial governments succeeded in establishing dependence on imported foodstuffs. In 1647 an observer in the West Indies wrote to Governor Winthrop of Massachusetts: "Men are so intent upon planting sugar that they had rather buy foods at very deare rates than produce it by labor, so infinite is the profit of sugar workers . . ."[20] By 1770, the West Indies were importing most of the continental colonies' exports of dried fish, grain, beans, and vegetables. A dependence on imported foods made the West Indian colonies vulnerable to any disruption in supply. This dependence on imported food stuffs spelled disaster when the thirteen continental colonies gained independence and food exports from the continent to the West Indies were interrupted. With no diversified food system to fall back on, 15,000 plantation workers died of famine between 1780 and 1787 in Jamaica alone.[21] The dependence of the West Indies on imported food persists to this day.

■ ■ ■ SUPPRESSING PEASANT COMPETITION

We have talked about the techniques by which indigenous populations were forced to cultivate cash crops. In some countries with large plantations, however, colonial governments found it necessary to *prevent* peasants from independently growing cash crops not out of concern for their welfare, but so that they would not compete with colonial interests growing the same crop. For peasant farmers, given a modicum of opportunity, proved themselves capable of outproducing the large plantations not only in terms of output per unit of land but, more important, in terms of capital cost per unit produced.

In the Dutch East Indies (Indonesia and Dutch New Guinea) colonial policy in the middle of the nineteenth century forbade the sugar refineries to buy sugar cane from indigenous growers and imposed a discriminatory tax on rubber produced by native smallholders.[22] A recent unpublished United Nations study of agricultural development in Africa concluded that large-scale agricultural operations owned and controlled by foreign commercial interests (such as the rubber plantations of Liberia, the sisal estates of Tanganyika [Tanzania], and the coffee estates of Angola) only survived the competition of peasant producers because "the authorities actively supported them by suppressing indigenous rural development."[23]

The suppression of indigenous agricultural development served the interests of the colonizing powers in two ways. Not only did it prevent direct competition from more efficient native producers of the same crops, but it also guaranteed a labor force to work on the foreign-owned estates. Planters and foreign investors were not unaware that peasants who could survive economically by their own production would be under less pressure to sell their labor cheaply to the large estates.

The answer to the question, then, "Why can't people feed themselves?" must begin with an understanding of how colonialism actively prevented people from doing just that.

Colonialism:

- forced peasants to replace food crops with cash crops that were then expropriated at very low rates;
- took over the best agricultural land for export crop plantations and then forced the most able-bodied workers to leave the village fields to work as slaves or for very low wages on plantations;
- encouraged a dependence on imported food;
- blocked native peasant cash crop production from competing with cash crops produced by settlers or foreign firms.

These are concrete examples of the development of underdevelopment that we should have perceived as such even as we read our history schoolbooks. Why didn't we? Somehow our schoolbooks always seemed to make the flow of history appear to have its own logic—as if it could not have been any other way. I, Frances, recall, in particular, a grade-school, social studies pamphlet on the idyllic life of Pedro, a nine-year-old boy on a coffee plantation in South America. The drawings of lush vegetation and "exotic" huts made his life seem romantic indeed. Wasn't it natural and proper that South America should have plantations to supply my mother and father with coffee? Isn't that the way it was *meant* to be?

■ ■ ■ NOTES

1. Radha Sinha, *Food and Poverty* (New York: Holmes and Meier, 1976), p. 26.
2. John Stuart Mill, *Political Economy*, Book 3, Chapter 25 (emphasis added).
3. Peter Feldman and David Lawrence, "Social and Economic Implications of the Large-Scale Introduction of New Varieties of Foodgrains," Africa Report, preliminary draft (Geneva: UNRISD, 1975), pp. 107–108.
4. Edgar Owens, *The Right Side of History*, unpublished manuscript, 1976.
5. Walter Rodney, *How Europe Underdeveloped Africa* (London: Bogle-L'Ouverture Publications, 1972), pp. 171–172.
6. Ferdinand Ossendowski, *Slaves of the Sun* (New York: Dutton, 1928), p. 276.
7. Rodney, *How Europe Underdeveloped Africa*, pp. 171–172.
8. Ibid., p. 181.
9. Clifford Geertz, *Agricultural Involution* (Berkeley and Los Angeles: University of California Press, 1963), pp. 52–53.

10. Rodney, *How Europe Underdeveloped Africa*, p. 185.

11. Ibid., p. 184.

12. Ibid., p. 186.

13. George L. Beckford, *Persistent Poverty: Underdevelopment in Plantation Economies of the Third World* (New York: Oxford University Press, 1972), p. 99.

14. Ibid., p. 99, quoting from Erich Jacoby, *Agrarian Unrest in Southeast Asia* (New York: Asia Publishing House, 1961), p. 66.

15. Pat Flynn and Roger Burbach, North American Congress on Latin America, Berkeley, California, recent investigation.

16. Feldman and Lawrence, "Social and Economic Implications," p. 103.

17. Special Sahelian Office Report, Food and Agriculture Organization, March 28, 1974, pp. 88–89.

18. Alan Adamson, *Sugar Without Slaves: The Political Economy of British Guiana, 1838–1904* (New Haven and London: Yale University Press, 1972).

19. Ibid., p. 41.

20. Eric Williams, *Capitalism and Slavery* (New York: Putnam, 1966), p. 110.

21. Ibid., p. 121.

22. Gunnar Myrdal, *Asian Drama*, vol. 1 (New York: Pantheon, 1966), pp. 448–449.

23. Feldman and Lawrence, "Social and Economic Implications," p. 189.

READING **14** ■

The End of Easter

Jared Diamond

introduction ■ ■ ■ ■

A favorite topic of science fiction writers—and one that piques our imagination—is the end of the world, or at least of civilization as we know it. Reflection on the end of the world is not something that arose recently. Even people who lived long ago pondered this possibility, as evidenced by the end of the world being one of the major topics of Revelation, the last book of the New Testament.

Will the Earth last millions of years, ending only when the sun loses its heat? Or will it come to a screeching halt at some earlier point, perhaps quite soon? If so, what could possibly bring our world to an abrupt end? Apart from the action of a God who says "The time has come," there is human action, folly so great that it leads to the destruction of the environment on which humans depend for their survival. But certainly humans, as bright as they are—and also as careless and self-serving as they are—could never be so thoughtless as to destroy their environment and, with it, their civilizations and themselves.

One would think not. We certainly must be more intelligent and future-oriented than to do something as foolish as this. Yet some past human groups did precisely this, as Jared Diamond recounts in this selection. As George Santayana said, "Those who cannot remember the past are condemned to repeat it." Knowing what happened at Easter Island can go a long way to making certain that we don't repeat their error.

Thinking Critically

As you read this selection, ask yourself:

■ With humans so short-sighted and industrialization proceeding at such a furious pace around the globe, what will prevent us from destroying our environment?

Among the most riveting mysteries of human history are those posed by vanished civilizations. Everyone who has seen the abandoned buildings of the Khmer, the Maya, or the Anasazi is immediately moved to ask the same question: Why did the societies that erected those structures disappear?

159

Their vanishing touches us as the disappearance of other animals, even the dinosaurs, never can. No matter how exotic those lost civilizations seem, their framers were humans like us. Who is to say we won't succumb to the same fate? Perhaps someday New York's skyscrapers will stand derelict and overgrown with vegetation, like the temples at Angkor Wat and Tikal.

Among all such vanished civilizations, that of the former Polynesian society on Easter Island remains unsurpassed in mystery and isolation. The mystery stems especially from the island's gigantic stone statues and its impoverished landscape, but it is enhanced by our associations with the specific people involved: Polynesians represent for us the ultimate in exotic romance, the background for many a child's, and an adult's, vision of paradise. My own interest in Easter was kindled over 30 years ago when I read Thor Heyerdahl's fabulous accounts of his *Kon-Tiki* voyage.

But my interest has been revived recently by a much more exciting account, one not of heroic voyages but of painstaking research and analysis. My friend David Steadman, a paleontologist, has been working with a number of other researchers who are carrying out the first systematic excavations on Easter intended to identify the animals and plants that once lived there. Their work is contributing to a new interpretation of the island's history that makes it a tale not only of wonder but of warning as well.

Easter Island, with an area of only 64 square miles, is the world's most isolated scrap of habitable land. It lies in the Pacific Ocean more than 2,000 miles west of the nearest continent (South America), 1,400 miles from even the nearest habitable island (Pitcairn). Its subtropical location and latitude—at 27 degrees south, it is approximately as far below the equator as Houston is north of it—help give it a rather mild climate, while its volcanic origins make its soil fertile. In theory, this combination of blessings should have made Easter a miniature paradise, remote from problems that beset the rest of the world.

The island derives its name from its "discovery" by the Dutch explorer Jacob Roggeveen, on Easter (April 5) in 1722. Roggeveen's first impression was not of a paradise but of a wasteland: "We originally, from a further distance, have considered the said Easter Island as sandy; the reason for that is this, that we counted as sand the withered grass, hay, or other scorched and burnt vegetation, because its wasted appearance could give no other impression than of a singular poverty and barrenness."

The island Roggeveen saw was a grassland without a single tree or bush over ten feet high. Modern botanists have identified only 47 species of higher plants native to Easter, most of them grasses, sedges, and ferns. The list includes just two species of small trees and two of woody shrubs. With such flora, the islanders Roggeveen encountered had no source of real firewood to warm themselves during Easter's cool, wet, windy winters. Their native animals included nothing larger than insects, not even a single species of native bat, land bird, land snail, or lizard. For domestic animals, they had only chickens.

From Jared Diamond, "Easter's End." *Discover Magazine*, pp. 63–69. 1995. Reprinted by permission of Jared Diamond.

European visitors throughout the eighteenth and early nineteenth centuries estimated Easter's human population at about 2,000, a modest number considering the island's fertility. As Captain James Cook recognized during his brief visit in 1774, the islanders were Polynesians (a Tahitian man accompanying Cook was able to converse with them). Yet despite the Polynesians' well-deserved fame as a great seafaring people, the Easter Islanders who came out to Roggeveen's and Cook's ships did so by swimming or paddling canoes that Roggeveen described as "bad and frail." Their craft, he wrote, were "put together with manifold small planks and light inner timbers, which they cleverly stitched together with very fine twisted threads. . . . But as they lack the knowledge and particularly the materials for caulking and making tight the great number of seams of the canoes, these are accordingly very leaky, for which reason they are compelled to spend half the time in bailing." The canoes, only ten feet long, held at most two people, and only three or four canoes were observed on the entire island.

With such flimsy craft, Polynesians could never have colonized Easter from even the nearest island, nor could they have traveled far offshore to fish. The islanders Roggeveen met were totally isolated, unaware that other people existed. Investigators in all the years since his visit have discovered no trace of the islanders having any outside contacts: not a single Easter Island rock or product has turned up elsewhere, nor has anything been found on the island that could have been brought by anyone other than the original settlers or the Europeans. Yet the people living on Easter claimed memories of visiting the uninhabited Sala y Gomez reef 260 miles away, far beyond the range of the leaky canoes seen by Roggeveen. How did the islanders' ancestors reach that reef from Easter, or reach Easter from anywhere else?

Easter Island's most famous feature is its huge stone statues, more than 200 of which once stood on massive stone platforms lining the coast. At least 700 more, in all stages of completion, were abandoned in quarries or on ancient roads between the quarries and the coast, as if the carvers and moving crews had thrown down their tools and walked off the job. Most of the erected statues were carved in a single quarry and then somehow transported as far as six miles—despite heights as great as 33 feet and weights up to 82 tons. The abandoned statues, meanwhile, were as much as 65 feet tall and weighed up to 270 tons. The stone platforms were equally gigantic: up to 500 feet long and 10 feet high, with facing slabs weighing up to 10 tons.

Roggeveen himself quickly recognized the problem the statues posed: "The stone images at first caused us to be struck with astonishment," he wrote, "because we could not comprehend how it was possible that these people, who are devoid of heavy thick timber for making any machines, as well as strong ropes, nevertheless had been able to erect such images." Roggeveen might have added that the islanders had no wheels, no draft animals, and no source of power except their own muscles. How did they transport the giant statues for miles, even before erecting them? To deepen the mystery, the statues were still standing in 1770, but by 1864 all of them had been pulled down, by the islanders themselves. Why then did they carve them in the first place? And why did they stop?

The statues imply a society very different from the one Roggeveen saw in 1722. Their sheer number and size suggest a population much larger than 2,000 people. What became of everyone? Furthermore, that society must have been highly organized. Easter's resources were scattered across the island: the best stone for the statues was quarried at Rano Raraku near Easter's northeast end; red stone, used for large crowns adorning some of the statues, was quarried at Puna Pau, inland in the southwest; stone carving tools came mostly from Aroi in the northwest. Meanwhile, the best farmland lay in the south and east, and the best fishing grounds on the north and west coasts. Extracting and redistributing all those goods required complex political organization. What happened to that organization, and how could it ever have arisen in such a barren landscape?

Easter Island's mysteries have spawned volumes of speculation for more than two and a half centuries. Many Europeans were incredulous that Polynesians—commonly characterized as "mere savages"—could have created the statues or the beautifully constructed stone platforms. In the 1950s, Heyerdahl argued that Polynesia must have been settled by advanced societies of American Indians, who in turn must have received civilization across the Atlantic from more advanced societies of the Old World. Heyerdahl's raft voyages aimed to prove the feasibility of such prehistoric transoceanic contacts. In the 1960s the Swiss writer Erich von Däniken, an ardent believer in Earth visits by extraterrestrial astronauts, went further, claiming that Easter's statues were the work of intelligent beings who owned ultramodern tools, became stranded on Easter, and were finally rescued.

Heyerdahl and Von Däniken both brushed aside overwhelming evidence that the Easter Islanders were typical Polynesians derived from Asia rather than from the Americas and that their culture (including their statues) grew out of Polynesian culture. Their language was Polynesian, as Cook had already concluded. Specifically, they spoke an eastern Polynesian dialect related to Hawaiian and Marquesan, a dialect isolated since about A.D. 400, as estimated from slight differences in vocabulary. Their fishhooks and stone adzes resembled early Marquesan models. Last year DNA extracted from 12 Easter Island skeletons was also shown to be Polynesian. The islanders grew bananas, taro, sweet potatoes, sugarcane, and paper mulberry—typical Polynesian crops, mostly of Southeast Asian origin. Their sole domestic animal, the chicken, was also typically Polynesian and ultimately Asian, as were the rats that arrived as stowaways in the canoes of the first settlers.

What happened to those settlers? The fanciful theories of the past must give way to evidence gathered by hardworking practitioners in three fields: archeology, pollen analysis, and paleontology.

Modern archeological excavations on Easter have continued since Heyerdahl's 1955 expedition. The earliest radiocarbon dates associated with human activities are around A.D. 400 to 700, in reasonable agreement with the approximate settlement date of 400 estimated by linguists. The period of statue construction peaked around 1200 to 1500, with few if any statues erected thereafter. Densities of archeological sites suggest a large population; an estimate of 7,000 people is widely quoted by archeologists, but other estimates range up to 20,000, which does not seem implausible for an island of Easter's area and fertility.

Archeologists have also enlisted surviving islanders in experiments aimed at figuring out how the statues might have been carved and erected. Twenty people, using only stone chisels, could have carved even the largest completed statue within a year. Given enough timber and fiber for making ropes, teams of at most a few hundred people could have loaded the statues onto wooden sleds, dragged them over lubricated wooden tracks or rollers, and used logs as levers to maneuver them into a standing position. Rope could have been made from the fiber of a small native tree, related to the linden, called the hauhau. However, that tree is now extremely scarce on Easter, and hauling one statue would have required hundreds of yards of rope. Did Easter's now barren landscape once support the necessary trees?

That question can be answered by the technique of pollen analysis, which involves boring out a column of sediment from a swamp or pond, with the most recent deposits at the top and relatively more ancient deposits at the bottom. The absolute age of each layer can be dated by radiocarbon methods. Then begins the hard work: examining tens of thousands of pollen grains under a microscope, counting them, and identifying the plant species that produced each one by comparing the grains with modern pollen from known plant species. For Easter Island, the bleary-eyed scientists who performed that task were John Flenley, now at Massey University in New Zealand, and Sarah King of the University of Hull in England.

Flenley and King's heroic efforts were rewarded by the striking new picture that emerged of Easter's prehistoric landscape. For at least 30,000 years before human arrival and during the early years of Polynesian settlement, Easter was not a wasteland at all. Instead, a subtropical forest of trees and woody bushes towered over a ground layer of shrubs, herbs, ferns, and grasses. In the forest grew tree daisies, the rope-yielding hauhau tree, and the toromiro tree, which furnishes a dense, mesquite-like firewood. The most common tree in the forest was a species of palm now absent on Easter but formerly so abundant that the bottom strata of the sediment column were packed with its pollen. The Easter Island palm was closely related to the still-surviving Chilean wine palm, which grows up to 82 feet tall and 6 feet in diameter. The tall, unbranched trunks of the Easter Island palm would have been ideal for transporting and erecting statues and constructing large canoes. The palm would also have been a valuable food source, since its Chilean relative yields edible nuts as well as sap from which Chileans make sugar, syrup, honey, and wine.

What did the first settlers of Easter Island eat when they were not glutting themselves on the local equivalent of maple syrup? Recent excavations by David Steadman, of the New York State Museum at Albany, have yielded a picture of Easter's original animal world as surprising as Flenley and King's picture of its plant world. Steadman's expectations for Easter were conditioned by his experiences elsewhere in Polynesia, where fish are overwhelmingly the main food at archeological sites, typically accounting for more than 90 percent of the bones in ancient Polynesian garbage heaps. Easter, though, is too cool for the coral reefs beloved by fish, and its cliff-girded coastline permits shallow-water fishing in only a few places. Less than a quarter of the bones in its early garbage heaps (from the period 900 to 1300) belonged to fish; instead, nearly one-third of all bones came from porpoises.

Nowhere else in Polynesia do porpoises account for even 1 percent of discarded food bones. But most other Polynesian islands offered animal food in the form of birds and mammals, such as New Zealand's now extinct giant moas and Hawaii's now extinct flightless geese. Most other islanders also had domestic pigs and dogs. On Easter, porpoises would have been the largest animal available—other than humans. The porpoise species identified at Easter, the common dolphin, weighs up to 165 pounds. It generally lives out at sea, so it could not have been hunted by line fishing or spear-fishing from shore. Instead, it must have been harpooned far offshore, in big seaworthy canoes built from the extinct palm tree.

In addition to porpoise meat, Steadman found, the early Polynesian settlers were feasting on seabirds. For those birds, Easter's remoteness and lack of predators made it an ideal haven as a breeding site, at least until humans arrived. Among the prodigious numbers of seabirds that bred on Easter were albatross, boobies, frigate birds, fulmars, petrels, prions, shearwaters, storm petrels, terns, and tropic birds. With at least 25 nesting species, Easter was the richest seabird breeding site in Polynesia and probably in the whole Pacific.

Land birds as well went into early Easter Island cooking pots. Steadman identified bones of at least six species, including barn owls, herons, parrots, and rail. Bird stew would have been seasoned with meat from large numbers of rats, which the Polynesian colonists inadvertently brought with them; Easter Island is the sole known Polynesian island where rat bones outnumber fish bones at archeological sites. (In case you're squeamish and consider rats inedible, I still recall recipes for creamed laboratory rat that my British biologist friends used to supplement their diet during their years of wartime food rationing.)

Porpoises, seabirds, land birds, and rats did not complete the list of meat sources formerly available on Easter. A few bones hint at the possibility of breeding seal colonies as well. All these delicacies were cooked in ovens fired by wood from the island's forests.

Such evidence lets us imagine the island onto which Easter's first Polynesian colonists stepped ashore some 1,600 years ago, after a long canoe voyage from eastern Polynesia. They found themselves in a pristine paradise. What then happened to it? The pollen grains and the bones yield a grim answer.

Pollen records show that destruction of Easter's forests was well under way by the year 800, just a few centuries after the start of human settlement. Then charcoal from wood fires came to fill the sediment cores, while pollen of palms and other trees and woody shrubs decreased or disappeared, and pollen of the grasses that replaced the forest became more abundant. Not long after 1400 the palm finally became extinct, not only as a result of being chopped down but also because the now ubiquitous rats prevented its regeneration: of the dozens of preserved palm nuts discovered in caves on Easter, all had been chewed by rats and could no longer germinate. While the hauhau tree did not become extinct in Polynesian times, its numbers declined drastically until there weren't enough left to make ropes from. By the time Heyerdahl visited Easter, only a single, nearly dead toromiro tree remained on the island, and even that lone survivor has now disappeared. (Fortunately, the toromiro still grows in botanical gardens elsewhere.)

The fifteenth century marked the end not only for Easter's palm but for the forest itself. Its doom had been approaching as people cleared land to plant gardens; as they felled trees to build canoes, to transport and erect statues, and to burn; as rats devoured seeds; and probably as the native birds died out that had pollinated the trees' flowers and dispersed their fruit. The overall picture is among the most extreme examples of forest destruction anywhere in the world: the whole forest gone, and most of its tree species extinct.

The destruction of the island's animals was as extreme as that of the forest: without exception, every species of native land bird became extinct. Even shellfish were overexploited, until people had to settle for small sea snails instead of larger cowries. Porpoise bones disappeared abruptly from garbage heaps around 1500; no one could harpoon porpoises anymore, since the trees used for constructing the big seagoing canoes no longer existed. The colonies of more than half of the seabird species breeding on Easter or on its offshore islets were wiped out.

In place of these meat supplies, the Easter Islanders intensified their production of chickens, which had been only an occasional food item. They also turned to the largest remaining meat source available: humans, whose bones became common in late Easter Island garbage heaps. Oral traditions of the islanders are rife with cannibalism; the most inflammatory taunt that could be snarled at an enemy was "The flesh of your mother sticks between my teeth." With no wood available to cook these new goodies, the islanders resorted to sugarcane scraps, grass, and sedges to fuel their fires.

All these strands of evidence can be wound into a coherent narrative of a society's decline and fall. The first Polynesian colonists found themselves on an island with fertile soil, abundant food, bountiful building materials, ample lebensraum, and all the prerequisites for comfortable living. They prospered and multiplied.

After a few centuries, they began erecting stone statues on platforms, like the ones their Polynesian forebears had carved. With passing years, the statues and platforms became larger and larger, and the statues began sporting ten-ton red crowns—probably in an escalating spiral of one-upmanship, as rival clans tried to surpass each other with shows of wealth and power. (In the same way, successive Egyptian pharaohs built ever-larger pyramids. Today Hollywood movie moguls near my home in Los Angeles are displaying their wealth and power by building ever more ostentatious mansions. Tycoon Marvin Davis topped previous moguls with plans for a 50,000-square-foot house, so now Aaron Spelling has topped Davis with a 56,000-square-foot house. All that those buildings lack to make the message explicit are ten-ton red crowns.) On Easter, as in modern America, society was held together by a complex political system to redistribute locally available resources and to integrate the economies of different areas.

Eventually Easter's growing population was cutting the forest more rapidly than the forest was regenerating. The people used the land for gardens and the wood for fuel, canoes, and houses—and, of course, for lugging statues. As forest disappeared, the islanders ran out of timber and rope to transport and erect their statues. Life became more uncomfortable—springs and streams dried up, and wood was no longer available for fires.

People also found it harder to fill their stomachs, as land birds, large sea snails, and many seabirds disappeared. Because timber for building seagoing canoes vanished, fish catches declined and porpoises disappeared from the table. Crop yields also declined, since deforestation allowed the soil to be eroded by rain and wind, dried by the sun, and its nutrients to be leeched from it. Intensified chicken production and cannibalism replaced only part of all those lost foods. Preserved statuettes with sunken cheeks and visible ribs suggest that people were starving.

With the disappearance of food surpluses, Easter Island could no longer feed the chiefs, bureaucrats, and priests who had kept a complex society running. Surviving islanders described to early European visitors how local chaos replaced centralized government and a warrior class took over from the hereditary chiefs. The stone points of spears and daggers, made by the warriors during their heyday in the 1600s and 1700s, still litter the ground of Easter today. By around 1700, the population began to crash toward between one-quarter and one-tenth of its former number. People took to living in caves for protection against their enemies. Around 1770 rival clans started to topple each other's statues, breaking the heads off. By 1864 the last statue had been thrown down and desecrated.

As we try to imagine the decline of Easter's civilization, we ask ourselves, "Why didn't they look around, realize what they were doing, and stop before it was too late? What were they thinking when they cut down the last palm tree?"

I suspect, though, that the disaster happened not with a bang but with a whimper. After all, there are those hundreds of abandoned statues to consider. The forest the islanders depended on for rollers and rope didn't simply disappear one day—it vanished slowly, over decades. Perhaps war interrupted the moving teams; perhaps by the time the carvers had finished their work, the last rope snapped. In the meantime, any islander who tried to warn about the dangers of progressive deforestation would have been overridden by vested interests of carvers, bureaucrats, and chiefs, whose jobs depended on continued deforestation. Our Pacific Northwest loggers are only the latest in a long line of loggers to cry, "Jobs over trees!" The changes in forest cover from year to year would have been hard to detect: yes, this year we cleared those woods over there, but trees are starting to grow back again on this abandoned garden site here. Only older people, recollecting their childhoods decades earlier, could have recognized a difference. Their children could no more have comprehended their parents' tales than my eight-year-old sons today can comprehend my wife's and my tales of what Los Angeles was like 30 years ago.

Gradually trees became fewer, smaller, and less important. By the time the last fruit-bearing adult palm tree was cut, palms had long since ceased to be of economic significance. That left only smaller and smaller palm saplings to clear each year, along with other bushes and treelets. No one would have noticed the felling of the last small palm.

By now the meaning of easter Island for us should be chillingly obvious. Easter Island is Earth writ small. Today, again, a rising population confronts shrinking resources. We too have no emigration valve, because all human societies are linked by international transport, and we can no more escape into space than the Easter Islanders could flee into the ocean. If we continue to follow our present course, we shall have exhausted the world's major fisheries, tropical rain forests, fossil fuels, and much of our soil by the time my sons reach my current age.

Every day newspapers report details of famished countries—Afghanistan, Liberia, Rwanda, Sierra Leone, Somalia, the former Yugoslavia, Zaire—where soldiers have appropriated the wealth or where central government is yielding to local gangs of thugs. With the risk of nuclear war receding, the threat of our ending with a bang no longer has a chance of galvanizing us to halt our course. Our risk now is of winding down, slowly, in a whimper. Corrective action is blocked by vested interests, by well-intentioned political and business leaders, and by their electorates, all of whom are perfectly correct in not noticing big changes from year to year. Instead, each year there are just somewhat more people, and somewhat fewer resources, on Earth.

It would be easy to close our eyes or to give up in despair. If mere thousands of Easter Islanders with only stone tools and their own muscle power sufficed to destroy their society, how can billions of people with metal tools and machine power fail to do worse? But there is one crucial difference. The Easter Islanders had no books and no histories of other doomed societies. Unlike the Easter Islanders, we have histories of the past—information that can save us. My main hope for my sons' generation is that we may now choose to learn from the fates of societies like Easter's.

15 ■

Child Soldiers

Mike Wessells

introduction ■ ■ ■ ■

War is so barbaric that it should be a relic of the past, something related only in stories of how humans "used to be" before they woke up to the folly of organized killing. Such, at least, is the thinking of many, based on their hopes of a better way of life and ideas of morality—of the way life should be. As we all know so well, however, such well-intentioned thinking is far from reality. War seems to be a regular part of U.S. life. It seems that we are always sending troops to some nation somewhere. Prompted by our politicians, our news media trumpet some new enemy, some country to which we need to "bring democracy." Fortunately for those of us who live in the wealth of this nation and enjoy its freedoms—for as long as they last—these wars are someplace "over there." Some other people constantly need our form of democracy, which in some Orwellian fashion can be brought to them at the end of a gun.

If I sound jaded or disenchanted by these statements, it is because I am. For years I have been hoping to see the end of this process, and it never comes. The reasons for this are not our need to bring democracy to some people, or to bring justice to despots, or anything of this kind. We are willing to work with bloodthirsty despots, with governments that brutally repress their citizens—as long as they cooperate with us. The reasons for our sending soldiers to other nations, rather, is the geopolitical structure that we currently have, an attempt to maintain the global balance of power.

After soldiers return home, they have to be reintegrated into civilian life. This is especially difficult for soldiers who have seen close-up, prolonged warfare. They have learned a way of viewing the world that does not match the civilian view, and they have seen and done things they would rather forget. This selection by Mike Wessells focuses on the reintegration of soldiers into civilian life, but with a different twist—that of child soldiers.

Thinking Critically

As you read this selection, ask yourself:

■ How do you think child soldiers, with all their horrifying experiences, can best be reintegrated into their societies?

*W*hile in Sierra Leone a couple of summers ago, I visited Grafton Camp, a facility for recently demobilized child soldiers operated by UNICEF and local partners. Many of the boys, ranging from nine to 16 years of age, had killed people as they fought in a civil war.... The camp director said that when the youths had been given drugs—most likely, amphetamines—while soldiering, they "would do just about anything that was ordered." Some, he added, were proud of having been effective killers.

These boys, who had shortly before been willing to kill and who had never received an adequate foundation of moral development, danced with enormous energy and played cooperative games under the supervision of the camp's counselors. As I watched, it was sobering to think that under certain conditions, practically any child could be changed into a killer....

■ ■ ■ A SOLDIER AT SEVEN

The nature of armed conflict has changed greatly in recent years. The end of the Cold War ushered in an era of ethnopolitical conflicts that are seldom fought on well-defined battlefields. Conflicts are increasingly internal, and they are characterized by butchery, violence against women, and atrocities sometimes committed by former neighbors. More than 80 percent of the victims are noncombatants, mostly women and children.

Increasingly children serve as combatants or as cooks, informants, porters, bodyguards, sentries, and spies. Many child soldiers belong to organized military units, wear uniforms, and receive explicit training, their lethality enhanced by the widespread availability of lightweight assault weapons. Other children participate in relatively unstructured but politically motivated acts of violence, such as throwing stones or planting bombs.

The use of children in armed conflict is global in scope—a far greater problem than suggested by the scant attention it has received. Child soldiers are found from Central America to the Great Lakes region of Central Africa, and from Belfast in the north to Angola in the south.

The problem defies gender boundaries. Girls are often forced into military activity—in Ethiopia, for instance, girls comprised about 25 percent of opposition forces in the civil war that ended in 1991. Typically, sexual victimization is a part of soldiering for girls, many of whom are forced to become "soldiers' wives." After the conflict ends, families and local communities may reject the girls as impure or unsuitable for marriage. Desperate to survive, many former girl soldiers become prostitutes.

The use of child soldiers violates international norms. The U.N. Convention on the Rights of the Child (CRC), signed in 1989 and ratified by more than 160 nations, establishes 15 years as the minimum recruitment age. In fact, most countries have endorsed an optional protocol that boosts the minimum recruitment age to 18

From Mike Wessells, "Child Soldiers." *The Bulletin of the Atomic Scientists*, 53, 6, 1997, pp. 32–39. Reprinted by permission.

years. But in the face of armed conflict, military units in some nations—whether governmental or rebel—often pay little attention to age.

In Grafton Camp, children were encouraged to draw, and many drew pictures that reflected their war experiences. One showed a house being shelled by artillery. Soldiers fired at the house and at people in the street, who were fleeing.

Inside the house was a man who had been shot. Blood flowed from his midsection. I asked the artist, a small-for-his-age boy of nine, to tell me about the picture and what it showed. He explained that soldiers (the rebel forces) attacked his village, bombed his house, and came inside and shot his parents. The bleeding man was his father. I did not ask why he had not painted his mother, who had also been murdered.

How old was he when his parents were killed? "Seven," he said. I asked him what happened after the attack. "My parents died—the soldiers told me to go with them so I did."

I asked what he had done in the military. He had "carried things." When I asked if he had killed anyone, he said "No." But when asked if he would have killed someone if told to do so, the strength of his desire to survive showed. "Yes," he said. He would have done "what he had to do."

When asked what he wanted for the future, he said, "I only want to go to school."

■ ■ ■ CHILD SOLDIERS AND INSECURITY

Child soldiering violates the fundamental rights of children, exploits youth for political purposes, subjects them to slaughter and the ravages of war, and immerses them in a system that sanctions killing. And it also poses formidable security risks for others. A society that mobilizes and trains its young for war weaves violence into the fabric of life, increasing the likelihood that violence and war will be its future. Children who have been robbed of education and taught to kill often contribute to further militarization, lawlessness, and violence.

The use of child soldiers also threatens fragile cease-fires and blocks reconciliation and peace. Not infrequently, conflict continues at the local level even after a cease-fire has been signed. Child soldiers are pawns in local conflicts because they provide a ready group for recruitment by warlords, profiteers, and groups that foment political instability.

The problem is especially severe in developing countries, in which children constitute nearly half the population and in which children are often reared in a system that mixes war, poverty, violence, hunger, environmental degradation, and political instability....

■ ■ ■ GLOBAL AND SYSTEMATIC

How widespread is child soldiering? Numbers are hard to come by. The destruction and turmoil of war make it difficult to create and preserve accurate records. Particularly in Africa, many countries have no history of keeping precise birth records.

Beyond that, many military groups, governmental and rebel, make no attempt to document or accurately report the ages of the children they recruit. And former child soldiers are often reluctant to identify themselves because they fear rejection by their communities or retribution from their former commanders—or from those whom they once attacked.

The best estimate—which is admittedly soft—is that in the mid-1990s, there were about a quarter of a million child soldiers, current or recently demobilized.[1] This figure comes from a series of 26 country case studies conducted by Rädda Barnen (Swedish Save the Children) as part of a larger U.N. Study on the "Impact of Armed Conflict on Children."[2]

Because the U. N. study was led by children's rights activist Graça Machel, the former first lady of Mozambique, it is typically referred to as the "Machel Study." One of the main conclusions of the study... is that child soldiering is a global problem that occurs more systematically than most analysts had previously suspected.

The Machel Study showed that in some countries, children constitute a significant percentage of the combatants. In Liberia, for instance, about 10 percent of an estimated 60,000 combatants in the civil war that began in 1989 were children. In El Salvador, children composed 20 percent or more of the FAES (Fuerzas Armadas de El Salvador). In Afghanistan, 10 percent of the Mujahadeen forces are estimated to have been children under 16 years. In Palestine during the Intifada, nearly 70 percent of Palestinian children are believed to have participated in acts of political violence such as stoning Israeli troops.[3]

Numerical estimates, however, only hint at the damage done to children and to the fabric of the societies in which they live. Children often become part of a system of hatred and killing, even if they do not participate in military activity themselves. In Rwanda, many Hutu children were informants, disclosing the locations of Tutsis and their supporters, who were then slaughtered in the 1994 genocide.

■ ■ ■ ■   **FORCED RECRUITMENT**

Children usually become soldiers through coercion, either through mandatory conscription or forced recruitment. When national armies have a manpower shortfall, they may find it convenient not to search too carefully for the accurate birthdate of a conscript. Rebel forces seldom have use for birth records, either. In countries covered by the case studies, government forces as well as rebel forces were often equally likely to use child soldiers.

In Cambodia, says the Machel Study, children who stood as tall as a rifle were often deemed eligible for military service. In Bhutan, local authorities instructed village headmen to bring forward a specified number of people from their respective villages. Children were among the "voluntary recruits."

Manpower-hungry militias often abduct children at gun point. In Afghanistan, Bhutan, Burma/Myanmar, El Salvador, Ethiopia, and Mozambique, soldiers have recruited children forcibly from schools. According to one underage Burmese recruit, government soldiers surrounded his school and arrested 40 to 50 youths between 15 and 17 years of age:

"Our teachers all ran away in fear," says the recruit, quoted in the Burma/Myanmar case study. "We were all terrified. I didn't know what was going on and they didn't explain anything to us."

In Ethiopia, armed militias would surround a public area such as a marketplace, order every male to sit down, and then force into a truck anyone deemed "eligible." At particular risk of abduction were teenagers who worked on the streets selling cigarettes or candy.

Forced abductions, says the Machel Study, were commonly one element in a larger campaign to intimidate communities. Armed groups that abduct children for soldiering are also inclined to go on rape-and-looting rampages while in the villages.

Abductions also can be used as an instrument of war. In Guatemala, for instance, the army singled out young members of the indigenous population for recruitment during its long civil war, thereby pitting them against their cohorts among the rebels. The Mayan community called it "the new genocide."

Militias often use brutish methods to weaken resistance to forcible recruitment. The case study for Uganda reports that people who resisted attacks by the Lord's Resistance Army "would be cut with pangas [machetes]. Quite a number of victims had their lips and ears chopped off in macabre rituals."

To seal off possible avenues of resistance from the children's communities, recruiters may deliberately destroy the bonds of trust between child and community. In Mozambique, for instance, recruiters from RENAMO forced boy recruits to kill someone from their own village.

■ ■ ■ FEAR AND OBEDIENCE

Abduction is only the first step in a process that uses fear, brutality, and psychological manipulation to achieve high levels of obedience, converting children into killers.

In many, countries, child recruits are subjected to beatings, humiliation, and acts of sadism. In Honduras, boys wearing only underwear were exposed by government troops to "the ram," in which they were forced to roll nearly naked on a stony or thorny surface while being beaten or kicked by a squad leader.

In Paraguay, government military trainers beat children with sticks or rifle butts and burned them with cigarettes while verbally mocking them. Those who resisted or who attempted to escape were further brutalized or killed.

A frequently used tactic is to have children learn by doing, which may mean exposing them progressively to violence, numbing them so they might someday commit acts of sadism on fellow humans. Child recruits in Colombia, for example, were forced to cut the throats of domestic animals and drink the blood.

A 14-year-old Mozambican boy, quoted in Mozambique's case study, said of RENAMO forces: "I was told to train. I would run, do head-over-heels, and climb trees. Then they trained me to take guns apart and put them back together again for four months. Every day the same thing. When it was over they did a test. They put someone in front of me for me to kill. I killed."

Few constraints exist on what trainers can do to children, and children themselves may lack the internal constraints against violence that ordinarily develop through exposure to positive role models, a healthy family life, the rewards for so-cially constructive behaviors, and the encouragement of moral reasoning.

Weakened psychologically and fearful of their commanders, children can be-come obedient killers, willing to take on the most dangerous and horrifying assign-ments. In countries such as Uganda, Liberia, and Honduras, child soldiers have served as executioners, and in some countries—notably in Colombia, Peru, and Mozambique—they have been required to perform ritual acts of cannibalism on their victims, acts calculated to instill contempt for human life.

Adolescents are often selected for suicide missions, and some commanders view adolescents as mentally predisposed for such duty. In countries such as Sri Lanka and Burma/Myanmar, child soldiers were given drugs—such as amphet-amines and tranquilizers—to blunt fear and pain and then used for "human wave" attacks that resulted in massive casualties. In Guatemala, underage soldiers were used as scouts and land mine "detectors."

Although some commanders complain that child soldiers take excessive risks, slow operations down, and do not seem to understand the dangers they face, many commanders prefer child soldiers because they are highly obedient and willing to follow the most unacceptable orders. As one person said in the Burma/Myanmar case study, "Child soldiers are always very eager to go to the front lines."

■ ■ ■ ■ UNFORCED RECRUITMENT

Coercion aside, children may join the military for security, a pressing need for unac-companied children who are vulnerable to nearly every kind of threat. Desperation for food or medical care often drives children into military life. The military may of-fer children the only path to wages to support themselves or their families. For these reasons, it is meaningless to ever speak of children's involvement in the military as strictly "voluntary."

The quest for national identity, liberation, and a secure homeland animates many armed conflicts. Typically, identity conflicts are saturated with an ideology of liberation struggle that draws a sharp line between Us and Them, glorifies the in-group while denigrating the out-group, and honors high levels of commitment to "the cause." Particularly in conflicts influenced by strong religious ideologies, youth may view the cause as having divine sanction, making it a clear-cut struggle between Good and Evil.

For adolescents still defining their identity, ideology provides direction that is otherwise lacking. In apartheid South Africa, black township youth—the Young Lions—adopted an ideology of liberation, which gave meaning to the harsh realities of their existence and conferred a clear sense of identity and direction.

In Guatemala, many children of landless peasants living in extreme poverty and victimized by repressive regimes embraced an ideology of revolution and joined the liberation struggle. In Rwanda during the early 1990s, the Hutu-dominated gov-ernment used radio to spread hatred of the Tutsis, who were demonized as murder-ous outsiders. This helped prepare children for roles as killers in the youth militias in the 1994 genocide.

Many communities glorify war and teach children at an early age to view military activity as prestigious and glamorous. Militaristic values may be transmitted via parades, ceremonies to honor war heroes, and the martyrdom of soldiers.

Media images may also play a part. In Sri Lanka, opposition forces have broadcast Rambostyle TV movies of live combat training.[4] In such contexts, boys learn machismo and come to associate military activity with respect and power—compelling attractions for children who otherwise feel powerless.

While some boys join the military for adventure or to win fame and the respect of other males, others bask in the praise of mothers who express pride in seeing their sons in uniform.

In places such as Northern Ireland, Palestine, or South Africa, now as in the past, peer pressure animates participation in political violence. Youths expect and encourage each other to take part in violent activities, and they attach great value to group loyalty.[5] Having been arrested and tortured are regarded as badges of courage and commitment.

In states such as Chechnya and Ethiopia, families have encouraged sons to join opposition groups as a means of avenging the deaths of family members or of seeking "blood revenge." Families may also encourage sons to join the military for economic reasons, seeing the salary from soldiering as the most likely route to survival.

Children who engage in political violence often have witnessed deaths, torture, or executions. Others have lost parents, had their homes and even their communities destroyed, or have been sexually abused. Even children who have not been physically attacked may feel victimized by assaults on relatives or on their ethnic group.

Psychologically, people who have been victims of violence are at great risk of becoming perpetrators of violence. It's a familiar pattern. I recall a recent visit with three women whose husbands had been shot execution-style while working in the fields in the early 1980s, during a long and brutal civil war. The women now live as a group. One of their sons, now 16, said he did not remember the killings. He was too young. But if the war, which ended in a cease-fire, should resume, he would join a military unit—if it would enable him to avenge his father's death.

In 1992, while I was visiting the Occupied West Bank, a Palestinian father told me how his six-year-old son had gone up the street to the home of an Israeli settler who had recently moved in. The son had no involvement in political violence. But when the son tossed small stones into the settler's garbage can, as if shooting basketballs, the settler stormed out of the house with an automatic weapon and threatened to shoot if the boy returned.

The following month, the father said, his son joined a group of Palestinian youths in throwing stones at Israeli soldiers. "I worry," said the father, "he will be arrested and tortured."

■ ■ ■ HEALING

In Angola, restoring spiritual harmony through traditional healing is an essential step in helping child soldiers demobilize and reintegrate into their home communities. In many Bantu cultures, people believe that when one kills, one is haunted by the unavenged spirits of those who were killed. Spiritually contaminated, a former child soldier who has killed puts an entire community at risk if he re-enters without having been purified.

In one community, a traditional healer told me a few years ago of a ritual he ordinarily conducts to purify former child soldiers. First, he lives with the child for a month, feeding him a special diet designed to cleanse. During the month, he also advises the child on proper behavior and what the village expects from him.

At the end of the month, the healer convenes the village for a ritual. As part of the ceremony, the healer buries frequently used weapons—a machete, perhaps, or an AK-47—and announces that on this day the boy's life as a soldier has ended and his life as a civilian has begun.

Anecdotal evidence suggests that this kind of purification ceremony helps decrease the stress and fear that gnaws on former child soldiers and helps communities accept young people back. The preliminary evidence also suggests that once young people have been accepted, the community often succeeds in teaching them nonviolent modes of behavior.

Such ceremonies seem to be relatively common in rural areas, not just in sub-Saharan Africa but in indigenous cultures around the world. The healers who practice them are on to something. It is premature and without scientific justification to assume that former child soldiers who have killed or done terrible things are forever "damaged goods" and beyond rehabilitation.

Traditional healing methods may work, in part, because they fit local beliefs. For example, in Guatemala, Mayan people believe that when someone dies, the spirit cannot go to the next life until a burial ritual has been conducted. This is why the exhumations of mass graves now under way in Guatemala are so important to the Mayans.

Many humanitarian assistance and development efforts overlook traditional healing methods, which are dismissed as unscientific. I discovered while working in Sierra Leone that local people were initially reluctant to talk about traditional healing with me, a Western Ph.D. Although traditional methods should not be romanticized or viewed as a panacea, they can be important tools for assisting former child combatants.

Nevertheless, a variety of obstacles impede attempts to address the problem of child soldiering. Warring factions, desperate for more troops, continue to exploit children. In addition, non-state actors such as armed opposition groups are not signatories to key instruments such as the Convention on the Rights of the Child. Typically, cease-fires and peace treaties include no provisions for the demobilization of child soldiers. Further, cultures van in their definition of "childhood"; many African societies regard a 14-year-old boy as a man if he has participated in the traditional rite of passage.

Labeling is also a significant problem.[6] Some people, even psychologists and psychiatrists, have written off entire groups of severely traumatized child soldiers as "lost generations." In Nicaragua, according to that country's case study, workers at a center to assist former child soldiers initially feared the children they work with, believing they were "born assassins," "bloodthirsty children," or "human tigers" who "take out people's eyes."

Stigmatizing labels, however, should not obscure the fact that there are tremendous individual differences in children's responses to war experiences, and that many methods—Western and traditional—exist for assisting former child soldiers.

■ ■ ■ ■ DEMOBILIZATION AND REINTEGRATION

The most immediate healing steps, which generally cannot be taken until after armed conflict ends, involve demobilizing everyone under the age of 18 years, reintegrating them with families and communities, and assisting them in making the transition into civilian life.

Effective demobilization programs provide basic needs, such as food, water, shelter, and security. This is most often accomplished by locating members of the child's immediate or extended family and then reuniting them as soon as possible.

To offer opportunities for healthy development and life in the community, reintegration programs often attempt to place former child soldiers in schools or to provide vocational training that can lead to jobs and financial conditions that mitigate against re-enlistment.

Effective demobilization and reintegration also requires attention to psychological adjustment. Depending on their experiences, former child soldiers may experience flashbacks and nightmares about traumatic events, causing difficulties in concentration that can impair judgment and performance in school. Some former soldiers carry heavy burdens of guilt and worry about what will happen to them.

War-affected children may act out aggressive impulses, creating problems and continuing the spread of violence. Inability to control aggressive behavior is often a problem for children who have been reared in a system of violence, who have few skills for handling conflict nonviolently, and whose moral development may have been limited by early immersion in the military.

It is important to heal the psychological wounds of war, to assist children in coming to terms with their experiences concerning death and violence, to reestablish daily routines that provide a sense of normalcy and continuity, and to develop values and skills of nonviolent conflict resolution. Nongovernmental organizations and U.N. agencies such as UNICEF have developed several effective programs for achieving these aims.

In Angola, for instance, I work with a multi-province program that enables adults in local communities to address the emotional needs of war-affected children through a mixture of Western and traditional healing methods.[7]

In the past year, a team organized by Christian Children's Fund and UNICEF has, with funding from the U.S. Agency for International Development, located the families of and successfully demobilized and returned home 83 percent of 2,925 child soldiers in UNITA-controlled areas.

To prepare the communities, the team trained local church people—*Catequistas*—to help parents, teachers, and community leaders understand and deal with the kinds of problems the returning children would face. The *Catequistas* also helped arrange traditional healing ceremonies. About half of the former child soldiers helped by the program are in vocational training, and about a fourth are in school.

■ ■ ■ STRENGTHENING THE CRC

Although community-based approaches are valuable, the world cannot wait for child soldiering to occur and then try to pick up the pieces afterward. Prevention ought to be the top priority

An immediate step would be to raise the minimum age of recruitment to 18 years. Although Article 38 of the Convention on the Rights of the Child establishes 15 years as the minimum recruitment age, the U. N. Commission on Human Rights is drafting an optional protocol to the CRC that sets 18 years as the minimum age for compulsory recruitment or for participation in hostilities. Because this protocol enjoys strong support, there is hope for its adoption by the General Assembly.

A key step toward strengthening the CRC is to pressure non-state actors to respect its provisions even though they are not signatories. If only governments adhere to the norms set by the convention, the door is left open to abuses of children's rights by opposition or rebel groups. Pressure to adhere to the standards set by the convention may be applied to both state and non-state actors through careful monitoring by U.N. agencies, nongovernmental organizations, and international media.

Another crucial step is to build commitment to the CRC, the most comprehensive instrument for the protection of children's rights. Although more than 160 nations are parties to the convention, there are several noteworthy exceptions—primarily the United States, which signed it in 1995, but has not ratified it.

The fact that the United States has not ratified the convention, the most widely endorsed human rights instrument in the world, is puzzling to its allies and damaging to its ability to lead on human rights questions. [The United States has ratified the Protocols to the Convention, however, and there is a campaign to get the U.S. Senate to ratify the Convention.] The ratification effort in the United States has been short-circuited by questionable concerns over whether setting the minimum recruitment age at 18 would compromise national security or limit sovereignty.

Another issue in the Senate centers on the fact that the convention outlaws capital punishment for anyone under 18. That raises the concern that ratification of the convention would limit the ability of states to use capital punishment. But perhaps the biggest obstacle to ratification is simply the lack of public awareness. Most people in the United States do not know about child soldiers, which means there has not been much public discussion about the CRC.

Around the world, nations that are parties to the convention must invoke it, not ignore it. They must point out the massive violations of children's rights that occur as a result of armed conflict. There must be enforcement of its basic provisions for safeguarding the physical, social, and psychological integrity of children and for guaranteeing basic rights such as the right to education.

To succeed, prevention efforts need to work toward structural changes that address poverty and oppression, fundamental sources of armed conflict and of much child soldiering.

Connections must also be built between children's rights, arms transfers, and militarization, issues that the peace community and the world at large have tended to address in a fragmentary manner. Only a holistic approach will succeed in ending child soldiering and building healthy social systems that protect children and orient them toward peace.

■ ■ ■ ■ THE TUNNEL

While visiting the Grafton Camp in Sierra Leone last year, I watched these former soldiers, these boys, these children, at play. They had been robbed of their childhood, exposed to death and suffering at an early age, and some had been made into killers.

And yet, as I observed and as I talked with the boys' counselors, I acquired a new appreciation for human resilience and potential for change. Some of the boys had once cooperated in killing, but now they cooperated in games such as running "the tunnel."

The boys stood in two lines facing each other, with partners in the line joining hands and raising their arms, creating a tunnel through which the first two boys would run.

When they reached the end, they faced one another and locked their hands in the air, becoming part of the tunnel through which the next pair at the front of the line ran.

A child's game, yes. You probably played it, or something like it, yourself. At Grafton Camp, there was much laughter as the boys ran faster and faster through the tunnel and as the tunnel snaked its way around trees and through gardens.

On another level, however, it was a serious game with a psychological dimension. The tunnel existed only through cooperation, the joined hands symbolizing human interconnectedness. The game required trust, because the boys forming the tunnel could have easily collapsed the tunnel, tripping the runners. Or they could have harassed the runners in myriad ways.

However modestly, the game was rebuilding the fabric of trust that the war had ripped apart. While no single game could rehabilitate a former child soldier, the camp itself seemed to offer hope that rehabilitation was possible. After all, some of the counselors were themselves former child soldiers who had been demobilized and who were now working to help younger children make the adjustment back to everyday civilian life.

And yet, what is done in a facility like Grafton is only a drop in an ocean of violence. In fact, Grafton Camp itself closed last summer, a victim of the revived violence in Sierra Leone. Some of the child soldiers at Grafton have been "remobilized." The laughter is long gone.

Children in Sierra Leone are being drawn back into the renewed conflict. Much the same is true in other countries locked in cycles of violence. Although the immediate goal is to protect children in areas of armed conflict, the longer-term goal must be to prevent the wars that lead children to the slaughter.

■ ■ ■ NOTES

1. Except where noted, figures are from current studies conducted by a variety of nongovernmental and governmental organizations. These studies are available from Rädda Barmen, and are summarized in Rachel Brett and Margaret McCallin, *Children: The Invisible Soldiers* (Vaxjo, Sweden: Swedish Save the Children, 1996).

2. The official title of the Machel Study is "Report of the Expert of the Secretary-General, Graça Machel, on the 'Impact of Armed Conflict on Children' Document A/51/306 & Add 1." It may be ordered from the Public Inquiries Unit, Department of Information, United Nations, New York, NY 10017. Fax: (212) 963-0071.

3. Samir Quota, Raija Punamäki, and Eyad el-Sarraj, "The Relations Between Traumatic Experiences, Activity, and Cognitive and Emotional Responses Among Palestinian Children," *International Journal of Psychology*, 1995, vol. 30, p. 291.

4. Guy Goodwin-Gill and Ilene Cohn, *Child Soldiers : The Role of Children in Armed Conflicts* (Oxford: Clarendon, 1994), p. 31.

5. Ed Cairns. *Children and Political Violence* (Oxford: Blackwell, 1996), p. 114.

6. Gillian Straker, *Faces in the Revolution* (Cape Town: David Philip, 1992), p. 13.

7. Michael Wessells, "Assisting Angolan Children Impacted By War: Blending Western and Traditional Approaches to Healing," in *Coordinators Notebook: An International Resource for Early Childhood Development*, vol. 19 (West Springfield, Mass: Consultative Group on Early Childhood Care and Development, 1996), pp. 33–37.

Name Index

Subject Index